Shyness
Shyness

A Bold New Approach

The Latest Scientific Findings,
Plus Practical Steps for Finding Your Comfort Zone

Bernardo J. Carducci, Ph.D.,
WITH SUSAN K. GOLANT, M.A.

RESEARCH IN COLLABORATION WITH
LISA KAISER, M.A.

HarperCollins*Publishers*

HarperCollins books may be purchased for educational, business, or sales promotional use. For information please write: Special Markets Department, HarperCollins Publishers, Inc., 10 East 53rd Street, New York, NY 10022.

FIRST EDITION

Designed by Elina D. Nudelman

Library of Congress Cataloging-in-Publication Data

Carducci, Bernardo J.

  Shyness / Bernardo J. Carducci. — 1st ed.

    p. cm.

  Includes bibliographical references.

  ISBN 0-06-018247-4

  1. Bashfulness. I. Title.

  BF575.B3C37   1999

  155.2'32—dc21   98-18482

99 00 01 02 03 ❖/RRD 10 9 8 7 6 5 4 3 2 1

*This book is dedicated to
Edward, my father, and to the memory of Mary, my mother,
Jan, my wife, and
Rozana, my daughter,
all of whom have never been shy
about giving me their love and support*

Contents

Acknowledgments

In addition to the thousands of individuals who have written to and talk with me about their shyness over the past twenty years, there are some special individuals whose personal involvement made *Shyness* possible. These "friends of *Shyness*" are: Marie Benz, Jan Carducci, Rozana Carducci, the Carducci Family, Jane Clark, Sue Campo, Mark Clark, Melissa Clark, Kathie Festo, Kimberly Gonzales, Joan Goldstein, Robin T. Marks, Nicole Moodie, Neil Pergament, Andrew Riconda, Michelle Wendy Vorob, Sara Whitely, Gayle "Kremer" Sallee, Melvyn M. Koby, J. David Lynch, Nancy Gores, Lauren Kennedy, the Kaiser Family, The Writer's Room, Vito Scalfani, Lateefah Torrence, Bernard Dunleary, John Burke, the Wheatly Family, Nancy Totten, and Hillary J. Epstein. Finally, no mention of this list of friends would be complete without acknowledging *Shyness*'s "best friend" Lisa Kaiser. As my research associate, Lisa's played a major role in helping to develop many of the important conceptual and pragmatic elements of *Shyness*. Whenever it was needed, Lisa kept asking these thought-provoking questions that helped me clarify my ideas. From her involvement with the initial book proposal and early drafts of the manuscript, Lisa's literary and intellectual contributions to *Shyness* were limitless. Shy individuals for many years to come will benefit from Lisa's creative and insightful participation with *Shyness*.

There are two other very special individuals who have become a major part of my life since I began working on *Shyness*. Elyse Cheney, my agent, was the first person to suggest the possibility of *Shyness*. Elyse guided me through the preliminary stages of this project with all of the skill, energy, and authority required to get *Shyness* up and running. At Harper-Collins, I offer my deepest gratitude to Megan Newman, my editor. Megan provided the type of support, feedback, and confidence you would hope to find in an editor, but always expect in a true friend. It pleases me to say that while working on *Shyness*, Megan exceeded my expectations in the former and has also become the latter. To work with such a friend has been a joy.

All of these friends have contributed to *Shyness* in their own special way. To all of them I say, Thanks. I couldn't have done it without you.

—BJC

Introduction

If you are shy, you're not alone. One of the tricks shyness plays on the mind is that it creates feelings of isolation. But shy people are not alone. They make up almost half of the population, and about 95 percent of us know first-hand what it means to be shy in some situations. We also know that shyness is not simply defined as "the failure to respond appropriately in social situations," as it once had. It's not introversion, being tongue-tied, having stage fright, or being a wallflower. *Shyness* addresses these and many other myths and misinformation about shyness by examining and synthesizing what is known about shyness in a practical manner that will make it possible for you to use this information in your own everyday living experiences. By providing a deep understanding of shyness and explaining now to use this information, *Shyness* will enlighten and empower people who feel they're cut off from the world.

Shyness will also challenge shy people to speak for themselves. Along with explanations of real-life shy experiences, I'll provide coping strategies for shy people to expand their comfort zone in the most common but significant interactions, such as parenting, dating, public speaking, working, traveling, and exploring the Net. *Shyness* will provide you with the basic principles of understanding the unique expression of your shyness.

Part I of *Shyness* presents a personalistic view of shyness by focusing on the general experience of shyness. It will deal with the most frequently asked questions about shyness, help you assess your own shyness, unravel common myths and misconceptions about shyness, present a new view on shyness to help you understand your shyness, and provide you with strategies to respond successfully to your shyness.

Part II presents a holistic view of shyness by addressing shyness of the body, mind, and self. It discusses how the body can create shy symptoms, the errors in thinking associated with shyness of the mind, the personal misconceptions that contribute to shyness of the self, and effective alternative responses to these three dimensions of shyness.

Part III presents a life cycle view of shyness by exploring the possibility of being born shy, the expression of shyness during childhood and adolescence, and the turmoil of shyness in adulthood. Strategies for parenting the shy child, understanding and helping the shy teen, and navigating those social situations that most often produce shyness in adults are presented.

Part IV presents a world view of shyness by discussing shyness in the context of love, work, culture, and technology. Strategies for establishing and maintaining intimate relationships, responding to daily interactions with coworkers, adjusting to cultural diversity, and meeting the challenges of rapid changes in technology are presented.

As you can see, *Shyness* is not just about shyness. It is about *your* shyness and how to understand and respond successfully to it personally, holistically, developmentally, and globally. Such an approach demonstrates an appreciation for the true complexity of shyness and reflects my belief that shy individuals can live, work, and love successfully by continuously expanding their comfort zone in an ever-changing global environment.

If you are shy or live, work, or are in love with a shy person, *Shyness* has much to offer you. Let's begin your journey into *Shyness: A Bold New Approach.*

Welcome to the Successfully Shy Life

"When I speak to someone, I usually get nervous and uncomfortable. I talk very fast, mumble my words, stutter. I don't talk loud enough for others to hear, so I'm constantly repeating myself."

"I egotistically take other people to be noticing and criticizing my behavior much more than they probably do. I set excessively high standards for myself, expecting a smoothness, quality, and ease of interaction that a nonshy person wouldn't dream of expecting."

"When I was younger, I was very quiet with strangers and in social situations. I was a completely different person when I was with my family and friends. I have a great sense of humor and a lot of personality that seemed to disappear in public. Today there is an ongoing struggle and inner badgering during social situations."

"Life is hell, when you cannot even talk because of fear of saying something dumb."

"When I was younger, people thought I was stuck-up, and they didn't like me. That hurt a lot."

"A couple of years ago, I had gum surgery. I found this prospect less nerve-wracking than going to a party that was held at about the same time!"

These are the voices of people whose shyness causes them pain and limits their choices. But shyness is a multidimensional, multifaceted personality trait. Since no two shy people are alike, your experience of shyness need not be as distressing. Throughout this book, you will hear from other individuals who, like yourself, are trying to understand their shyness in order to live a successfully shy life.

How does one lead a successfully shy life? It doesn't mean becoming an extrovert. Rather it means understanding how shyness influ-

ences the most important aspects of your daily life and what you can do about it. Living the successfully shy life is no different from other successes; it is full of risks and possibilities, new experiences and defeats, challenges and rewards.

Part I of this book will give you a basic understanding of shyness in general and help you interpret your own unique experience. In Chapter 1 we will deal with the most frequently asked questions about shyness in order to penetrate its mysteries. In Chapter 2 the Shy Life Survey will help you explore the various dimensions of your own shyness; such self-awareness is the first step toward self-confidence and living a successfully shy life.

In Chapter 3 we will investigate and debunk the most common myths and misconceptions about shyness. Interestingly, I have found that shy individuals in particular give these much credence, seriously hindering their ability to live successfully shy lives.

Chapter 4 offers a new view of shyness based on three underlying principles. These principles can form the basis for decisions you make to ensure that you live a successfully shy life.

Shyness is not about changing you; it's about helping you understand the unique experience of your shyness. Reading it will be like any other life-altering journey—starting a new job, visiting a foreign country, moving to a new neighborhood, initiating a romance. You may feel a sense of uncertainty but also hope and excitement. I am here to offer you a road map and serve as your guide.

Welcome to Shyness: A Bold New Approach.

Penetrating the Mysteries of Shyness

Shyness, one of the most common of human experiences, is fraught with mysteries. Consider the following little-known facts:

- Shy children tend to have narrower faces than their extroverted peers.

- Shy people are more likely to suffer from allergies and hay fever than nonshy people. They also have a more highly attuned sense of smell.

- Shy people are more apt to be conceived during August and September, when the days get shorter and the nights longer.

- Shy Caucasian children are more inclined to have blue eyes than brown eyes, and outgoing Caucasian children are more inclined to have brown eyes than blue.

- We humans aren't the only species to experience shyness. Scientists have been studying shy cattle as well as shy cats, shy fish, and shy dogs.

- Shyness varies from country to country. Israeli children seem to be the least shy, while Japanese and Taiwanese kids are the most.

- Most shyness is hidden. Only a small percentage of shy people appear to be obviously ill at ease. Hiding one's shyness, however, does not lessen the suffering it causes.

- People as diverse and successful as Robert Frost, Eleanor Roosevelt, Bob Dole, Al Gore, Carol Burnett, Johnny Mathis, Barbara Walters, Johnny Carson, David Letterman, Barbara Hershey, Jennifer Jason Leigh, Sting, Prince Albert of Monaco, and the late Princess Diana—the smart, the bold, the beautiful, the rich, the royal, and the famous—have all identified themselves as shy.

These are among the most perplexing and fascinating aspects of this complex human trait. Most of us have encountered shyness in our everyday lives—hating the first few days of kindergarten, sulking in our rooms as teenagers because we were afraid to ask a girl on a date, getting tongue-tied when meeting someone new, suffering a bad case of the jitters before a big presentation. Shyness impacts all of us—nearly half the population describes itself as being shy—and between 75 and 95 percent of us have been shy at some point in our lives.

Shy tendencies are universal because it's human nature to be cautious; to fear rejection; to want love, affection, and acceptance; and to retreat into isolation when we're pressured by the demands of the outside world. Many shy people have found ways to lead successfully shy lives despite these inhibiting tendencies, while others continually choose to act on their shy feelings and lament their dwindling social lives.

Although shyness can be alienating, it doesn't make us Martians. In fact, shyness is so pervasive that it can no longer be considered a "social disease" as it once was; rather it is a complex personality trait that is part of our humanness.

But pervasive as it is, it is still steeped in mystery and often in pain. Indeed, whether it's at a wedding reception, on an airplane, or at a casual dinner party, when people discover that I am a shyness expert, they confess their own shyness and then invariably besiege me with questions: What is shyness? What causes it? Are we born shy, or do we acquire it later in life? Is there a cure?

Based on my twenty-plus years of research in the field of personality psychology, my reading and understanding of the research of others, and my correspondence with thousands of people who call themselves shy, *Shyness* will attempt to penetrate some of the mysteries of shyness by answering these and many other questions.

What Is Shyness?

Although there are many theories, nobody knows exactly what shyness is. And despite studying this trait for more than two decades, I too continue to be baffled and awed by its power. Shyness can evolve through the life span and permeate all aspects of your existence: career plans, aspirations, and performance; courtship and marriage; child rearing; even your use of technology. It changes as you mature and encounter new challenges and, for many, is simply a way of life.

What we commonly identify as shyness is usually the discomfort and behavioral inhibition that occurs in the presence of others. It appears most obviously as silence. Bashfulness. Blushing. Stammering. Anxiety. The term *inhibition* describes the overt shy behavior that we can actually observe: being quiet and staying away from people and stimulating environments.

According to Harvard scholar Jerome Kagan, shy people become inhibited when they get stuck on the newness, the unfamiliarity of social situations. They worry about how they'll perform and how strangers will perceive them in these uncontrollable, unpredictable settings. In fact, many shy people adhere to strict routines made up of the tried and true in order to reduce the uncertainty and novelty in their daily lives. This evasive tactic creates safety, but it also limits life experiences and does nothing to alleviate shyness.

Social anxiety is another aspect of shyness. This is the apprehension provoked *before* a social situation when you want to make a good impression on a real or imagined audience but doubt that you can. Although shyness includes this preperformance anxiety (a kind of social stage fright), it also encompasses behavior, thoughts, and feelings during and after interactions.

People often confuse shyness with introversion, but introverts are not necessarily shy. They have the conversation skills and self-esteem necessary for interacting successfully with others but simply prefer being by themselves. They feel energized by solitude, and they don't become anxious or self-critical when they're with others. The performance anxiety, self-consciousness, and self-defeating thoughts so common among the shy may not occur in introverts. Shy people, on the other hand, want desperately for others to notice and accept them, but they seem to lack skills and the thoughts, feelings, and attitudes that could help them manage social interactions.

This desire to be with other people is called sociability. Just because you are shy doesn't mean that you're not sociable; in fact, this is where many problems arise. It is the conflict between the desire for social contact and the inhibition that causes so much pain. Your sociability may influence how much you *want* to be with others but not how you handle that contact.

Shyness is also not a social disease such as social phobia or avoidant personality disorder. These mental illnesses interfere with daily life; people who suffer from them simply cannot be with others and are usually treated with medication and psychotherapy. Shyness is not listed in the *Diagnostic and Statistical Manual of Mental Disorders–IV* (which mental health professionals use when diagnosing their patients) because it's not a mental illness, merely a normal facet of personality. Shy people do not, for the most part, try to avoid others but

rather seek them out despite having difficulty making connections.

In truth, shyness is so much more than not being able to
make small talk at a cocktail party, or being afraid of public
speaking, or having low self-esteem. It affects an array of behaviors, thoughts, and emotions. It goes far deeper and feels
more intense than its rather simple end result—reticence.

Shyness affects your whole being—your body, your mind,
and your self. When you are feeling shy, your pulse races and
your hands become cold and clammy while your cheeks flame
with embarrassment and your stomach churns. Your mind is
also working overtime. Your thoughts turn obsessively on how
you are handling the current social interaction—to such a degree that you can't pay attention to what is actually being
said, and so you can't participate. Shyness influences how you
think about yourself, your identity. You feel a wall between
yourself and others. It becomes a defining characteristic, a
part of your self.

Jenny, a Canadian homemaker, described to me in painful
detail her experience of shyness:

> My shyness is expressed in the most agonizing way. I
> want to reach out and make contact, and be acknowl-
> edged as a member of the human race, but I just don't
> seem to be able to break through the barrier. Even when
> people try to be friendly and reassuring, I have a hard
> time making eye contact. When it comes to friendly con-
> versation, my mind goes blank. I stand there mute, filled
> with misery. If any words are jarred loose, they come out
> fragmented or incoherent. Most of the time I don't say
> anything, and then I come home ready to explode with
> all the things that were left unsaid. My frustration is so
> great at times.

Because so much of shyness is infused with the human
soul, scholars may never really understand it through standard

research procedures. We may only be able to grasp it by listening to shy people like Jenny. In fact, the best definition of shyness is completely subjective: *if you think you're shy, you are.* When it comes to shyness, perception is reality, and each perception is as unique as each individual.

What Causes Shyness?

There is no one cause of shyness but many diverse causes including brain chemistry and reactivity (we could think of this as inborn temperament), harsh treatment from teachers or classmates, overprotective parents, faulty self-perceptions, poor adaptability, intolerance for ambiguity, physical appearance, life transitions (such as going away to school, divorce, a new job), and even cultural expectations. And some people are simply more sensitive about their behavior and are more easily embarrassed than others—I call this the embarrassability factor.

Shyness comes from an interweaving of nature and nurture; it evolves as we grow older and face new circumstances and challenges. Some people go through shy phases; some grow out of it; others, through disappointment, loss, or other turbulence, simply give up hope and withdraw.

Shyness will explore all of the known causes of shyness, identify what they have in common, and help you seek out the deeper meaning of shyness for yourself in the real world.

Are People Born Shy?

Absolutely not. And there's no "shy gene," either. Since shyness is related to self-consciousness, the earliest it can emerge is at about age two, when children become aware of themselves as distinct entities. Psychologists call this realization having a "sense of self." Infants don't yet have a sense of self, so they cannot be shy.

Some babies, however, are highly reactive. They are extremely sensitive to stimulation and become distressed when they feel overwhelmed by unfamiliar people, objects, or situations. But even this innate temperamental tilt toward shyness doesn't doom you to a life of social aversion. Much depends on parenting and life experience. Shyness has its roots in neurobiology—the functioning of the brain. At least three brain centers orchestrate the whole-body response we recognize as feeling shy. You can think of it as an overgeneralized fear response. I will cover these issues in greater detail in Chapters 5 and 8.

Is There a Cure?

There is no pill or magic therapy to cure shyness because it is not a disease. Nor is shyness a character defect that should be repaired. There is no specific cause of shyness that can be identified and eliminated. Still, you can overcome shyness at your own pace and don't need to be clinically diagnosed and treated—even if you think your case is more acute than anybody else's. Once you put your shyness in perspective you will have more confidence in your ability to cope with it.

At worst, shyness is a source of personal discomfort stemming from the choices you make. Throughout this book I will explain how you can make choices that will reduce your shyness and its corresponding discomfort, and how you can help your children, loved ones, friends, and coworkers if they are shy.

To fully understand shyness, we need to consider its consequences—its costs and its value.

The High Cost of Shyness

Shyness seems un-American. We are, after all, the land of the free and the home of the brave. From the first settlers and explorers who came to these shores five hundred years ago to our leadership in space exploration, America has always been associated with courageous and adventurous people ready to go where others fear to tread. Our culture still values rugged individualism. Personal attributes held in high social esteem include leadership, assertiveness, dominance, charisma, independence, and courage. Hence, the stigma associated with shyness.

In our society we give the most attention to people who are verbally expressive, active, and sociable. We single out as heroes and heroines athletes, politicians, television personalities, rock stars—experts at calling attention to themselves: Madonna, Howard Stern, Roseanne, Dennis Rodman. People who are most likely to be successful are those who are able to grab attention and feel comfortable with it.

What shy people want least is to be the center of attention. The shy elementary schoolchild may not ask the teacher for help. The shy college student is reluctant to pose a question in class. In adulthood the shy employee is too embarrassed to make a formal presentation to those who grant promotions and the shy suitor is too mortified to be the first one out on the dance floor. In every case, shyness undermines the ability to access the attention of those who could contribute to success. In a culture where everybody loves a winner, being shy is like entering a foot race with lead insoles.

Consider the findings of Stanford Business School professor Thomas Harrell. To figure out the best predictors of success in business, he gathered the records of Stanford Business School graduates, including their transcripts and letters of recommendation. Ten years out of school, the graduates were ranked from most to least successful based on the quality of their jobs.

Harrell found that the only consistent and significant predictor of success (among students who were, admittedly, bright to begin with) was verbal fluency—exactly what the typical tongue-tied shy person can't muster. The verbally fluent are able to sell themselves, their services, their companies—all critical skills for running a corporation. Think of Lee Iacocca. Shy people are probably those behind the scenes, designing the cars, programs, and computers—impressive feats but jobs that don't pay as well as CEO.

But the costs of shyness cut deeper than material success, and they take on different forms throughout your lifetime.

A shy childhood may result in a series of lost opportunities. Consider the youngster who wants to play soccer but can't muster the wherewithal to become part of a group. If his parents don't find a way to help him overcome his apprehension around others, he may slip into more solitary activities, even though he wants to be social. This further reduces the likelihood of his developing social skills and self-confidence.

Shy kids often endure teasing and rejection. Because they are so reactive, they make perfect targets for bullies. Who better to taunt than someone who gets scared easily and cries?

Shyness can predispose one to distorted thinking. Isolated people allow their fears and feelings to fester or escalate. There is no one around to correct their faulty thinking.

Loneliness is a natural consequence of having spent decades shunning others due to the angst of socializing. Isolation can lead to mental and physical decline. In fact, recent research has shown that having a diverse social network may boost the immune system and even prevent colds!

Shyness brings with it the potential for abusing alcohol and drugs as social lubricants. Philip Zimbardo of Stanford University has found that shy adolescents feel more peer pressure to drink or use drugs than do less shy adolescents. They abuse these substances in order to feel less self-conscious and to achieve a greater sense of acceptance.

Shyness is linked to sexual difficulties. Since shy people have a hard time expressing themselves, communicating sexual needs and desires is especially difficult. Performance anxiety may also make the prospect of sex overwhelming. Because shy people tend to avoid seeking help, any problems created by embarrassment or self-doubt will likely go untreated.

Shy people waste time deliberating and hesitating in social situations. As a post office clerk in his late forties told me, "When I feel shy I can't think, and if I do think of something to say, I want to say it at exactly the right time, and by then the right time has passed." According to Zimbardo, part of the problem lies in the fact that those who are shy don't live in the present but are obsessed with the past and the future. A shy person in conversation is likely to be thinking about how past conversations have initially gone well and then deteriorated. As Dr. Zimbardo says, "These are people who cannot enjoy the moment because everything is packaged in worries from the past—a Smithsonian archive of the bad—that restructures the present." They may also worry about the future consequences of their words: "If I ask him where he's from, will he get bored and think I'm stupid?"

Sadly, many shy people settle for less in life because they don't know how to break free. One fifty-year-old woman wrote to me, "I am afraid to get a new job because then I will have to prove myself, and I'm afraid the employers and employees will not like me. Also, because I don't think I will get hired, I stay in a job that is boring and unfulfilling. I am being stifled."

And a young psychology student in Canada wrote, "Shyness is basically ruining my chances of being happy and successful, of having a good job and getting married. It's depressing and painful."

A "stifled" or "ruined" life is a terrible price to pay for a personality trait that can be modified. And, with different choices, it *can* be modified. As a retired secretary in New York wrote to me, "Age has given me wisdom to mostly overcome my shyness. Many years ago, I realized that I was blessed with an angel husband, terrific family and friends, and was healthy, good-looking, clean, honest, decent, intelligent, and a loyal person. So to heck with this shyness!"

The Hidden Value of Shyness

Despite the pain it causes, shyness must have had some positive function for the evolution of mankind or it would not have endured as a personality trait.

Some scholars have tied shyness to the fight-or-flight instinct, our physical reaction to threat. Eons ago, this instinct helped us respond to physical predators—a charging buffalo or a roaring bear. Our ancestors had two options: they could throw a spear or they could flee. While a more aggressive individual might attack the threatening beast, the caution inherent in fleeing has an important survival function. No doubt, shyness has pulled us out of many a confrontation with dangerous beasts.

While the fight-or-flight instinct still benefits contemporary, highly evolved humans by protecting us from modern physical threats like an out-of-control, swerving car, it also affects our responses to mental or emotional threats that could harm our personal identity or self-esteem. For example, we might feel threatened by a grouchy boss, a beautiful woman at a nightclub, a snooty wine steward in a fancy restaurant, or a new coworker. We may fear that these people could reject us or make us feel inadequate, and so we are cautious around them. Instinctively, we sense that approaching them is in some way perilous to our self-image and dignity.

According to psychologist Jonathan Cheek of Wellesley College, situational shyness (such as being shy when first encountering a new coworker or a beautiful woman) "can help to facilitate cooperative living; it inhibits behaviors that are socially unacceptable." In short, it keeps us in line. Most of us show some degree of social inhibition; we think about what we are going to say or do and the consequences of our behavior in advance. This prevents us from making fools of ourselves or hurting others' feelings.

Shy people seem to be highly attuned to their mistakes and

the effects of their behavior and words, but this too may be valuable. Consider what happens when people are insensitive to these issues: they offend others, dominate conversations, and disclose too much of their personal lives. They may even lie while looking you in the eye because they don't care about the consequences of their actions. Frankly, our society would be a free-for-all if we didn't have some sense of personal accountability and a healthy fear of shame.

Upon making a faux pas, a shy person may retreat. This can be beneficial too, especially if he retreats to spend time with people he's comfortable with, those who accept him unconditionally. If he confides in them about his mistakes and insecurities, he builds intimacy. He can ask for advice, rehearse an apology or strategy, or perhaps just get a reality check. Who knows—maybe a friend will tell him that the "mistake" was not a mistake after all.

A retreat can be helpful if used wisely and constructively, as an opportunity to privately evaluate what we did wrong, regroup, and evolve a new plan of action. It can be a chance for learning and self-reflection. None of us wants to repeat our mistakes. It should not, however, be a time to berate ourselves.

Shy people are often gifted listeners. If they can get over their self-induced pressures for witty repartee, they can be great at conversation because they may actually be paying attention. (The hard part comes when a response is expected.) Doreen Arcus at Harvard University explains that shy children are likely to be especially responsive. Parents of the children she studies tell her that "even in infancy, the shy child seemed to be sensitive, empathic, and a good listener. They seem to make really good friends, and their friends are very loyal to them and value them quite a bit."

A thirty-two-year-old library technician in Indiana wrote to me about how she finds shyness a desirable trait. "While I don't like shyness in myself, I think it's an attractive quality in others. I like shy people, perhaps because they're easier for me to approach and relate to."

For any society to function well, a variety of roles need to be played. There is a place for the quiet, more reflective shy individual who does not jump in where angels fear to tread or attempt to steal the limelight from others. Not all of us can be leaders or explorers—the majority of us must hang back and be part of the crowd. Shy people, for the most part, make up the rational, cautious mass of us that puts the brakes on the wild impulses of our society. Shy people such as Robert Frost or Eleanor Roosevelt watch and wait and analyze, and their observations help us understand our public selves and our souls.

A little bit of shyness may be good for you and society. But too much of it benefits no one.

How This Book Can Help

Shyness is about the choices and chances, the possibilities and opportunities, the risks and rewards that are part of life not only for shy people but for all of us. I will emphasize choices that will help you lead a successfully shy life. But let's make a distinction between changing yourself and changing your choices. I am not asking you to put on a mask in public or ignore your instincts. However, I do want you to make wise choices. Right now, shyness may be in control of your life; it makes all of your decisions. That is neither fair nor honest. More important, it's not the way life has to be lived.

Changing lifelong shy behavior is not an easy task, and you should expect some initial discomfort. But success is possible. I've seen it time and again. You can make better decisions in your everyday life by using strategies that will help you with immediate challenges and long-term dreams.

To do so, follow the steps I call the Four *I*'s: identification, information, incorporation, and implementation.

Identification

If you go to an auto mechanic and simply complain, "My car is broken," he won't be able to fix it. "Broken" could mean anything from the transmission to the carburetor to the timing belt. How can he change what he does not understand or recognize? If you explain, however, that the car doesn't start, it narrows the possibilities so he can take some course of action—he'll check the battery, the starter, and the fuses.

The same can be said for helping yourself overcome your shyness. How can you change what you don't understand? Before you begin, you need to be sure you're trying to fix the right thing. The first step is to identify how shyness affects your life and personality.

One shy man told me, "I'm socially incompetent. I'll never get anywhere. I've just given up on women." He then launched into a lengthy discussion of his shyness-induced frustrations: women start to fidget and look around the room after a few minutes of conversation with him, he never gets a second date, and he's lonely.

After listening to him go on about his problems, which he believed were inborn and intractable, I realized that he wasn't socially incompetent at all. He knew how to converse with people at work, he had many male friends and seemed to get along well with others. He simply wasn't good at talking to women he found attractive. In these situations he became obsessed with impressing them and sounded like a brash yet tongue-tied know-it-all. No wonder women rejected him.

I told him, "As I see it, you're trying too hard to make a good impression. You want to live up to some ideal so that you'll be liked, but the side effect is that you're also plagued by evaluation apprehension. You're anxious and think that you're socially incompetent because you're *acting*. Face it, if you're putting on an act just to make a good impression, you'll have to continue acting throughout the relationship. It's just not worth it. Besides, it's an impossible task. You can't act all the time."

The Shy Life Survey in Chapter 2 will help you identify the areas in your life most affected by shyness. This is a great first step in your quest for understanding and change.

Information

You need dependable information, such as the research I'll be presenting in this book. Shyness is not immutable. You can work with it and change your behavior, thoughts, and emotions. Information that dispels the myths about shyness can help you sort through what is real about your situation and what is not. Ultimately, appropriate information will help you make decisions about how to change your behavior.

Incorporation

It's important to incorporate the truth about shyness into your life decisions, no matter how big or small. Incorporation means increasing your self-awareness. You don't want to deny, run away from, or be obsessed with your shyness. Rather, it's most helpful to incorporate shyness into who you are—your sense of self. Once you have this self-awareness you will be in a better position to make good choices.

Implementation

Once you have identified the problem, obtained reliable information, and created potential strategies, you are ready for the final step—taking action to put yourself in control of your shyness. Indeed, it's not enough to know what to do and how to do it; you also have to tolerate change.

Change can be difficult at first, but throughout the book I will tell you how to take action. I will also show how the Four *I*'s apply to real-world situations that may create problems for you on the job, at parties, in the classroom, and in intimate relationships.

A Word About Change

When we try a new way of being—quitting smoking, going on a diet, starting a new job—we may get off to a fast start because we're motivated, but find that within hours or days the going gets rough. This is when we experience nicotine fits, chocolate cravings, or anxiety and reach for the cigarette or Hershey bar or retreat to our cubicle. Such regressive behavior is easy, but it's often a bad idea.

In dealing with shyness, it's important to remember that behavior and feelings can worsen before they improve. It's natural to feel uncomfortable as we warm up to a new way of being. If we try to speak to new people, we may feel even more self-conscious than usual because we're attempting an activity that feels different and unfamiliar.

We regress not because our willpower is weak or because we don't know what to do. We just don't expect our new lease on life to be so difficult. Because our expectations are unrealistic, we don't anticipate problems and consequently fail to create coping strategies to get us through the rough times. When our intense discomfort catches us by surprise, we simply give up and scurry back to the relative safety of our old ways.

With time and determination, however, you will find that if you make it past these initial setbacks, change becomes easier. Perhaps you should take a lesson from toddlers who are learning how to walk. It would be so much easier for them to continue crawling than to keep falling down when they pull themselves up on wobbly legs and take those first faltering steps. But, with support from a loving family and the sense of perseverance at the core of all our beings, babies learn to walk and then to run. Crawling, although relatively effortless, is much less satisfying.

If you are determined to deal effectively with your shyness, you may make it through your first encounter with a stranger without overwhelming anxiety. But the second or third encounter may feel uncomfortable and awkward. You shouldn't stop there, however, because you've just been through the worst. The fourth conversation may be easier, but you'll never know until you *get there*. Unfortunately, many shy people give up before they make it that far.

Hope for a Successful Shy Life

It's time for you to begin living a successful shy life—a life that does not ignore the pain and suffering that shyness can create but that incorporates realistic and rational alternatives. We will consider the complexity and pervasiveness of shyness in its entirety, from infancy through your adult relationships with family, friends, teachers, lovers, coworkers, bosses; from issues of career, culture, and technology.

This book is a dose of reality, an antidote to the misperceptions of shyness. I'll bring together a range of perspectives—historical, academic, medical, cultural, and psychological—to give context to practical advice. I will explain shyness from its possible genetic origins to its broadest social ramifications, using sources ranging from scientific studies to the personal accounts of shy individuals. I will dispel misunderstandings about this pervasive, almost universal feature of personality and give you the information, insights, and strategies to better understand and accept yourself. Together we will solve many mysteries about shyness so that you can break its cycle and begin living a healthy, successful shy life.

I will speak for people who are too shy to speak for themselves. This book is a lesson in life for all shy people and those who live, work, and play with them; who counsel them; who love them. I'm confident that once you understand the truth about what it means to be shy, you will be better equipped to break free.

I would like you to become more aware and accepting of yourself and your shyness, to trust your own perceptions and value your feelings. Shyness is not about who you are or what others believe about you. It is about the choices you make and the actions you take. Above all, to lead a successful shy life, you must trust yourself to make new choices and act with confidence.

Identifying Your Shyness

As you read this book, you might wish to keep a Shy Life journal. This can help you pinpoint when you feel most shy and note what you do about it. You can analyze situations, rehearse alternative behaviors and thoughts, and track your triumphs as you take steps to achieve a successfully shy life. Throughout the book, I will suggest writing exercises for your journal. You can begin by jotting down your answers to the Shy Life Survey.

Shyness is too rich, complex, and personal an issue to capture in a single score. The purpose of this survey is to help you understand your shyness, rather than to rate, categorize, or classify it.

This survey first appeared (in a shorter form) in an article I wrote for *Psychology Today* in 1995, in collaboration with Philip Zimbardo. We brought together the most recent findings on shyness to date, and asked readers to complete this questionnaire and mail it to me.

Quite simply, the article hit a nerve. Between 1979 and 1994, I had collected data on shyness from more than 1,800 individuals. Suddenly, as a result of this article, more than 1,000 responses flooded into my office within a month. They were full of startling, visceral insights and were often accompanied by personal notes begging for help. My analysis of the information gathered from all of these surveys forms the backbone of this book.

The Shy Life Survey can be your first step in coming to grips with your shyness. By answering the questions truthfully, you will begin to identify how shyness affects your life and personality. As you read further in this book, refer back to this survey as both a means of identification and a resource for information to help with your incorporation and implementation.

The Shy Life Survey

Please answer the following questions as honestly as possible.

Part I

Circle the answer that best fits your situation.

1. Do you consider yourself to be a shy person?
   yes   no

2. If yes, have you always been shy (were you shy previously and still are)?
   yes   no

3. If no to question 1, was there ever a prior time in your life when you were shy?
   yes   no

4. How often do you experience (or have you experienced) feelings of shyness?
   a. Every day
   b. Almost every day
   c. Often, nearly every other day
   d. Once or twice a week
   e. Occasionally, less than once a week
   f. Rarely, once a month or less

5. Compared with your peers (of similar age, sex, and background), how shy are you?
   a. Much more shy
   b. More shy
   c. About as shy

   d. Less shy

   e. Much less shy

6. How desirable is it for you to be shy?
   a. Very undesirable

   b. Undesirable

   c. Neither

   e. Desirable

   f. Very desirable

7. Is (or was) your shyness ever a personal problem for you?
   a. Yes, often

   b. Yes, sometimes

   c. Yes, occasionally

   d. Rarely

   e. Never

8. What types of people make you shy? Circle all that apply.
   a. My parents

   b. My siblings

   c. Other relatives

   d. Friends

   e. Strangers

   f. Foreigners

   g. Authorities by virtue of their knowledge (intellectual superiors, experts)

   h. Authorities by virtue of their role (police officers, teachers, superiors at work)

   i. Elderly people (who are much older than me)

   j. Children (who are much younger than me)

   k. Persons of the opposite sex, in a group

   l. Persons of the opposite sex, one-to-one

m. Persons of the same sex, in a group

n. Persons of the same sex, one-to-one

9. What do you believe is the cause of your shyness? Circle all that apply.

    a. Born shy

    b. Emotional abuse

    c. Physical abuse

    d. Overprotective parents

    e. Faulty/inconsistent parental discipline

    f. Negative emotional experience(s) involving peers during my childhood

    g. Negative emotional experience(s) involving individuals of authority (teachers, coaches, etc.) during my childhood

    h. Being forced to engage in certain public activities as a child (dance or music recitals, sports, plays)

    i. Family disruption (death of a parent, frequent moves)

    j. Other siblings

    k. Parents' divorce

    l. Parent(s) remarrying

    m. Negative emotional experiences during my young adulthood involving peers (roommates, classmates, sororities/fraternities, coworkers)

    n. Being easily embarrassed

    o. Negative emotional experiences during my young adulthood involving individuals in positions of authority (professors, supervisors)

    p. Lack of social skills

    q. Lack of confidence

    r. Being easily overwhelmed

    s. Shy parents

    t. Excessive self-consciousness

    u. Perfectionistic, critical, or demanding parent(s)

    v. Withdrawn or disinterested parent of the opposite sex

   w. Withdrawn or disinterested parent of the same sex

    x. Other explanations not listed above

Explain:_____

_____

_____

    y. Do not know what caused my shyness

10. In what areas of your personal life has shyness created a problem for you?
- a. Meeting new people
- b. Making friends
- c. Dating
- d. Establishing intimate relationships
- e. Other areas of my personal life:

_____

_____

_____

11. In what areas of your educational life has your shyness created problems for you?
- a. Speaking up in class
- b. Participating in student organizations/sports
- c. Planning or attending school-sponsored events (dances, games, rallies)
- d. Asking for letters of recommendation
- e. Seeking advice/assistance from teachers outside of class
- f. Asking questions during class
- g. Participating in group discussions, projects
- h. Giving a presentation to the class
- i. Making friends with classmates
- j. Asking for help from other classmates

     k. Studying with other classmates

     l. Other areas of my educational life:

     _____

     _____

     _____

12. In what areas of your professional life has shyness created problems for you?

     a. Talking to coworkers

     b. Speaking up at meetings

     c. Asking for a promotion and/or raise

     d. Socializing with coworkers at lunch or after work

     e. Socializing with clients

     f. Expressing my ideas privately to coworkers or clients

     g. Public presentations to coworkers or clients

     h. Participation in professional organizations and/or networking groups

     i. Outreach. Promoting my business or services among those who do not know me

     j. Other areas of my professional life:

     _____

     _____

     _____

13. Do you think your shyness can be overcome?

     yes   no   uncertain

14. Are you willing to seriously work at overcoming it?

     a. Yes, definitely

     b. Yes, perhaps

     c. Not sure

     d. No

15. What actions have you already taken to overcome your shyness? Circle all that apply.

a. Tried to go out to meet people (nightclubs, dances, singles events, parties, coffeehouses, bookstores)

b. Tried to make conversation with individuals I don't know but would like to

c. Read self-help books

d. Had individual therapy

e. Joined a fitness or recreational club or organization (tennis club, softball team, sailing club, gym, hiking group such as the Sierra Club)

f. Had group therapy

g. Visited Internet chat rooms and/or discussion groups

h. Self-medicated (consumed alcohol and/or illegal drugs)

i. Tried to change the way I think about myself

j. Changed my physical appearance

k. Attended seminars or workshops on shyness

l. Served as a volunteer

m. Joined professional organizations related to my job or career

n. Signed up with a dating or matchmaking service

o. Joined a religious or spiritual group

p. Attended self-esteem workshops or seminars

q. Underwent relaxation, meditation, or biofeedback training

r. Took prescription medications

s. Attended stress-management training

t. Other actions:

_____

_____

_____

Part II

You might wish to explore your shy experiences in greater detail. In your journal or on a separate piece of paper, answer the following questions as completely as you can.

1. Describe factors you believe have contributed to your shyness.

2. Describe how your shyness is expressed.

3. Describe what problems your shyness has created for you in your personal, social, and/or professional life.

4. Describe what you have tried to overcome your shyness.

5. Describe if and how you use the Internet to deal with your shyness.

6. Is there anything regarding your shyness that you want to know more about?

7. What else would you like to say about your shyness?

Part III

I would love to hear about your experiences with shyness. If you are willing to add to our growing body of knowledge about shy people and their lives, please send your survey results to me. Please include the following demographic information for research purposes. Of course, your responses will be kept confidential.

Age:

Date of birth:

Gender: male   female

Occupation:

Ethnic identification:

Education:

Please forward your responses to:
Bernardo J. Carducci, Ph.D.
The Shy Life Enrichment Institute
P.O. Box 8064
New Albany, IN 47151-8064
E-mail/website: www.carducci.com/shylife

Shyness Myths and Misinformation

Throughout my many years of studying and working with shy people, I've found that many are limited by their own misperceptions. Their thinking often follows along these lines: "I'm shy, I can't help acting this way, and there's nothing I can do about it. It's my destiny to be wary and nervous around people. I have no alternative but to feel shy, an alien in human society who cannot be among others. And forget about meeting new people! I can't function when I'm with them; I can't reveal who I really am. It's too risky, so I keep to myself. Why set myself up for the inevitable rejection when other people realize that I'm not very good company? The best option is to withdraw."

This is just not true. If you are shy, you have options—*including the option not to act on your shyness*. You aren't an antisocial weirdo; you're merely opting to act on your shy tendencies and buying into the many myths about shyness that abound in our society.

These myths confuse all of us about shyness. More important, when you believe them and incorporate them into your sense of identity, they become the source of much pain and discomfort. These myths can turn you into a "shy person," someone who must behave in a certain way and live a certain lifestyle to remain true to them. And that hurts you because it's dishonest and limiting.

By exposing some of the most common myths about shyness, we can begin to repair the damage they cause and replace them with the truth.

"Quiet, complacent babies are shy. They will always be shy because they were born that way."

You may conjure up images of docile, subdued babies and believe they are shy, but they aren't. In truth, those most likely to grow up shy are highly reactive and quite vocal infants. Moreover, there are no "natural-born shy people." People can be *predisposed* to shyness, but it's not necessarily their fate to be shy all their lives.

As I explained in Chapter 1, shyness involves a sense of self, otherwise known as a self-concept, identity, or self-awareness. To be shy, you must have an identity that you can compare with other people. This is a complex intellectual task, because you must think: "I'm me, and I've got certain features that some people have and others don't; you're you, and some of your features are the same as mine while others are different."

This inkling of an independent self must be present before a child can be shy or, for that matter, have any other personality characteristic. It emerges when a youngster is about fifteen to eighteen months old. That's when she looks in a mirror and realizes that the image she sees is, in fact, her. She is no longer an extension of her parents or siblings.

But having a sense of self and being able to make comparisons are only the first steps toward acquiring shyness. Self-consciousness—concern about others' evaluations of you and your actions—appears at about two or three years of age. Before this, an infant will burp whenever she wants to, or cry whenever she feels sad or frustrated. She doesn't care how others react to her outbursts, so she lets loose when she feels she must. Young toddlers are not little savages, they're merely people free of self-consciousness.

As every parent knows, kids get into a battle of the wills when the terrible twos arrive. This is not stubbornness but the child's emerging understanding of what it means to be self-conscious. Two-year-olds are trying to assert their will and control their actions when they become aware of how others react to their behavior. They're getting used to living by others' rules after being unencumbered by self-consciousness.

Once youngsters establish a sense of self and self-consciousness, they can be considered shy if they stay away from new people or places and become reticent about their concerns because their minds, bodies, and souls are telling them to react in this way.

"Shy children are destined to be shy adults."

Shyness is not like having blue eyes or growing to be as tall as other family members. Height and eye color are genetic—purely physical—while shyness is physical, intellectual, and emotional. The dynamics of the body, mind, and self mean that shyness is not fated.

We are all made up of various characteristics that seem intrinsic to our identity, self-expression, and view of the world. But if you look closely, you will find that some of these characteristics can be altered even though they may seem indelible and predestined.

Consider the Olympic runner. His physical makeup gives him the potential to be a champion, but that potential can't be realized without the drive and determination (from his self) and the ability to respond to his coach's training (through his mind). A runner isn't just long legs and pumping adrenaline. The best athletes are smart and dedicated, too.

The same is true for shyness. Even if one has a physical predisposition to be shy, the other elements—a shy mind and self—must also be present for a seemingly shy child to grow into a shy adult.

"Shyness is stronger than I am."

The detailed, often painful confessions and recollections of the thousands of shy people I've heard from in the course of my research reveal that many believe shyness controls their lives. Here's just a sample of what they tell me:

- "It limits me and my possibilities. I feel afraid and at the same time I know how silly it is, but I can't control the feeling of fear."

- "Shyness is like a bubble that I can't break out of."

- "Sometimes I feel like I'm trapped in a mental prison."

- "It is very unfortunate that people in our society look down on shyness. Many of us cannot help the way that we were created or raised."

Not only do many shy people believe shyness is more powerful than they are, but they feel that they're alone or that there's something inherently wrong with them. More important, they believe that they can't change.

But here is what one shy person, a sales manager, wrote to me about how she controls her shyness and anxiety: "To overcome my shyness, I started my own business and started doing retreats and workshops. I have no fear when I'm doing what I love. I'm not preoccupied with my shyness. I don't feel I suffer all that much. When I feel ill at ease, I look for a comfort zone. When I feel real nervous and blush, I smile and say I am a bit shy. Once I say it, I don't feel so alone."

You are stronger than shyness, and you can set it aside when you need to by changing how you think, feel, and behave.

"I am the only shy person I know."

Shyness is extremely common. In fact, almost half of our population claims to be shy, a percentage that has increased in the past twenty years. Perhaps more astounding is the finding that between 75 and 95 percent of us have felt shy at one point in our lives. No matter what its context or definition, almost everyone has experienced shyness. So if you're shy, you are not alone. In fact, if you stand on a crowded bus or in a movie theater and look to your left or right, chances are one of the people next to you is also shy. From my research, I have compiled some statistics on the pervasiveness of shyness:

- Almost 50 percent of our population say that they're shy.

- About 89 percent of shy people claim that they've been shy all their lives.

- Of people who are not shy now, 75 percent have been shy at some point in the past.

- Only 11 percent of our population claim that they are not shy now and have never been shy in the past.

- About 21 percent of shy people feel shy daily or almost daily, while almost 60 percent of the people who say that they're shy feel shy at least once a week.

- About 78 percent of shy people believe that they can overcome shyness, while 3 percent say that they can't.

The pervasiveness of shyness in our busy society surprises us because it's often invisible. The three most common shyness-provoking situations are

- Being around strangers

- The presence of people in positions of authority by virtue of their role or knowledge

- Being with members of the opposite sex, either one-on-one or in a group

You may think that you're the only one in the world who is shy because shyness can cause you to isolate yourself. But if you don't talk about your doubts and fears with friends, you may not realize that other people have the same feelings you do. And since you don't open up, you may not get the support you need from loved ones.

In addition, when you look at a room full of strangers, you may not notice the more reticent individuals. Instead, you zero in on the more outgoing and chatty people who seem to be able to talk to anyone, anywhere. Because you compare yourself with extroverts, you feel like a failure. So you clam up instead, never allowing yourself to relax and warm to new people.

These misperceptions and faulty comparisons can stop you in your tracks. But they are *choices*. You *choose* your thoughts, and you *choose* the people with whom you compare yourself. You can select other thoughts and courses of action to reduce the discomfort of shyness.

"Shyness is all in your head."

Shyness is not a mental defect, a personality flaw, a neurosis, or an emotional disorder. It is a characteristic feature of personality that involves the body, mind, and self of each shy individual. In fact, during uncertain situations, it arouses the whole being, right down to the smallest neurons in the brain. Because you feel uncomfortable when in the grip of shyness, you may question yourself and have conflicting emotions about your identity and self-esteem.

If shyness only occurred in your head, it would be easy to alleviate. All you would have to do is think different thoughts to put an end to your misery. But because shyness is so deeply ingrained, quick-fix remedies such as breathing exercises or thinking positive thoughts ("Go to your happy place") will never work because they are superficial. They fail to address your deepest thoughts and emotions.

You need long-term approaches that will help you get through the inevitable rough times. You need a plan that you can incorporate into your mind, body, and self to help you with the unique way in which you experience shyness.

This book does not offer simple solutions that are ultimately doomed to fail. Rather, I provide correct information and strategies that do work. I appreciate the complexity of life in the long run. I don't want to merely help you become a "social sprinter"—capable of only performing in a limited number of situations for a brief period. I want you to be like a long-distance runner who can handle any social terrain you encounter, no matter how rough or for how long.

"All shy people are alike."

Most people think they know the stereotypical shy person: the wallflower at the high school dance; the coworker who never meets your gaze; perhaps yourself, moments before you enter a party that's in full swing. But shyness has many faces.

You can feel shy inside yet present a different face to the outside world. One woman in her thirties said to me, "My shyness comes and goes depending on the situation. Most people I know refuse to believe I am shy, but I know myself well—and apparently they do not. It is at times difficult, but I deal with it and conceal it pretty well. If I were to say to someone, 'I was a nervous wreck,' they always reply, 'Well, you didn't look or act nervous.' I may not have shown it, but my insides were twisting."

Many shy people report that they're apprehensive about their behavior in public but confident about their performance on the job or their parenting skills. They just feel at sea during social situations.

They also tell me that others often mislabel them as aloof, snobby, cold, bitchy, or stuck-up. These prejudicial perceptions can make it even harder for one to express oneself with new people. For instance, a graduate student in Hawaii said,

"People say I come across as disliking them when we first meet instead of seeing me as being shy."

And a female college student in Nebraska wrote, "I know that I'm perceived to be unfriendly or even a snob. I've been told I'm attractive and look like the type who should be outgoing and confident, but that contrasts with how I am. I think of a snob as being someone who believes she is better than everyone else, and I think of a shy person like myself as being someone who thinks everyone else is better than her."

We know that shy people can be bold because we have numerous examples of "shy extroverts," a term coined by Philip Zimbardo. Consider David Letterman of late-night television fame. Although his performance in front of a live studio audience and countless viewers seems relaxed and spontaneous, Letterman is known to be relentless in the planning and orchestration of each nightly performance. He spends little time socializing outside a small circle of friends and rarely attends social functions.

Inappropriate boldness is also often a coping mechanism for shy people. As one man explained, "I attempt to hide my shyness by exhibiting hostility. I often do silly, outrageous things." Many shy people choose such self-defeating strategies. I've found that the most common is what I call forced extroversion. This means pushing yourself to go to parties or be in the company of others without having first set in place appropriate strategies to help you through.

A twenty-six-year-old male college student tried this self-defeating approach to little avail. "I tried to overcome shyness by joining clubs, going to dance clubs, walking with my head up. Nothing works. When I try to overcome my shyness, something inside of me will not let me break out."

The short-term solution of forced extroversion is often counterproductive. Going to parties will get you around people, but it doesn't give you a way to cope with your shyness in a crowd. Consequently you may become more shy and leave the situation with a sense of disillusionment and failure. You may even stop attending parties altogether and assume that you're just not meant to have a social life.

Researchers have identified several types of shyness. Each of these is associated with contrasting thoughts, behaviors, and emotions.

The Publicly Shy

"I've always been this way," said Chrissie, a wife, mother of two, and data-entry worker in the Midwest. "Ever since I was very little I was never able to talk easily. My mind goes blank, and I can't think of anything to say."

Chrissie finds it easiest to be inconspicuous. "People already know me as being quiet. It would be a big deal if I spoke up, so sometimes I just don't say anything. If I'm in a group, I feel apprehensive, nervous, and I can't sit still and relax."

Chrissie admitted that even when she does participate in conversation, she's unhappy with how she comes across. "I'm afraid of disagreeing with someone or offending them. I'm afraid of rubbing them the wrong way, I guess. It's really hard for me to make phone calls, too. I have to force myself."

Chrissie's life accommodates and reinforces her shyness. Her husband is fairly extroverted, and although she gets uncomfortable when she's with his friends, she appreciates his gregariousness. "I need someone to help me along and get me to be more talkative and outgoing," she said.

She spends her days with her kids, who are extroverted. (She's glad about that.) She works the second shift, keeping to herself most of the time. "I don't have to be outgoing at work. I can sit at my desk and not have to deal with other people. We're allowed to wear headphones so we can listen to music or the TV while we work. I don't converse too much. They're used to it, and they don't expect me to hang around with them."

Publicly shy people like Chrissie are visibly anxious. They

choose not to speak, engage in crippling internal dialogue, refuse to make eye contact, and use their shyness as an excuse to withdraw from challenges. They can be spotted a mile away. Interestingly, publicly shy people actually have more in common with attention-seeking extroverts who are overly focused on themselves and their needs. I'll explain why in Chapter 6.

The Chronically Shy

Another way to look at Chrissie's experience is to say that she is chronically shy. The chronically shy are the people who say they've been shy for as long as they can remember. In fact, they claim it's the only way they know how to live. Their lifelong recollections contribute to the myth that people are born shy because they can never recall a time when they weren't. They face shyness during most social encounters and are labeled shy by teachers, parents, friends, and loved ones. It's impossible for them to imagine a life free of shyness because it permeates everything they do, from standing in line at the grocery store to making career decisions.

Chronically shy people often lead a pained existence. From my research I have found that they experience shyness more frequently than other shy people and report being shy in significantly more situations. They perceive themselves as being more shy than their peers. They experience shyness as a personal problem more frequently and believe that they are less capable of overcoming their shyness than other people.

Although many chronically shy individuals believe that they can never change, I have found that they can.

The Privately Shy

Patrick is a fun guy. He has a lot of friends, a quick wit, and a wide smile. He was the president of his class in college, landed a good job, and is a talented swing dancer to boot.

Patrick is so good at talking; he gets paid to speak as a seminar facilitator in the public schools. But sometimes words fail him. "I just have nothing to say," he told me. "It doesn't mean that I don't like someone. I just don't want to talk when I'm feeling shy. I wonder, 'Why would they want to talk to me? I have nothing to say that would interest them.'"

Patrick's shy moods, as he calls them, follow a pattern. He likened it to what basketball players experience when they know they're going to lose. They throw the game to deny the other team the pleasure of winning. Patrick withdraws when he wants to deny himself the pleasure that he usually gets from being with others. "I'm shy when I have a bad day," he explained. "I'll get in a mood that makes me shy if something goes wrong at work, because I'll think about it a lot, and it'll just perpetuate itself."

Even though he does have some insight into why he feels shy, it still baffles him. On the one hand he claims that he has "always been extroverted," but on the other, he knows that he's shy. His friends don't understand his true feelings, either, probably because he hides them.

"If I'm in one of those moods and people notice that I'm not being outgoing and funny, I'll say, 'I'm really tired.' If I'm in a group, it's usually easier because then I'm not forced to talk. I always have something to read with me, and everyone knows that I'm an avid reader so they excuse that. If I'm at someone's apartment, I'll scan the bookshelves, and I'll even read a book if it has caught my eye. It's rude, I know, but I do it."

Privately shy people like Patrick—the shy extroverts mentioned above—can be boisterous when they're not crippled by shy thoughts. Nobody around them would suspect that they're shy, but they feel it under their skin. Many actors, talk-show hosts, politicians, teachers, and comedians are privately shy and only feel comfortable when they're playing a role with scripted dialogue.

The privately shy have learned to act outgoing—as long as they are in a controlled environment. A politician who can speak from a prepared text at a political rally may get tongue-tied during the question-and-answer period. A professor may feel comfortable as long as she is discussing her area of expertise but may freeze at a faculty meeting. As one amateur actor told me, "When I'm offstage, I am completely withdrawn. I am unable to shake the dread, and I am a nervous wreck. When onstage, I am exuberant and shot full of confidence."

The Transitionally Shy

These individuals act and feel shy during certain periods of their lives, usually when they leave one phase and begin another, such as entering college, starting a new job, or beginning to date after a divorce. This is a common and normal response to uncertain, insecure, and unpredictable situations. In these threatening circumstances, they display all of the characteristics of the publicly shy. But once they have habituated and are able to cope with their new challenges, they become less shy and more confident about themselves and their abilities.

Steve is transitionally shy. "I don't consider myself closed off to interacting," he explained while we sat in the park. "It's just that it's difficult. I can't show myself right off the bat to someone. I doesn't work for me."

Shyness is both an old and a new problem for him. He has always been shy but hasn't been troubled by it for years. On the day we spoke, however, he was feeling a bit confused. Just getting over a breakup, he was finding it hard to make connections on dates, a difficult task for anyone. He explained:

> First dates can throw me for a loop. Take last night. I had
> a first date with someone I barely knew. Initially there
> was a lot of nervousness because I was sitting there think-
> ing, "I can't connect with Wendy." In some cases, I feel a
> connection and either I think that the woman doesn't feel

it or that she's not attracted to me. I generally feel that I'm not connecting the way I ought to be, even when I know we have a lot in common, at least superficially.

But eventually, the nervousness went away. I settled down and had a good time. I think Wendy probably relaxed, too.

People who are transitionally shy are able to move in and out of their shyness as they become more comfortable with their situation.

The Successfully Shy

The successfully shy person is in control. He is aware of his shyness but doesn't let it hold him back from living a full life. He incorporates his shyness into his everyday experiences by anticipating when he'll feel shy, accepting that sometimes he will, and resolving his feelings by using strategies that will get him through the rough times. He doesn't feel bad about being shy and doesn't let it stop him from pursuing his dreams.

Matthew, a writer in his early thirties, is a successfully shy person. He has been shy for as long as he can remember. "I don't know if it's self-fulfilling or if I was just born this way," he said. "My mother claims that early on, in kindergarten, I stayed by myself and did puzzles in the corner and didn't interact with the other children. I started grade school a year late because when she first brought me in to school, I threw such a fit that I was kept out for a year."

But Matthew's tendency to be happily isolated shifted as he got older. As a teen, he needed to break out. He went from being what his mother thought of as an easygoing "sweetheart" to a wild and crazy guy just so he could abandon his shyness. "I acted like a crazy man when I was drunk," he said, "and people seemed to enjoy me more. I got a reputation in high school as being nutty and wild when I drank, so I showed a side of me that nobody really saw before."

Although they were fun, Matthew's partying days didn't last. In college he discovered that he loved to write; it enabled him to express his feelings freely. "Writing was sort of like drinking but without the alcohol. It was an outlet for me that didn't involve that much self-abuse—at least physical self-abuse," he said, laughing.

Although he considers himself to be shy in adulthood, Matthew has found ways to get through most of the rough spots. He excelled in school and won awards for his writing, found jobs in the publishing industry that fit his personality type, hung on to his good friends from the old neighborhood, and has had a string of long-term, monogamous relationships throughout his twenties. Shyness hasn't materialized much in his personal life; if he isn't writing, he is with people who understand him and accept his ways.

He also learned how to prepare himself to deal with his shyness, especially when it came to his first public reading of his work. "I practiced reading my short story out loud at home for a few weeks," he confided. "Once in the morning and once at night. I read it for some of my friends, and it was awful. The actual reading went wonderfully, in comparison. After the first page, I wasn't nervous at all. Actually, it was one of the most positive experiences I've had all year. I was terror-stricken only for the first few minutes."

Matthew was surprised to receive a lot of positive feedback from the audience, because he believed he hadn't done well. "I don't think I'm ever going to completely get over all of my nervousness, but the reading wasn't so bad, and it's something I'll have to do if I want to be a writer."

Matthew is just as philosophical about his shyness in general and how it affects his self-image. "I don't think that I'm so absorbed by shyness that it completely ruins or hurts my life," he said. "I think I've pretty much accepted that this is how I am. It's not awful. It's not the worst thing in the world."

In fact, Matthew can see the value of shyness, since he feels that his insights as a shy person help his writing and deepen his understanding of human nature. "I think it has made me more self-aware, more self-analytical, and that's a good thing. It has probably made me more compassionate, too."

My goal in this book is to help you understand that you can be shy sometimes but that you don't have to let your shyness limit your life. Just like Matthew, you can realize that shyness isn't a curse that will burden you for the rest of your days.

"My shyness comes from low self-esteem."

An artist in New York wrote to me, "I feel my low self-esteem has more than a little to do with the debilitating effects of my shyness. I would give anything to be outgoing and financially and socially successful."

A twenty-five-year-old Georgia cashier had similar feelings: "My shyness has made me feel very bad and alone in the past. There's nothing that I would like more than to have the self-confidence and self-esteem to be able to talk to anyone at any time in any place. I think it would enable me to live not only a happier life, but a better, more fulfilling life."

Shy individuals often point to low self-esteem as the cause of their discomfort. And low self-esteem does come into play when they reflect on their social skills. However, sometimes this negative self-concept is of their own making.

I have found, for instance, that shy individuals set impossible standards for themselves. If you have unreasonably high expectations, you may feel that anything less than being the life of the party won't do. When you haven't won over the crowd, you believe you've failed miserably. You become hypercritical of your performance and unable to fully relax in conversation.

Indeed, you become so caught up in self-criticism and so focused on your inner dialogue that you're incapable of listening to anyone else. And so you get left behind. As one woman put it, "Sometimes words spill out, but they are inappropriate because the conversation has moved on to something else." Your liveliest conversations may be within yourself.

Moreover, in some situations it isn't low self-esteem but an overblown sense of oneself that keeps shy people from interacting with others. I have found that for the most part, they don't believe they are unworthy of being talked to, but they do complain that others don't realize how interesting and wonderful they are. They expect others to discover the hidden, fascinating aspects of their personalities—others must make the introductions, draw them out in conversation, do the work in social situations. They have difficulty meeting others halfway —to initiate contact and keep up their end of the conversation. The burden of social facilitation is on others.

"Shyness is a life sentence."

A gardener in his midthirties wrote this sad letter to me:

> I live a rather lonely and comparatively isolated life. I've been afraid to leave my parents' home to live on my own, because although I don't have a real close relationship with them, I am relatively comfortable around them and don't feel so lonely. Also, I'm extremely hesitant about pursuing my dream of being a teacher, due to this infernal shyness. In short, shyness crimps virtually every aspect of my life that has a social dimension to it.

Shy people have said to me repeatedly, "I can't help it! I was just born shy, and there's nothing I can do about it." This is just not so. Shyness is not a life sentence or an indelible birthmark. *It is a series of choices that gradually cement into a lifestyle.* This young man, for instance, has chosen to continue to live with his parents, to forgo the company of others, and to abandon his dream of becoming a teacher. These choices were not preordained.

Shyness becomes an entrenched habit only after you have

surrendered to it too often. If you want to be happier, you do not have to overhaul your identity. You merely must make different choices so you won't get trapped.

I like to think of shyness as having much in common with allergies. Hay fever is not a fatal disease, but it is a source of discomfort. Once diagnosed, however, those who are allergic to pollen can make appropriate choices about their behavior and minimize their suffering. They don't have to live in sanitary, plastic bubbles, but they will stay away from gardens in bloom, springtime fields, and florists' shops. They can enjoy life once they learn to control their exposure to what makes them uncomfortable.

Think of *Shyness* as your antihistamine for shyness, a remedy for sweaty palms and racing heart. Just as allergic people are still allergic after taking their medication, you will still be shy after reading this book. You just won't suffer through your shyness—you will be successfully in control of it.

Successfully shy people understand how shyness impacts their lives, just as people with hay fever understand how allergies affect theirs. They measure out their exposure to difficult situations and build resistance by being more self-aware. They chart their life course with more clarity when they understand the role that shyness plays. They accept their shyness—body, mind, and self.

The key to their success comes from their choices. Instead of going to loud nightclubs or parties because that's "the thing to do," they spend time in more intimate settings: a friend's house, a neighborhood coffee shop or café, or a special-interest meeting. They also don't isolate themselves in home offices or in front of the television. Instead, successfully shy people develop friendships slowly so that a sense of comfort and mutual trust can grow naturally. They take on responsibilities based on their capabilities instead of letting their fears and self-doubt hold them back.

At the core of the successfully shy individual is a genuine, hard-won understanding of what it means to be shy in a world that promotes the myths and misconceptions of shyness.

"Only extroverts are happy."

Perhaps the most powerful myth of all is that only sociable, outgoing people are happy and have fulfilling lives. As a shy high school student in Florida wrote to me, "I want to burst out and let everyone know I'm here! I want to be like my crazy friends who get super grades, super guys, super friends, *success in all they do and say*! Happiness!"

People who accept this myth believe that shyness is stopping them from living the life they were meant to live:

"If I weren't shy I could . . . "

"If I weren't shy I would . . . "

"If I weren't shy I should . . . "

Like Chrissie and the frustrated gardener, they believe they are doomed to lives of quiet isolation. They assume that they are less interesting or competent than nonshy people. They excuse themselves from life by declining invitations, avoiding risk, and fleeing social situations that make them uncomfortable. They view their shyness as a disease or an inherited disposition over which they have no control. They know that shyness will haunt them all of their days.

Successfully shy people can see through this myth. They recognize that most people feel shy occasionally and that these feelings are temporary and normal. They reclaim their power from shyness when they concentrate on whatever faces them—from a situation as minor as introducing themselves to a new coworker to one as overwhelming as having to make a new set of friends because of a cross-country move. Most important, they do not focus on the problems and symptoms of shyness. Instead, they concentrate on solutions and strategies.

Successfully shy people are honest with themselves. They can identify their fears and insecurities and develop strategies to work through them. Conversely, those who give in to their shyness can't see themselves clearly. They get trapped in a web of false perceptions.

Once you buy into one myth, others must follow. You may tell yourself that you simply aren't good with people and never try to disprove it. Eventually the myths take over. You can't reach out to friends and loved ones because the myths silence you. You don't understand yourself and become preoccupied with covering up your shyness, so you don't expect that anyone else will understand or accept you.

These myths not only separate you from others, they separate you from your true self; your myth-based perceptions of yourself are vastly different from who you want to be. For example, you may want to feel comfortable while speaking to new people but think of yourself as incapable of engaging them in conversation. Psychologist Carl Rogers noted that this separation of the ideal self from the real self creates anxiety.

You may interpret your anxiety as fear and self-doubt, and that might cause you to stop doing whatever makes you anxious. But anxiety isn't in and of itself a bad thing. In fact, Rogers believed that anxiety is merely a warning sign that you should take action to alleviate it. The best way to do this is by expressing your true self.

How would you, a socially anxious, shy person, do that? You could observe other people who are good conversationalists and imitate them. Focus on your previous social successes instead of dwelling on your failures. And you could use your anxiety as a stepping stone to self-awareness instead of seeing it as an insurmountable hurdle.

In fact, throughout this book, I will explain how you can reframe your anxiety so it won't constantly hamstring you. To break away from these myths that bind and restrict you from your true potential, you need to reexamine your assumptions about yourself and your shyness. Indeed, the assumptions of people who suffer from shyness are radically different from those of successfully shy people.

Assumptions of the Unhappily Shy

- I get nervous when I'm with new people because they're judging me.

- I don't talk much because the less said, the less that can be criticized.

- I want to be with others, but I don't have anything to say.

- Nobody else gets nervous or anxious—I'm the only one who is miserable at parties. Everyone is having fun except me.

- All the people in the room can see how uncomfortable I feel inside.

- I'm to blame whenever there's a pause in conversation or the conversation goes nowhere.

- I'm not good at joining in conversations already in progress. When I interrupt, everyone stops talking and stares at me.

- I have a hard time talking to new people, so I'm a failure in general.

- I've messed up past conversations; I should have said this, but instead I said that . . .

With this magnitude of internal pressure, you can see how it might be impossible to have social success—or a happy life, for that matter. Overgeneralizations that create doomsday scenarios blow out of proportion any minor faux pas. When you believe them, you shoulder all the blame for whatever may go wrong in an interaction whether or not it's your fault. You put so much pressure on yourself to refrain from saying anything untoward that you begin to act as if you're a diplomat trying to negotiate a delicate cease-fire.

Not only do these assumptions create catastrophes out of every "Ahem," but they turn conversations into evaluations. Indeed, your words aren't on trial here—you are. Instead of merely carrying out a fundamental social exchange, you set out to prove yourself in every interaction. You put your whole self on the line each time you open your mouth. Rather than passing the time chatting about how stuffy the room is, you may be thinking, "I really, really want you to like me while I'm talking to you about atmospheric conditions in here."

As you will see, the successfully shy have quite different assumptions about their social interactions.

Assumptions of the Successfully Shy

- I have interesting things to say, and most people will realize it.

- Most people are friendly and will give me the benefit of the doubt if I blush, get tongue-tied, or can't come up with a snappy reply.

- I don't have to win over every person I meet or be the life of the party to have a good time.

- Just about everyone gets anxious about meeting new people or speaking in public. Most of the rest of the people here must be nervous, too.

- I know how to make myself comfortable in an uncomfortable situation.

- I look forward to joining an ongoing conversation. There is so much to learn from the repartee.

- I'm a good listener, and I try not to get distracted by my blushing, anxiety, or the pressures that can come from talking to someone who I feel is somehow superior to me.

- When I admit to others that I'm feeling shy or nervous, it makes the feeling simmer down.

- A normal conversation has a lot of give-and-take and is full of silences, stops and starts, and misstatements.

- I don't expect to have instant rapport with most people. I'm willing to get to know someone by asking questions, sharing information about myself, and taking time to let a relationship develop.

- If I don't hit it off with someone, I don't dwell on it. You can't be friends with everyone.

- I prepare myself for new encounters by setting realistic expectations for myself.

- I try to follow my heart because I've learned that my dreams are important to my happiness.

Successfully shy people have more realistic, fair, forgiving, and accurate views of shyness and their control over it. They understand that they must create workable strategies to alter a specific situation. They don't let their fears and insecurities run wild because they know they have choices.

Consequently, successfully shy people are no longer victims of shyness or of a cruel world that doesn't understand them. They're merely real people who have found their own power. It is my intention to help you find yours.

In Your Shy Life Journal

Reflect on which myths you have believed over the years. How might you change your view of shyness, based on your new knowledge? How can you help yourself be successfully shy?

A New View of Shyness

Many great minds have attempted to understand the enigma of shyness. Charles Darwin, the genius behind evolutionary theory, linked the physical responses of shyness, such as blushing, to shame. He claimed that when we feel shy we "retreat into the shadows" of silence and isolation to cover up what we've done wrong and feel ashamed about.

Interestingly, however, Darwin expressed tender concern for his young daughter who became shy with him when he returned from a long expedition. To help her out, Darwin felt that he and others in his household should refrain from calling attention to it. He believed the fuss would make her more self-conscious and less able to express herself freely. Instead, he recommended showing her compassion and gave her time to get used to him.

Freud also interested himself in the phenomenon of shyness. According to the psychoanalytic view, the problem isn't so much that shy people think too little of themselves, but that think too much of themselves. Freud believed shy people are narcissists—they interpret everything in light of themselves. They don't speak because their attention is focused within, not on those with whom they should be talking. They feel all eyes are on them and fail to realize they're just a face in the crowd.

Psychoanalytic theory traces the roots of narcissistic shyness to frustrated attempts to satisfy universal primal, subconscious urges for food, sex, companionship, and love during childhood. Shy people didn't get what they needed from their parents, so they dote on themselves to make up for the early emotional abandonment. They don't express themselves because they're so busy loving themselves and making sure that they're perfect at all times. Consequently, they live in their heads even when surrounded by a throng.

I disagree with this theory. There is nothing inherently, seriously, or neurotically wrong with shy people. If their parents weren't nurturing enough, that's not their fault. And if they can't resolve their conflicts—and we all have internal conflicts—then the *resolution* is faulty, not the person. I agree that it is valuable to look at your internal and early experiences—the body, mind, and self—but it's erroneous to blame shy people for being shy.

Carl Jung, who broke away from Freud and developed his own theory of personality, was also concerned with how people express themselves. Instead of blaming stern parents or a hidden neurosis for shyness, Jung argued that we all have two "attitudes" about our place in the world: "introverted" and "extroverted." These orientations exist within us in a variable ratio; some people are more extroverted, while others are more introverted.

Jung felt that to achieve a healthy personality we must create a rough balance between the two attitudes that allows us to express both. Not surprisingly, shy people have more introverted tendencies, so their energy is directed away from others and toward themselves in isolation. But they are rarely completely introverted because, like everyone else, they also feel motivated to be part of the social world.

The Dilemma of Shyness

Darwin, Freud, and Jung were all trying to resolve the basic dilemma of shyness: Why is it that certain people yearn to be with others yet cannot do so? After years of research, I have found their explanations fascinating but limited. Shyness, rather than being the result of shame, narcissism, or introversion, seems to have three themes. These run through the many testimonies and the research I have read, and they make sense of all the disparate information regarding shy interactions:

1. Shy people get caught in an approach/avoidance conflict.

2. Shy people are generally slow to warm up to new people, places, and situations.

3. Shy people need to establish and expand their comfort zones in their daily lives.

These issues explain shy behavior during interpersonal interactions. They apply to the most mundane tasks, such as making small talk with a coworker, as well as to life-altering decisions like starting a family or deciding on a career path. They're the basic ground rules that you should keep in mind as you navigate difficult social encounters.

Once you understand how shy behavior operates and when it's most likely to surface, you can plan ahead, make choices about which action to take, and empower yourself to break free of the myths. You will become successfully shy because you will comprehend the mechanics of shy behavior and make choices to liberate yourself from its tyranny. Let's explore these themes more fully.

The Approach/Avoidance Conflict

Some people have a fairly easy time being with others. They can approach friends, neighbors, and even strangers because they're interested and curious about people, feel comfortable in a crowd, and learn about themselves and the world by exchanging information socially.

Others gather information by observing their neighbors. They don't get involved with people because they're happiest alone. These classic introverts exult in their isolation. An introverted college student in Pennsylvania wrote to me, "Social situations are not that important to me. Small talk at a party is not my idea of a good time; I'd rather be at home reading a good book or hanging out with good friends."

But sometimes these two desires—to approach and to avoid people—meet in the same individual (especially when tackling an unfamiliar challenge such as looking for a new job, starting a new program, or meeting new people), and that creates an internal battle of wills. Your heart tells you to be with others, while simultaneously your head orders you to actively avoid them. You need social contact but doubt your ability to succeed at it. You want to be accepted and understood but hold back from expressing yourself fully. You are afraid of being judged, so you refrain from revealing yourself at all. You can't figure out what to do, so you become frozen in your colliding wishes. You are caught in the grasp of the approach/avoidance conflict.

Amy found herself in this uncomfortable situation when she attended her friend's wedding. She knew that she should talk to some of the other guests but wasn't sure how. First she looked around the room for a familiar face and was disappointed to discover that she couldn't find one. Yet, if she didn't introduce herself to at least one stranger, she felt doomed to spend the whole evening by herself. Even though she didn't want to be alone, she was still afraid of what would happen if she started talking to the handsome man standing next to her in the receiving line. The following thoughts rolled around in Amy's mind: *Do I look all right? How is my hair? My dress? I shouldn't have worn these shoes. They're old and make me feel dumpy. I wonder if he noticed. Should I talk to him? What should I say? Isn't he the groom's big-shot cousin, the one who makes a ton of money? Why would a guy like him pay attention to a person like me? What on earth could I say to him? I'm just Kathy's college friend. I'd never be able to interest this guy in anything I say. I'd like to talk to him; he's sort of cute. Maybe I could ask him for some stock tips. Oh, he'd probably just think I'm annoying.*

This internal dialogue stopped Amy from uttering a word, not only because it took most of her energy, but also because it affected her whole self. Filled with insecurity, nervousness, and doubt, she was too preoccupied with her internal state to initiate conversation. She remained silent because she feared looking foolish. Outwardly, she appeared bashful, uncomfortable, and anxious; inside she was roiling.

Several scholars have traced shyness to this approach/ avoidance conflict. To minimize your anxious preoccupation with this internal debate, you may become quiet and remote. But withdrawal can backfire because others may misperceive it as aloofness. One woman wrote to me, "I am a very friendly person once people get to know me, but that's just the problem. I'm afraid that I can come off looking like a snob or worse because I don't talk much. I'm not good at first impressions but rarely have a second chance to show that I am a nice person."

This woman is not alone. My research shows that shyness causes the most anguish when one contemplates the initial personal contact, the first step to developing a conversation. More than half of the two hundred respondents in one study claimed to have difficulty with this step, but less than 10 percent reported shyness as a problem in their intimate relationships. This leads me to conclude that for most shy people, once they get beyond the initial conflict, shyness ceases to hold them back from being themselves.

The Risk Factor

Why do people become caught in the approach/avoidance conflict? I believe it has to do, in part, with the fear of taking risks.

If you are shy, you may view others as dangerous and being with them a risk you can ill afford. They won't physically hurt you, but you've never been in this situation with this person and don't know what to expect. Like Amy, you may fear rejection; it would make you feel even worse about yourself.

Moreover, just as you can't predict what others will do, you can't foresee how you will react. You fear saying something stupid or offensive, being unable to conceive a witty comeback, stuttering, or otherwise embarrassing yourself. Why take the chance? The mere act of talking can be a big risk, so you avoid it by staying away from new people and interacting only with those you know well. As a doctor's assistant in her early thirties wrote to me, "In social situations I usually stand in a corner and only talk to those who approach me or those who are already friends."

The avoidance of risk can become an organizing principle in your daily life: you get your coffee at the same deli every morning, socialize with the regular crowd, talk to the same few coworkers, and so on. Unfortunately, protecting yourself from risk can become more important than your personal and social development. A CPA in New York was dominated by his fear of risk taking and rejection. He wrote, "Even though I've experienced plenty of real rejection and have survived just fine, I'm afraid of being rejected almost as soon as I've spotted anybody who appears to have the time and inclination to talk to me. That fear persists for the first two or more years that I know someone."

In truth, every accomplishment, every challenge involves some risk and provokes anxiety. Each step toward personal fulfillment means that you might have to take one and perhaps even two steps back. Unfortunately, while you may spend your time cautiously avoiding new social challenges, you may be too preoccupied to think about how you can help yourself. Anxiety grips you and slowly pulls you down.

It's only natural to want what you fear and to fear what you want, but it's not healthy to go on wanting while doing nothing to conquer those fears, like the thirty-seven-year-old North Carolina counselor who wrote: "I do not have a social life, and have never had one. When I see some lady I think

I'd like to meet, instead of introducing myself, my fantasy mind kicks in and I meet her that way. It's easier than an actual approach."

If you constantly tip the balance of your life in favor of avoidance, your anxiety, lack of accomplishments, and protective armor will eventually corrode your true self. Besides, the rewards of taking appropriate risks can be enormous. A high school student in Upstate New York who mastered her fear of risk taking explained, "I try to put myself in certain situations where I may not be comfortable. If I begin to stutter when trying to express myself, I'll slow down and relax. I have definitely noticed improvement. It is truly a feeling of liberation when the shyness starts to go away."

Everything in life involves risk; only death is certain and free of tension. To help you determine how you view social encounters, try this interpersonal-risk quiz.

Assessing Your Tolerance for Risk

On a scale of 1 ("Totally uncharacteristic of me") to 5 ("Totally characteristic of me"), rate yourself on the following statements:

1. It's easy for me to approach total strangers at social gatherings and begin a conversation.

Uncharacteristic   1   2   3   4   5   Characteristic

2. I enjoy being the center of attention.

Uncharacteristic   1   2   3   4   5   Characteristic

3. If I disagree with someone, I will let them know.

Uncharacteristic   1   2   3   4   5   Characteristic

4. I don't mind being one of the first people on the dance floor.

Uncharacteristic   1   2   3   4   5   Characteristic

5. I usually don't worry about being rejected for what I do or say in public.

Uncharacteristic   1   2   3   4   5   Characteristic

6. If I'm attracted to someone, I let them know.

Uncharacteristic   1   2   3   4   5   Characteristic

7. I don't mind going to social gatherings alone.

Uncharacteristic   1   2   3   4   5   Characteristic

8. I look forward to meeting new people at social gatherings.

Uncharacteristic   1   2   3   4   5   Characteristic

9. I don't worry about making a social faux pas because most people will forget what I do wrong.

Uncharacteristic   1   2   3   4   5   Characteristic

10. I usually don't hold my feelings back when I'm interacting with others.

Uncharacteristic   1   2   3   4   5   Characteristic

The higher your score (25–50), the more likely you are to take risks with other people. If you scored on the low side (10–24), you're probably avoiding new encounters because you believe they're too unpredictable and dangerous.

The key is to take calculated risks by planning for challenges. I will show you how below.

Anxiety Is a Powerful Teacher

If you fear taking risks and get caught in the approach/avoidance conflict, you may never prove to yourself that you can, in fact, meet new people successfully. One of the difficulties is that the conflict isn't resolved by merely backing off and remaining silent. Unfortunately, anxiety is added to the mix, and it may intensify the shyness, reinforce your with-drawal, and inhibit future interactions.

In Your Shy Life Journal

Write about the meaning of risk taking for you.

Explore situations in which you were afraid to take a risk but did. Perhaps they were in the business world or in sports. How did they come out? Can you draw inspiration from these examples?

Using the Four *I*'s—identification, information, incorporation, and implementation—write about the value of taking social risks. What would it mean to you in terms of meeting new people and conquering old fears?

- Identification: Visualize yourself in a "risky" situation where you would normally feel anxious.

- Information: Write out what you need to know about how to be successful in the situation. How would you need to act? What would your demeanor be like? Would you need to be well informed about certain issues?

- Incorporation: How will you put this information into your life? What will you do in this situation? How will you approach people? What style do you feel comfortable with? How would you comport yourself if you were no longer afraid of taking this risk? Hold that positive image in your mind, and see if you can act on it the next time you're in an anxiety-provoking situation.

- Implementation: Now become involved in the situation and achieve what you've prepared.

Here is how anxiety works. Thomas invited Scott, his pal at work, to a party. Scott showed up alone. He was nervous because he didn't know anyone there and felt he wasn't good at talking to new people. He stood off to one side of the room all night and didn't engage anyone except Thomas, who was busy being the host. Scott hung around, silently in terror, hoping that others would introduce themselves and carry the burden of making conversation. This is known as "social loafing."

After about an hour, the noise, crowd, chaos, and anxiety felt overwhelming to Scott, so he nodded good-bye to Thomas and left. At first he felt relieved that he had escaped the party and in so doing reduced his anxiety. But on the way home, he began to berate himself for being so bad with people. He hadn't met anyone. While he was attacking himself, he picked up a six-pack of beer and a video. He got home, still angry, and parked on the couch in front of the television.

When Thomas invited him to a baseball game the following weekend, Scott said he was busy. He spent that weekend surfing the Net and getting caught up in a personal film fest of his favorite Clint Eastwood movies.

Scott's anxiety, powered by three major learning strategies, weakened his approach behavior and strengthened his avoidant tendencies. Normally we use these strategies whenever we confront an obstacle we must conquer—dividing fractions, riding a bike, typing, practicing yoga. Scott, sadly, applied them to perpetuate his approach/avoidance conflict.

The Three Strategies of Learning

1. *Positive reinforcement.* This means rewarding yourself for doing what you set out to do. Scott compensated himself for reducing his anxiety by enjoying his beer, renting movies he loved, spending time on the Internet, and saving himself from another threatening situation—the baseball game. He patted himself on the back by making his time alone pleasurable.

2. *Negative reinforcement.* This means eliminating what bothers you. Scott removed anxiety-provoking situations from his life by steering clear of personal interaction. He loafed socially at the party, left early, and declined Thomas's invitation to the baseball game.

3. *Punishment.* This means taking yourself to task for behaving badly. Punishment hurts, but it is effective. Scott scolded himself for leaving the party, which underscored that he was a failure with people. He didn't allow himself the benefits of personal contact, no matter how innocuous (How threatening could a baseball game be?), because he believed himself undeserving. He thought he would just bungle any attempts, no matter what.

These learning strategies strengthened Scott's avoidant behavior by teaching him to shun social situations—they just weren't worth the uneasiness they caused—and by weakening his tendency to approach others. These tools can effectively turn one avoidant situation into a pattern of sustained shy isolation. A single bad experience grows into a habit as you repeatedly choose to flee when you feel uncertain. And since in social situations you only know how to be anxious and can't fulfill your desire to approach people, you label yourself shy and act accordingly.

But you can make different choices using these same three principles of learning. Scott, for example, could have used these tools to strengthen his approach behavior and unlearn avoidance.

Using positive reinforcement, Scott could realize that he doesn't have to be the center of attention at a party to be a success. He could reward himself for any social approach he does make. Just going to a party for an hour could be a cause for celebration compared to a night alone on the couch. Rather than ruminating, "I'm a loser because I was only there for an hour," he could think, "Hey, an hour is better than nothing, right? Maybe next time I'll stay an hour and a half."

Using negative reinforcement, Scott could choose to eliminating not what makes him uncomfortable, but what makes him comfortable: avoidance and short-term solutions to relieve his anxiety. He could resolve to say yes to social opportunities and stick with his purpose because the anxiety will eventually lessen as he acclimates. For instance, rather than waiting for a formal overture, he could have walked to the other side of the room where a card game was in progress. There he could have watched and eventually joined in or just commented. The pressure of meeting strangers would have diminished as he interacted with the group about the plays.

Scott could have also altered his expectations by minimizing the intensity of whatever he was trying to avoid. If he realized that he didn't *have to* make new friends every time he went out, his anxiety about introductions would also diminish.

Scott could then reduce punishment by being less serious about each interaction. Although his whole self-worth was not on the line each time he opened his mouth, he acted as if it were. He could have reminded himself that if he had blundered during one conversation, it really wouldn't matter; the other person probably would forget about it.

He could have also contained his negative self-talk to prevent it from spilling into his self-esteem. It's difficult to shut off these destructive tape loops, but it must and can be done. (I'll show you how in Chapter 6.)

Shyness is a dynamic process, not a self-fulfilling prophecy or a static label. The approach/avoidance conflict is powerful but only becomes debilitating when it is ingrained in your body, mind, and self. Scott wasn't shy by nature; he was merely making choices that reinforced shy behavior.

The Slow-to-Warm-Up Tendency

In addition to the clashing emotions aroused by the approach/ avoidance conflict, you may experience ambivalence about your sense of personal control. In fact, you may either feel that you have no control over yourself and the other person's attitude toward you, or you may try to overcontrol so that you can ensure you're making a good impression.

In Your Shy Life Journal

Explore how you use positive reinforcement, negative reinforcement, and punishment to keep you frozen in the approach/avoidance conflict. How might you use positive reinforcement and negative reinforcement to learn a new way of being? How might you stop punishing yourself? Could you take each social encounter less seriously?

I have found, for instance, that shy people often bear too much responsibility for making a conversation work. They are trying to manage the other person's impression of them even though there is only so much they can do. If the encounter fails, they feel defeated and they shut down. Or they may avoid making contact in the first place. That's the ultimate control! As one writer told me, "If I'm attracted to a man, he'll most likely never know it because he's the one man I won't talk to or be able to flirt with—the most I can do is make prolonged eye contact!"

If you find yourself in this situation, it is helpful to remind yourself of what you can and cannot control:

You *can* control
- Your thoughts
- Your feelings
- Your behavior
- Your attitude
- Your direction in life
- How you spend your time

- With whom you spend your time
- How long you stay in a social situation

You *cannot* control
- Others' attitudes toward you
- What another person will say
- How someone will treat you
- Social obligations

Rather than shutting down to gain control, it's helpful to recognize that everyone approaches a new situation by warming up to it. We humans just don't rush in and begin socializing immediately; shy or not, we investigate new or uncertain circumstances, listen to our instincts, determine how to behave, and eventually acclimate ourselves. The warm-up period gives us time to plan our approach.

You can grasp how the warm-up period works if you recall what happens at a party at which dance music is played. The band begins, but nobody dances. They play another song, and one brave couple glides out onto the dance floor. Everyone else watches. Soon another couple joins in, then another. Eventually the dance floor fills, and nobody notices what the others are doing—the dancers are completely immersed in the music. A few people may stand around the edges of the swaying crowd, observing, but once the pressure is off, they too relax and have a good time.

In Your Shy Life Journal

Reflect on what is within your control and what is not. Then focus on what you can do, and put the rest out of your mind. You'll be one step closer to being successfully shy when you recognize that your fate is your own.

Everyone needs to warm up; some can do it quickly. But researchers Stella Chess and Alexander Thomas of New York Medical Center have found that others are "slow to warm up" to new social situations, which seem like shocks to the system. These people are generally shy. They need extra time to sort out the approach/avoidance conflict, or perhaps they have a relatively small repertoire of social skills on which to rely. A seventeen-year-old high school student typified the slow-to-warm-up personality in her response: "I've always been well-involved socially, but I tend to become shy around different or unfamiliar people so I can see how they behave first."

However, although shy people may be slow to warm up, when given time and space in which to acclimate, they too lose their inhibitions. For instance, the writer who could only make eye contact with unfamiliar men had little trouble with those whom she got to know. She added, "When I've had the opportunity to see men on a regular basis (in school, at work, in my apartment building), I have managed to get to know them and have relationships."

Being slow to warm up is not a failing; it's just a part of human nature. The problem lies in ignoring this fact and in rushing through the warm-up period or in feeling bad about how long it takes. I've found that shy people often have unrealistic expectations. They anticipate that they will "turn on" socially as soon as they walk into a party. When they can't, they believe they are less socially skilled than everyone else.

Indeed, I have found that many shy people rush through the warm-up period in what I call "forced extroversion" because they feel anxious and want to be approached, welcomed, and appreciated as soon as they join the group. They observe a crowd that has already jelled and wonder why they're not part of it. They need to be reassured about their behavior—and themselves—by taking part in engrossing conversations. They forget that these revelers have already experienced their own varying warm-up periods.

If you are hurrying the warm-up period, you may also squander precious moments focusing on anxiety, self-doubt, and impending social disaster. You may calculate how best to avoid others rather than how to make your way through the crowd. Or you may drink to relax. This short-term strategy is counterproductive and self-defeating. The conviviality that may come from alcohol is artificial. For example, a painfully shy female college student wrote to me, "I do like drinking with my friends, but I notice that I tend to indulge myself in alcohol to feel more loose and talkative when it comes to meeting my boyfriend's friends. But then when I see them sober, I feel like a loser because the other night I was a happy, talkative drunk." Besides, it's most likely the warm-up period and not the alcohol that is making you feel more relaxed.

A better way to deal with your slow-to-warm-up tendencies is to find friends who have a similar rhythm. Rather than being stranded at parties because a pal can jump into the thick of it, invite along a more reticent companion who adjusts at a pace that more closely resembles yours. Or use your warm-up period to find people at the party who seem quiet but interesting. Given that half the population considers itself shy, there should be others there who are hanging back, too. Patience is key.

If you have slow-to-warm-up tendencies, you may also need extra time to adjust to the larger life passages that most of us navigate, such as entering a stable career, getting married, or having children. Making these life transitions isn't easy for anyone. Our minds, bodies, and selves react. We become anxious and uncertain of our capabilities. We have trouble sleeping, eating, and relaxing. Our thoughts race with plans to meet new expectations.

The adjustment can be even more intense for those who are shy. In fact, researchers have found that shy people tend to accomplish these developmental tasks later than others. You can see this slow adaptation in all phases of the shy life.

Consider the shy first-grader who hates the first few weeks of school, the teenager who doesn't start dating until long after her friends, the college sophomore who goes home every weekend to hang out with his high school buddies, or the assistant who, despite her competence, clings to her mentor and doesn't seek a more autonomous position.

These difficulties are the normal growing pains of someone who is slow to warm up. They will dissipate, however, once you become accustomed to your new situation. Besides, hanging back gives you time to cope; although you're not assimilating all of the changes at once, you are adjusting. Everyone has a distinct tolerance for change, and we each respond differently. Becoming aware of your slow-to-warm-up tendencies and giving yourself more space and time when confronting anxiety-provoking situations are the best ways to deal with them.

Because of this natural hesitation to adapt to new challenges, you may not benefit from the support of your peers since they're making these life transitions sooner. Your friends may all marry right after college, but you may hold back. When the time comes for you to plan your wedding, they may have moved to the next challenges in life such as having children, buying a home, or advancing in their careers.

You may lag behind, lacking confidants with whom you can share your experiences, but this doesn't mean that you will be less successful in the long run. You can and should accomplish all of life's passages that your nonshy friends do; you will just approach them at your own rate, once you've become comfortable with the new circumstances and expectations.

Above all, bear in mind that as you take the first steps on the road to a successfully shy life, you will put yourself in unfamiliar situations. Rather than decreasing at this point, the warm-up period may become even more prolonged because you are choosing to approach new situations rather than avoiding them. That's okay. Remember that you will get where you need to go even if you're in the slow lane. It's just in your nature to take your time.

The Comfort Zone

The comfort zone is a universal need that encompasses your physical, social, and psychological peace. When in your comfort zone, you feel content and in control. You know what's going to happen to you and feel understood. Nothing threatens you—not another person, not a situation, not even your most intimate feelings.

Awareness of the comfort zone will help you develop a strategy for finding personal fulfillment and leading a successful shy life. The first step is to understand its components:

The physical comfort zone. You establish a physical comfort zone by gravitating to places in which you feel calm—your work cubicle, couch, neighborhood, customary table at your favorite diner—wherever you can relax because you are safe.

The social comfort zone. You create a social comfort zone when you surround yourself with the people who understand and appreciate you, including, family members, close friends, coworkers, E-mail pals, and even the occasional anonymous individual on the train. They share varying degrees of intimacy with you, but whatever the degree, you can handle the relationships. Those in your social comfort zone like you, you like them, and you can count on them for unconditional acceptance. While you may not always agree, you know that they won't judge you unfairly or criticize you.

It may take a while for new people to become part of your social comfort zone; the warm-up period is necessary to build rapport.

The personal comfort zone. You forge a personal comfort zone while engaging in actions or using personal resources about which you feel confident. Perhaps skiing, reading Russian literature, telling jokes, staying calm under pressure, or being self-assured about your appearance all fit into your personal comfort zone, while public speaking, scuba diving, slurping spaghetti in a restaurant, and making small talk do not. Your personal comfort zone allows you to express yourself freely and without anxiety. Strengthening it increases your confidence in yourself, even in unpredictable circumstances.

Establishing a comfort zone renders the unfamiliar familiar. You do so when you take a friend to a party so you don't have to face a room full of strangers alone, when you read up on a restaurant before making reservations, when you talk on the phone before meeting someone in person, or simply when you let the warm-up process take its course. Some shy people and their friends create comfort zones instinctively by acknowledging shyness and allowing it to ebb naturally with time and understanding.

A graduate student in social work wrote to me about how she found her comfort zone among people of like interests. "I never really had any 'social life,'" she noted, "because of my shyness throughout high school and college. I avoided gatherings because I wouldn't know what to say. Grad school has been the turning point. All the students share a common interest, so I am opening up more and actually eat lunch with a group of classmates, which I didn't do before."

Your comfort zone has no limits and is constantly changing shape as you incorporate new people and situations and let go of those you haven't encountered in a while. Some people add to their comfort zone relatively easily because they're somewhat adventuresome.

Unfortunately, shyness can have the opposite effect. It can lead you to develop a stagnant, constricting, inflexible—or, in the worst case, shrinking—comfort zone. When in your restricted comfort zone, you may not feel shy because you're completely comfortable with your surroundings, your companions, yourself. But you may have a hard time expanding your zone to include new people and experiences. You may feel that you lack the psychological resources—social skills, belief in your physical attractiveness, or confidence in your unique gifts—to carry you into other environments.

You may isolate yourself so you don't have to be tested or rejected; you may retreat into your shy comfort zone to avoid the pressure emanating from critical people. Consequently, you may only feel comfortable at home, with a handful of people, and draw upon few personal resources. As you back away from challenges, your comfort zone may harden and contract despite your desire to expand it. You may feel confined and frustrated because life seems to be passing you by.

Many shy people complain that they can't break out and show the world who they really are. Their shyness becomes their comfort zone. At the other extreme are those who force themselves into overwhelmingly unfamiliar situations outside their comfort zone. They can physically get themselves to a social event, but they are unprepared for what will happen once they arrive. My research shows that these attempts at forced extroversion almost always fail.

Although you may want instant rapport with another person, you must experience a universal passage that can be frustrating, awkward, and time-consuming. Desperate for attention and connection, you may not allow yourself to hang back while making yourself comfortable. You may rush in when you should be merely experiencing a natural process of growth.

John, a college student, had this very problem. "I have forced myself to go to clubs and parties," he wrote, "but I always chicken out when it comes to actually having to approach anyone. I psych myself up to talk to people in my class, but always chicken out there, too." John has admirable intentions, but he is unequipped to make wholesale changes in his behavior—nor has he allowed for the possibility that others may be wary about accepting a total stranger into their comfort zones!

Expectations must be realistic. A friendship doesn't develop all at once. John must establish a commonality with another person before he can make a friend. Fortunately, college presents many opportunities to do so. He can draw upon shared experiences within the classroom. Keeping in mind his approach/avoidance conflict and his warm-up period, he can start slowly by talking to the student sitting next to him. They might continue the relationship as the semester progresses, studying together for exams and going out for coffee after class.

He might also adjust his expectations by deciding if he is comfortable at clubs or parties. He won't be able to express himself unless he's confident that he can handle the situation without becoming overwhelmed. And he should bear in mind that the majority of people he would meet at these social gatherings are probably the kind who like parties. If that's not what he's interested in, then he should look elsewhere.

Your goal should be to expanding your comfort zone, not by coercing yourself to act like an outgoing, seemingly fearless adventurer, but by gently widening your range of experiences. Slowly but steadily, you can add new endeavors that once made you uncomfortable. You expand your comfort zone by increasing your approaches to less familiar situations, surroundings, and people while you fortify your emotional and psychological resources.

A good way to do this is to build on what you already feel sure about. For instance, if you practice karate and a friend invites you to a boxing class, you may take this risk despite your initial hesitation by reasoning, "Well, I have a blue belt in karate, so I'm probably strong enough and have the stamina to box. Besides, Jennifer invited me, and I know her pretty well. She wouldn't lead me astray. What have I got to lose but some pounds and lots of sweat? I'll try one class to see if I like it." In this way, you gradually enlarge your comfort zone instead of breaking it open all at once.

Take into account your warm-up period, and make progressive changes that show steady progress. These can be incremental. Even the smallest step is helpful. Rather than reading at home, bring a book to a café and read there. Go to a movie theater instead of renting a video. Strike up a conversation with the person who also waits at the bus stop every morning. The weather is always a safe subject. Make small talk with the grocery-store cashier. Rather than staying home, bring a friend along to a benefit dinner.

As positive experiences accumulate, you will realize that you can achieve some of your goals—all it takes is sensing when your comfort zone has become too restrictive and making appropriate adjustments. As a formerly shy man who works in the electronics industry explained, "You have to be creative and use your imagination, develop a certain trust in yourself, take risks, and don't let failures and disappointments hang you up."

Each attempt will revitalize you. As your comfort zone expands, you will learn more about yourself and strengthen your identity. You will accomplish feats you never thought possible. You'll surprise yourself with courage and ambition and understand the world just a little bit better. Shyness can dissolve when you fully participate in life.

Bringing It All Together

Shyness is a conflictual cycle—a way of behaving that prevents you from connecting with others. But it can be resolved with time, insight, and self-acceptance. Awareness of the important role played by the approach/ avoidance conflict, the warm-up period, and the comfort zone will empower you to understand why you are shy in certain situations and how you can cope with it. These elements work synergistically to reinforce shy behavior, but you can also use them to overcome it. Never again must you believe that shyness controls your life or that you are powerless to break free.

Think back to your first day of kindergarten. Many adults claim they first realized they were shy when they were suddenly entrusted into the hands of a new caretaker in an unfamiliar building before a room full of peers. They cried, clung to their mothers, and developed a headache or stomachache to avoid going back the next day. But they eventually adjusted to the new environment and made a few friends, despite their shyness.

In Your Shy Life Journal

List who and what comprise your physical, social, and personal comfort zones right now. Next, re-create your comfort zone of five years ago. Compare the two lists. How different are the old and new zones? If they are quite different, you are relatively open to new experiences. If they aren't, explore ways to gently expand your current comfort zone.

You can interpret this common situation in light of the three principles of shyness. The approach/avoidance conflict rendered these children ambivalent: they were frightened and anxious despite their natural curiosity about school. They gave in to the avoidance by trying to stay home. But because they persisted in their education, the warm-up period took effect. They gradually became accustomed to the teacher and classroom and developed friendships. They established a comfort zone by relying on their friends and familiar surroundings for security.

The same can be said of adolescents attending their first dance (and planning what to wear down to every last detail), adults anxious about going on a first date, or workers unnerved by a job transfer. If you are shy, it may take you more time to acclimate to your new situation, but with patience you will eventually create a new comfort zone.

Consider the man who wants to befriend a few guys at his

gym but is too shy to approach them. Unsure whether they would speak to him, or perhaps fearing that they are more skilled than he is, he keeps to himself. The approach/avoidance conflict is effective. But soon the warm-up period does its work: the men acclimate to one another and eventually share information about weight training. Before long, they spot each other during workouts. The three principles that comprise shyness and its reconciliation help us to understand it as a dynamic, ever-evolving process.

But shyness isn't just behavioral. It is also influenced by our physiology, intellect, and emotions. How you understand these internal influences has an important impact on how you will deal with the overt process of shyness. In Part II, I will explain these internal functions, or what I call the body, mind, and self of shyness.

In Your Shy Life Journal

It's important for you to note when shyness appears in your life and how you respond to conflicting feelings. It's even more important to understand how you can change your responses so that you're more comfortable, confident, and successfully shy. Consider the following conflict-laden situations:

1. Feeling embarrassed at a party

2. Feeling anxious during a first date with someone you really like

3. Not knowing how to jump into an ongoing discussion

4. Being pressured by friends to get a tattoo

5. Asking a question in a seminar or class

6. Making a presentation in front of your department

7. Seeing an attractive stranger at the bookstore

For those situations that seem relevant to your life:

Record how you act when caught in the approach/avoidance conflict.

What do you feel is at risk?

What might be gained from participating fully in the interaction?

How might you try to cope with your anxiety?

What would be the consequence of that behavior?

How can you unlearn your shy response?

In what new ways might you approach the situation, taking into account the warm-up time you need?

How might you gradually enlarge your comfort zone?

What would you have to do to apply what you have learned?

Shyness of the Body, Mind, and Self

"It's like being alone all the time," Diana, a thirty-one-year-old, unmarried, unemployed woman in Ohio told me. "I don't know how to talk to people, and I always think that I'm different."

The feeling of suffering alone overwhelms Diana. Even a simple shopping trip makes her nervous. "If I have to go to the store, I do it as fast as I can. I don't look at other people, or I go when nobody's there. If I get stuck in line with other people, I almost have a panic attack while I'm waiting. I've just got to hurry up and get out of there."

Diana also has trouble navigating work because she feels distracted when surrounded by others. While her coworkers sometimes intrigue her, she mostly keeps her distance. "I have to avoid certain situations so I wouldn't be around people," Diana said. "Now that I think about it, it's a double stress. I'll be working but also thinking about how I can keep away from people; I think they're going to hurt me in some way. But then there are times when I want to be with people and they don't care. They don't understand."

At the root of Diana's shy feelings is fear: "They're judging me; they don't like me; they think I'm weird."

The isolation, self-criticism, and anxiety impact Diana's feelings of self-worth. "I usually don't like myself much of the time," she admitted sadly.

A Holistic View

I've spoken with many people like Diana. They're so buried in their shyness that they don't know how to repair their lives.

Shyness can affect the very core of your being. I call it holistic be-

cause it influences the body (physical reactions), the mind (thoughts), and the self (sense of identity). These dimensions influence and respond to one another and need to be understood in relationship.

When you are feeling shy, your body reacts with pounding heart, sweaty palms, churning stomach. Your mind interprets these uncomfortable bodily "symptoms" as a sign of danger and creates negative thoughts that eventually affect your self-esteem and self-confidence. The poor self-esteem, in turn, triggers the bodily reaction, and on it goes. This is the synergy of body, mind, and self.

In Part II we will study these three aspects carefully, but first let's take a brief overview at how Diana's body, mind, and self are impacted by her shyness.

Shyness of the body: Diana is overwhelmed by anxiety in the presence of others such as her coworkers and even total strangers at the supermarket. Although from an evolutionary standpoint these physical symptoms were meant to help her, they in fact paralyze her. I'll explain how and why the body creates these shy symptoms, as well as how you can cope with them, in Chapter 5.

Bear in mind, however, that attempts to reduce the physical symptoms of anxiety using prescribed medication (such as Prozac, Xanax, or BuSpar), alcohol, or deep breathing and relaxation techniques may lessen physical arousal so that you can feel more comfortable in awkward situations, but they do not cure shyness. You can get to a party in a physically relaxed state, but if your mind and self are still mired in shyness, you may remain withdrawn and self-critical.

To overcome shyness, you must also understand how your mind processes thoughts, why your social skills are lacking, and how you can better assess your role in social situations. While antianxiety medication can be a good first step if you suffer from high levels of general anxiety, it's not the only step you should take.

Shyness of the mind: Diana fears that other people are constantly judging her, but the only person judging Diana is Diana. This is the shy person's biggest "mind" problem. It can cause you to make other errors in thinking. I'll explain the specific thought patterns that may hinder you and how you can alter them in Chapter 6.

I'm intrigued by the shy mind because it is so powerful. Alleviating its negative focus and incorporating valid social skills can enable you to better cope with your shyness. Social-skills training, self-help books, and talk therapy can help, but it doesn't end there. If you understand your mind but not your body or self, the physical aspects of anxiety and the self-doubt may ambush you.

Shyness of the self: Diana believes that others don't understand or like her. But these are her perceptions, not those of friends or loved ones. Diana's shyness influences her sense of self, but she can rediscover her self-worth once she better understands herself. In Chapter 7 we'll explore how.

Some of the most popular ways of trying to reach the shy self are through hypnosis, affirmations, and support groups. Unfortunately, I find these techniques may reinforce a sense of victimhood. Instead of changing what they don't like about their shyness, people who follow these practices can embrace its negative aspects along with the positive.

The self grows by breaking free of shy myths, not by dwelling on affirmations such as "I'm shy and proud of it." Otherwise one may fall into this line of thinking: I'm a good person. Why don't others notice that and make life easier for me by approaching me and asking me questions about myself? I just need to be around people who will take the time to drag me out of my shell.

Throughout Part II, we will explore what happens within the body, mind, and self of a shy individual. I will provide suggestions for alleviating your discomfort and creating choices about strategies. When you understand the synergy of the body, mind, and self of shyness, you may no longer be held in its thrall.

Shyness of the Body

In the course of my research, I unearthed a one-hundred-year-old article by English scholar Harry Campbell that sums up the physical symptoms of shyness quite eloquently:

> Blushing, a feeling of heat all over the body with a sense of suffocation, pallor even to the lips, a sensation of cold water down the back; cardiac disturbances, such as palpitation, fluttering or tumbling sensation at the heart; faintness, giddiness; perspiration, especially of the hands; dryness of the mouth, stuttering, headache, mental confusion; flurry, the employment of wrong words, the making of ridiculous remarks, and the doing of ridiculous things; silence, garrulousness; wriggling, and choreic movements of the body; inability to hold the hands naturally and composed, resulting in the restless movements of them; restless movements of the fingers, twiddling of an object, such as a pencil or brooch, biting the nails, general tremor, bending of the legs, such as crossing and recrossing them—inability, as in the case of the hands, to dispose of them naturally; giggling, "nervous laugh," a "sheepish" expression, inability to look one straight in the face, the eyes glancing up, down, on one side, or askance.

Sound familiar? Since shyness is a part of human nature, the symptoms haven't changed for a hundred or even ten thousand years, but we may characterize them differently these days. For example, a train engineer in his forties described his shyness this way: "The skin on my entire head becomes red and feels very hot. I sweat profusely. I stammer. I feel as though the focus on me becomes intensified while

I'm embarrassed." And a woman wrote, "I express my shyness by lowering my head and looking up (simultaneously), by refraining from expressing my opinions in a group, remaining quiet and on the outskirts of a group, blushing easily."

Dr. Campbell and the train engineer are describing a physical state of arousal that we recognize as a stress reaction. Every bodily response has a function. The function of the stress reaction is to protect you from danger. After all, your body's primary purpose is to preserve itself. It makes you feel hunger pangs when it needs fuel; it renders you sleepy when it must replenish its energy stores; and it reacts to threats by trying to protect you from danger. The physical symptoms you experience when you feel shy exist for a reason, and it's up to you, as a highly evolved human with a highly evolved brain, to decipher the reason.

The original purpose of these uncomfortable sensations was to make you aware of peril in your midst and to produce the fight-or-flight response that protected you from trouble—most likely a predator. Once the stress reaction alerted you, you could advance toward the enemy (fight) or run and hide in order to escape notice (flight). These reactions are meant to prod you into action, to avert danger.

But rather than seeing the stress reaction as protective, you may interpret these sensations as meaning that something is amiss with you. Or you may assume that you should avoid certain people because your body is telling you they are dangerous. Indeed, you may be unable to cope with the physical symptoms associated with shyness because you're not at all sure about what you're dealing with.

That Out-of-Control Feeling

When you are feeling threatened in social situations, your body will act up first. You may even feel that it's out of control. It seems to have a mind of its own, flushing, fidgeting, and sweating.

In truth, your body becomes aroused when you are in frightening, intimidating, or unusual social situations. These seem threatening because you believe they can harm your sense of self. Remember Diana's fear that her coworkers were going to hurt her? She didn't worry about her physical self, but rather that her colleagues might make her feel inadequate.

Trembling hands and knees and stuttering are manifestations of internal overarousal that depend on your mind's focus. When delivering a speech and holding index cards, you fear that your hands will tremble. Consequently, they do. When you walk into a room full of strangers, you concentrate on being graceful, so your knees give out. When talking, you want to form words clearly, but when you try too hard, you stutter.

Your shy stress reactions may feel so overwhelming that you believe they prevent you from being yourself when you're with others. The symptoms may *seem* overwhelming, but bear in mind that they *are not.* Your reactions are temporary. They're designed to keep you alert while you're adjusting to new situations. But even though they are meant to be short-lived, you can easily transform them into long-term responses that spiral out of control. How? By allowing your mind to dwell on them.

Recently a young man wrote to me, "Usually I begin sweating a little on my forehead, and then I think about it and begin obsessing, which only makes me sweat more."

By understanding the nature of your stress reaction, you can control it instead of allowing it to control you.

Understanding Your Stress Reactions

Thanks to advances in our understanding of biochemistry, the way the shy body responds to threat is no longer a mystery. There are four general principles of stress reactions.

1. *Stress reactions are comprehensive.* They involve the whole

body—muscles, eyes, heart, lungs, mouth, and more—in an organized and purposeful manner. In fact, they affect the operation of the brain, including its creation of memories, perceptions, explanations, and emotions.

Stress reactions begin in the amygdala, a small almond-shaped structure deep in the brain that detects threats in the environment. (See Chapter 8.) When the amygdala senses danger, it sends warning signals to the cerebral cortex, the higher brain, which makes decisions about how it should respond, and also to the autonomic nervous system, which prepares the body for dealing with the threat before it fully knows what it is. Your reacting nervous system triggers the sweaty palms, shallow breathing, flushed cheeks, thumping heart, and parched mouth that you recognize as a shy response. I'll explain why the body uses these particular protective devices below.

Sometimes your body becomes so involved in a stress reaction that your mind has difficulty processing information. As a banker wrote to me, "When I speak in front of my colleagues, I cannot keep track of my thoughts. My outer appearance gives no indication of this. My face is calm, my voice is even, but mentally I am suffering." It's also common to become so overwrought with shyness during an introduction that you don't even hear the person's name. Your mind is preoccupied with the many sensations of the stress reaction and is trying to find a reasonable way to stop its physical manifestations while at the same time carrying on a decent conversation. Often the stress reaction is so powerful it will take precedence.

"I feel hot," you may be thinking when introduced to a new coworker. "I must be blushing. Do you think he notices? How am I going to stop it? Is there something clever I could say about it? Maybe I could cover my cheeks with my hands and pretend that I'm shocked by what he's saying. Ugh. Now it's even worse. This is awful. And I haven't a clue what he's saying to me. Did he just ask me a question?"

When this happens, you are dividing your attention between three mental activities: experiencing your physical discomfort, looking for ways to alleviate it, and conversing. Your inability to manage three disparate activities in your mind simultaneously is not your fault; the task is nearly impossible. (If you don't believe me, ask two friends to talk into each of your ears while you sing a tune. You'll find it hard to follow what either one says or keep the words to the song straight.)

Stress reactions are no fun, and they certainly are difficult to control when you misunderstand them. The following are strategies to help refocus your mind so that you can target your attention toward the social task you're facing and away from the physical arousal of your stress reaction.

- Remember, stress reactions are short-term responses to fear. If you ruminate over them, they can become long-term, out-of-control panic attacks. Don't dwell on them! Remind yourself that they will pass, and they will.

- Refocus your attention. Stop thinking about your clammy hands when you should be concentrating on what you're saying and hearing. The best way to do this is to force your attention on something else. For example, ask that new employee a question, or compliment her on her hairstyle.

- Give yourself enough time to warm up to new situations. Since you know that you will feel nervous in a new situation, remind yourself that you're in the warm-up phase of an encounter. Just don't let the warm-up period and your stress reactions go on forever. Refocus.

- Be realistic. You may believe that your nervousness is more visible than it really is. Stress reactions can feel intense, but as the banker made clear, they don't necessarily appear so. Unless your coworkers have x-ray vision, how will they know that your stomach is in knots?

- Go easy on yourself. If you're anxious at a big party, take a break. Step outside for air, duck into the rest room to wash your hands, or examine a painting. Move in and out of "threatening" situations. It's helpful to intersperse easy conversations with friends with more intimidating activities like meeting new people.

- Watch your interpretations. Above all, don't interpret your body's signals to mean that you don't belong or that you're just not meant to be with others. A stress reaction simply informs you that you're highly alert and will be able to pick up on anything "dangerous" that comes your way. That's all! Think of yourself as the most alert person in the room, not the most uncomfortable one.

2. *Stress reactions are economical.* They're the easiest bodily response during times of crisis; they require the least expenditure of thought, effort, and energy. It may seem paradoxical to view stress reactions as economical, since you seem to expend so much energy when caught in one. But actually, the body is directing energy to certain organs and withdrawing it from others in order to protect you from a perceived threat. Your discomfort stems from this lopsided physical arousal. But each symptom has a purpose.

- Dry mouth. You may have difficulty talking because you're thirsty, but during a crisis you're not supposed to use your mouth to talk or eat. Salivation is designed to break down food and increase its taste quality. The salivary glands temporarily shut down during stress to discourage these activities when you should be fighting, running, or keeping silent (while hiding).

- Clammy hands. You may become self-conscious about your sweaty palms, especially when greeting people and shaking hands. But your hands and the rest of your body are perspiring because heat is a side effect of the stress reaction. Oddly enough, clammy hands are meant to make you more comfortable by cooling you off.

- Upset stomach. It's hard to seem confident when your insides are twisting. But during stressful situations the stomach releases more acid so that it can quickly digest its contents to provide a swift burst of energy for fight or flight. Your discomfort also prevents you from eating when you have more urgent activities to attend to.

- Tension headaches. During a stressful encounter, all of your muscles are stretched for protection. The muscles in your forehead eventually become strained and start aching.

- Faintness. You may feel light-headed during an episode of extreme shyness because blood is rushing away from your head to other parts of your body that need more. Indeed, passing out is actually a protective defense. To avoid stress, the body shuts down and takes a time out. You don't have to cope with pain or bad news when you are unconscious.

- Stuttering, trembling, weak knees. These reactions inform you that the situation is getting out of hand. If you don't take action, you will be in trouble.

- Pounding heart. Because the stress reaction requires certain organs to receive more blood than usual, the heart works overtime to move blood to where it is needed the most.

- Sheepish grin, downcast eyes, head turned to the side. These body-language cues all indicate submission and may be inborn traits. Research has shown that juvenile rhesus monkeys grin when they're feeling intimidated. Perhaps this facial expression has evolved into the smile, a sign of appeasement and affiliation, although an element of nervousness can remain. (Just think back to your third-grade teacher scolding, "Wipe that foolish grin off your face" when she yelled at someone for misbehaving.) Turning away and looking down are other approaches to minimizing threat. These gestures create a psychological barrier. If you can't leave the room when you're uncomfortable, you cross arms and look down. These are ways of getting small, of avoiding.

- Silence. The inability to speak originates in an impulse that the amygdala sends to a region of the brain controlling the muscles and nerves in the face. With this signal, the facial muscles freeze and the jaw tightens, making it difficult to be articulate. So while the cat hasn't gotten your tongue, the amygdala *has* clenched your jaw. Silence allows energy to be diverted to more critical parts of the body.

- Speaking in an unnatural voice. This originates in another signal from amygdala to the part of the brain that controls your throat. The muscles of the larynx and vocal cords tighten to render your voice dull, strained, and flat. Your awareness of your stilted speech and unexpressive delivery can increase self-consciousness and make you even less willing to speak up.

These last two points deserve further comment. Silence, while allowing energy to be diverted to more critical parts of the body, is also a sign that you have surrendered to the stress reaction. This is a short-term response that fails in the long run. A better strategy is to make your alternative response more economical than the original one. This takes some time and practice, and I'll explain how you can do that below.

3. *Some stress reactions are automatic, some are semiautomatic, and some are strategic.* These three types of stress reactions comprise your personal arsenal of protective behaviors, and you need to stockpile all of them to fight social skirmishes.

Some stress reactions, like the release of extra adrenaline when someone is chasing you, or blinking rapidly during a dust storm, are inevitable. These automatic reflexes are the best solutions to bad situations.

Other stress reactions, such as crying when you're upset, are semiautomatic but feel automatic. These reactions are your *dominant responses*—deeply ingrained patterns of behavior to which you may revert when you don't know what else to do.

A twenty-six-year-old shy woman in Ohio described her semiautomatic dominant response as follows: "When I am in a situation where I am talking one-on-one with someone I do not know well, I start to feel like a shy little kid. My smiles feel frozen, I do not speak as articulately as I normally do, I get facial twitches, and my hands and voice sometimes shake. I am often outgoing and friendly, but if I feel someone is watching me or judging me (whether they are in reality or not), I become exceedingly self-conscious."

Frequently, silence is the shy individual's semiautomatic dominant response to difficult social situations. It seems to take far less effort to withdraw from a stressful encounter than to create an effective, long-term strategy to subdue the threat. Silence is easy; it requires little energy and seems to be instinctive. But it's not. You weren't born silent, but at some point you learned that silence is an easy way to deal with the agony you feel when with others.

Unfortunately, silence is also ineffective and can even be

detrimental. In the short run, it may relieve you of having to converse with others, but it creates frustration in the long term. Countless shy people have described to me the disappointments inherent in silence. As one woman wrote, "I can't think, and if I do think of something to say, I want to say it at exactly the right time, but by then the right time has passed." After leaving a social interaction, shy people suddenly find themselves brimming with what they could have and should have said. Or they fear others think of them as aloof snobs who are dreadful to be around.

Moreover, silence prevents you from meeting new people and learning about the world. When you expend most of your energy thinking about yourself, your nervousness, and your frustration, you have little left for those around you. (This is the source of the aloof label.) Very few people can break through and reach you when you are so withdrawn.

As a result of continued silence, you may berate yourself for failing to make contacts yet again. Eventually you may stop dealing with new people because, even though the silent treatment is unproductive, you don't know another strategy. As I explained in Chapter 4, this avoidance only exaggerates the feared situation.

Fortunately, you can modify your semiautomatic responses. In fact, you can reach for a new, strategic response that, with time and practice, will replace silence and become dominant. It's up to you to make contact with others—to stop focusing on yourself and start paying attention. This is the essence of being socially sensitive. With hard work and a commitment to change, these new behaviors will become reflexive and habitual. Here are some useful strategic responses:

- Give a compliment. This always works because people want to talk about what others find attractive or unique. Even a mundane comment such as "Great report!" will start a conversation.

- Perform a social grace. Get someone coffee, pass a bowl of chips, open a door, do whatever it takes to make the other person comfortable. At the very least, ask the individual next to you if she needs anything. She'll appreciate you for it.

- Ask questions. Open-ended questions are especially useful. They start conversation, encourage others to carry the ball for a while, and help you become involved. Simple questions like "What kind of work do you do?" "How do you know the host?" or "How's your presentation coming along?" are great ice-breakers.

- Have something to say. If you want to talk more, you must have something to talk about! Expand your mind and your conversational comfort zone by exploring what is likely to interest others. Read newspapers, observe your surroundings for signs of change (a new gallery opening, perhaps), and be aware of the hot issue of the day.

These socially sensitive acts always work. Not only will they help you break through your self-imposed silence and divert your attention from your anxiety, but they will also make you seem interested in—and eager to talk to—others. Just a few social successes can turn a strategic response into a new semiautomatic, dominant one. Success is highly reinforcing.

4. *Stress reactions involve emotions.* Because your mind is also engaged in stress reactions, it creates emotional explanations for your bodily sensations (the sweating, blushing, stammering, and so on). Indeed, when you find yourself in the midst of stress reaction, you may impose all sorts of meanings on it, even if your conclusions are misguided. The following are among the most common shy interpretations for stress reactions:

- I don't belong here.

- This situation is too much for me.

- I'm unattractive and unworthy of attention.

- I'm a hopeless case because I can't even handle a simple exchange with a cashier.

- Everyone around me notices my anxiety.

- My body is out of control.

These shy interpretations have two things in common: they're all negative, and they're all untrue. But, rather than thinking, "I wish my heart weren't pounding like that; I hate walking into parties," you can think instead, "Gee, my heart is pounding like mad; let's try to get *excited* about being at this party." Nothing is stopping you from relabeling your anxiety except habitual shy thinking.

We all create labels for our emotions. "Nervousness," for example, is made up of a pounding heart (physical arousal) and the sight of a beautiful person (the cue that triggers the arousal). But "attraction" is also made up of a pounding heart and the sight of a beautiful person. It all depends on how you frame your reaction.

You can relabel the symptoms of your arousal to transform negative concepts such as "anxiety," "fear," or "nervousness" into more positive ones such as "excitement," "anticipation," or "alertness." Even though they're ephemeral, these labels have an important impact on your actions. If you label something anticipation, the consequence is approach; if you label it anxiety, the consequence is avoidance. Here's how to relabel:

Reframe your feelings. Many stress reactions are not the result of anxiety; they're merely the consequence of trying something new. Rather than thinking of yourself as being anxious, why not call the emotion excitement?

Reinterpret your level of arousal, and be realistic. Are your feelings truly overwhelming and out of control, or is your experience less intense than that? Anything short of a full-blown panic attack is tolerable.

Identify the reason for your anxiety. Learn from your anxiety by identifying the reason behind it. Is there something tangible to fear? A real threat? An imagined threat? What evidence do you have that the threat is real? What is the magnitude of that fear?

Actually, far from being detrimental, it is good for you to be aroused. It means you're expanding your comfort zone and learning new life lessons. Without tension in your life, there is little growth. To be successfully shy, you must learn to tolerate situations that make you a little nervous, by taking incremental courses of action and by viewing your anxiety as a source of growth and learning.

The Hidden Value of Anxiety

A stress reaction can be quite uncomfortable, but under certain circumstances, I welcome this arousal. Even after twenty years of teaching, I still look forward to getting a bit nervous before addressing my students. I need the tension to deliver a good lecture. My reaction also tells me that I'm still excited about teaching after all these years.

However, I don't let my physical arousal get in the way of my instruction. I've learned a few tips from actors, professional orators, comedians, and athletes, who all *need* to get jittery before performing. The lesson: be prepared so you won't have to think about your speech, lines, jokes, or jump shots when you're nervous.

I prepare by writing down my lectures in advance. Orators recite their speeches in front of a mirror. Actors rehearse endlessly. Big-time comedians try out new jokes in small clubs.

Athletes practice, practice, practice. And all of us look forward to getting anxious because we know the nervousness we feel before showtime allows us to give great performances. That sense of excitement helps us deliver with a bit more zip.

It's useful for you to do the same thing. Prepare. But always look for that sense of excitement before you go to a party, deliver a speech, or greet your new boss. Rather than seeing it as an anxiety response that dampens your experience, allow it to give you a competitive edge that makes you feel more alive.

How Shyness Connects to Fear and Anxiety

Fear comes from a specific threat, perhaps an out-of-control car hurtling toward you or the thought of a blind date. It dissipates soon after that object or situation has disappeared. Anxiety, on the other hand, is more general and is not provoked by a specific threat. Rather, it creeps up slowly, and although less intense, it takes longer to fade.

Although they are distinct in origin, we experience fear and anxiety in much the same way: the body becomes aroused, alert, and ready to defend itself. But you can easily identify the situation that triggers fear, while the source of anxiety may be elusive. Moreover, anxiety symptoms are more diffuse than reactions triggered by fear. They may make you seem tense, edgy, or jumpy because you're always alert for unseen threats. Many anxious people find it hard to relax, even when they're alone.

Some individuals have difficulty ascertaining what causes their shyness-related physical reactions. Their symptoms are often bothersome—usually not intense enough to interfere with daily life—yet they seem to have no concrete cause. These mild, ongoing stress reactions are the result of anxiety, not fear.

Although we're all prone to feeling anxious at some point in our lives, there is a spectrum of anxiety sufferers and causes.

Some people are anxious only when anticipating a watershed event in their lives like a job interview, an important deadline, or a wedding. Just about everyone feels apprehensive and perhaps shy during these times, but after the big day has passed the anxiety level usually drops.

Others are anxious because their nervous systems are highly reactive. Their bodies seem constantly to be in overdrive, regardless of the situation. This kind of anxiety is a purely physical reaction. These individuals may be helped by consulting a doctor and taking medication to alleviate their anxious arousal.

Yet another group of people are unsure what causes their anxiety. They feel apprehensive in many situations but not all. Their reaction is due neither to a specific situation like a job interview nor to a highly reactive nervous system. On a continuum of anxiety responses, they fall between feeling anxious about a specific stressor and being anxious all the time.

Many shy people fit into this category; they suffer from anxiety triggered by a variety of broadly related situations that involve interacting with and being evaluated by others. It's not the job interview that provokes the response, but the room full of coworkers one must face every day. It's not the wedding, but the crowd of people who will be there.

Some people have so much social anxiety that they seek treatment from mental health professionals. Once they've entered a course of therapy and/or medication, their social anxiety decreases. As a New Yorker in the publishing industry wrote to me, "I am still capable of being paralyzed by shyness, and it's okay. Now I call my therapist or a good friend as soon as I realize what's going on. I just say, 'Help! I'm feeling shy and can't figure out why.' Usually there is an underlying anxiety, and just identifying it helps."

There are also those who have a normal level of social anxiety based on their desire to make a favorable impression on others. This kind of arousal can be beneficial and positive because it prompts you into taking action, such as preparing a speech.

But you can also handle normal social anxiety in ways that are hurtful. You may isolate yourself, become uncommunicative, and focus exclusively on your worries, thereby exaggerating the anxiety and becoming more deeply mired in it. You may come to believe that your level of anxiety is worse than anyone else's and that you'll never recover.

If you feel you are suffering from social anxiety, check with your doctor to determine if medication and therapy can help you. If your body isn't at the root of your anxiety, you may need to begin changing your perceptions, behaviors, and emotions about the social situations that trigger your nerves. As always, coming to terms with the cause of the problem is the best approach because it puts it into perspective and provides you with an opportunity to take control.

Reality Checks

It's natural to want a quick fix for anxiety—we all want out of uncomfortable situations. However, many short-term strategies just don't work. Some, such as imagining clouds, eating carbohydrates, being near or visualizing bodies of water, breathing deeply, taking medication, or drinking alcohol, can decrease intense arousal by slowing the brain's activity or diverting your attention. But these short-term solutions don't resolve the *cause* of the arousal; they temporarily divert you from your shyness and anxiety without getting at the heart of the problem.

You may feel anxious because of your perception that others threaten your self-esteem. While you can calm yourself by thinking about waterfalls or tropical beaches, when you open your eyes, you will still be shy, anxious, and perhaps even terrified about asking the boss for a raise or that woman for a date.

The following reality check will help you put the anxiety-provoking situation in perspective and address the cause of your fear so that you can overcome your inhibition.

Thinking through the answers to these questions can help you stare down your fears. With a dose of the truth, you will find that the worst will never happen.

In Your Shy Life Journal

The next time you feel nervous, give yourself a reality check. Answer the following questions:

Are my fears realistic, or am I just imagining the worst possible outcome?

Will I really be in the spotlight, or will it just feel that way?

Am I constantly avoiding this situation? If so, does my avoidance make it even more frightening?

What is causing me to feel so anxious? What is so threatening to me? What is my worst fear?

In what ways can I realistically control the situation?

In what ways can I prepare for the situation?

What areas are beyond my grasp? (See Chapter 4.)

Will I feel like a success if I just show up and have a good time, or am I putting pressure on myself to be the star of the show?

Long-Term Strategies

Just as there are ineffectual short-term strategies, there are many futile and even detrimental long-term strategies for alleviating the anxious arousal associated with shyness.

The most obvious one is avoidance—the elimination of the stressor altogether. As a young bookstore clerk wrote to me, "I have left social gatherings without telling people, no matter what the consequences, even if I had to walk all the way home in the middle of the night. I avoid social situations almost totally."

When you stop talking to new people, eating in new restaurants, or venturing into new territory, you may even stop believing that you ever wanted to do these things in the first place. Your personal life languishes as you strictly adhere to the tried and true.

A second highly detrimental and even dangerous long-term strategy is self-medication—the use of alcohol or any other substance except those drugs specifically prescribed to alleviate symptoms of anxiety. The perils of this strategy are many. You can become dependent on these substances. You will limit your interactions to the times when you're under the influence. You may believe the substances make you "talkative." You will doubt your ability to manage your shy symptoms without these chemicals. They can interfere with your ability to think of things to say (i.e., shyness of the mind) and/or your ability to say it (e.g., slurred speech).

Although effective long-term strategies vary from individual to individual, the basic rules apply to everyone. They will encourage you to reach a better understanding of the causes and effects of your shyness and help you use your anxiety as a new source of self-awareness. Consequently, you will gain a fuller appreciation of how anxiety fits into the big picture of your life. These strategies are both general and flexible enough to apply to any situation that creates a shy stress reaction.

- Persist. Remember, keep repeating your new behaviors because they will get easier and make you less anxious over time. Don't give up.

- Stop avoiding. If public speaking makes you nervous, create plenty of opportunities to do so. Practice at home, in front of close friends, or join a speech-making club such as Toastmasters. Your goal is to turn an anxiety-provoking activity into a routine one.

- Act now. When you learn new behaviors relatively early in life, your brain can incorporate them quite easily. While it is more difficult to change as you age, it's never too late. There is no time like the present; destructive habits will only become more entrenched as time goes on.

- Review the three principles of shyness: the approach/avoidance conflict, the slow-to-warm-up tendency, and the comfort zone. Understand how they affect your behavior in the feared situation. Are you avoiding an activity you really want to try? Are you expecting instant rewards instead of giving yourself adequate time to warm up? Are you nervous because the feared activity is outside your usual comfort zone? How can you help yourself? If you can apply the three principles, the new situation will no longer feel new.

- Befriend your anxiety. Welcome your stress reaction as a part of who you are. When you relax and think to yourself, "Oh, here you are again, anxiety, my old companion," it seems to lose its power to control you, especially if you add, "I'm not going to let you stop me from doing what I need to do!"

- Do "social reconnaissance." Plan your attack by gathering as much information as you can in advance. Check out a venue before delivering a speech. Inquire about appropriate attire for a dinner dance. When you orient yourself in advance, you are more prepared to be in the situation. There are fewer surprises.

Using Avoidance to Your Advantage

I've advised you to eschew avoidance. However, there is a good use for it, when you act with conscious intent. Let me explain.

Imagine a hungry lion coming toward you, an unarmed, solitary being in the jungle. Your reaction is simple: you run for safety. That's avoidance on the physical level, and there's nothing wrong with it. In fact, avoiding the hungry lion saved your life.

But avoidance is beneficial only when you spend your time in safety thinking about how you can reduce the threat in the future. Once you've caught your breath, you need to create a plan to help you deal with the lion the next time you encounter it. Perhaps you could take along your comrades because there's safety in numbers. Or you could develop weapons that would kill the lion. Or you could determine when the lion sleeps and only venture into its territory when it's safe.

Just like the jungle adventurer, you need to learn from your experience and develop strategies that will prevent you from avoiding threats in the future. Skipping a networking seminar once is permissible. But avoiding them every time they're scheduled will not only hinder your career, it will also render networking seminars all the more intimidating.

If you dodge one seminar, spend your time wisely. Strategically plan how you will get through the next one successfully. Bring a colleague along so you won't feel so alone. Obtain a list of attendees, and pick out the people you'd most like to meet. Develop your social skills so that you'll be prepared for spending a few hours in the company of strangers. Learn from your avoidance by planning ahead for your next challenge.

A Last Word About Shyness of the Body

In this chapter I have not recommended physical solutions such as deep breathing, relaxation techniques, regular massages, self-medication, or meditation for the shy body. The body knows what it's doing when it creates stress reactions. It signals your every nerve and hair follicle that there's danger lurking. If you experience those signals, the body has done its job successfully.

My strategy is to combat the shy body with the mind. Only the mind can direct the body to create stress reactions: it decides whether fighting or fleeing is in order; it seeks to reduce your physical reactions; it interprets the meaning of the arousal.

In Chapter 6 we will explore how the shy mind explains threats and why it often evolves the wrong solutions to deal with those threats. And I'll offer suggestions for how your shy mind can select better strategies.

6

Shyness of the Mind

"Socially, shyness has made me an isolationist. I am constantly worried about my ineptitude and inadequacies in social situations."

"I'm an awful communicator, which I think is connected with my shyness. I'm afraid of what people will think of me when I say something, or I'll be afraid of saying the wrong thing."

"There's a lot of internal dialogue. I can't quite explain it. I try not to behave shy, but I always feel that I am."

Ah, the workings of the shy mind. I'm fascinated by it. The shy mind is a trickster and a mythmaker. Still, it is only the *mind* of the shy individual (and not the shy body or self) that creates, believes, and eventually falls victim to the myths about shyness.

Although you may feel your thoughts are unique, I have found that shy minds often think alike. These predictable thought patterns allow the myths to creep in and find refuge. The shy mind is powerful—powerful enough to embrace these myths despite their falseness. But it is also powerful enough to break through to the truth. To borrow a phrase from my favorite movie, *Cool Hand Luke*, I want to help you "get your mind right." All it takes is a deep understanding of shy thought patterns and the determination to reconfigure them during social encounters.

There's a lot more to changing the shy mind than merely thinking positively, but it's not as difficult as it may first appear. Your task becomes easier once you break down the patterns into manageable pieces and recognize the progression of shy thoughts. Let's take a closer look at this progression.

The Paradox of Narcissism

It may be counterintuitive to conceive of a shy person as a narcissist. After all, the narcissist needs to be the center of attention, and that's the last thing on a shy person's mind. As a highly respected physician explained to me, "I was left back in the second grade because my teacher thought I couldn't read. I actually could read, but I was mortified of reading out loud." Shyness can obviate attention-seeking behavior.

However, in one sense shy individuals are narcissists. They are the center of attention in their own minds; during interactions with others, they star in their own dramas. Why? As we have seen, the volume of physical responses is turned up loud in the shy body and can become the source of much distraction and discomfort. When the body is so aroused, shy people feel tense and focus inward. They constantly check their reactions and measure their impact on others. In a conversation, they begin to believe that others are listening to their every word, watching their every gesture, evaluating their every pore.

This is a fallacy. Other people have their own issues to deal with and do not focus on you with such intensity. Once you let go of evaluating yourself and the myth that everyone else is watching you, you can be free to think about what others are saying. You can plan your next rejoinder and observe environmental cues. When you shift the focus away from your reactions, it's like turning off a radio inside your head; you can develop an outward view.

In the remainder of this chapter we will see how this paradoxical form of narcissism underlies many shy thought patterns and ultimately creates the framework for shyness of the mind.

Every Conversation Is an Evaluation

A social worker in Washington wrote the following to me: "WHAT A CURSE! To be so constantly self-centered and fearful! 'How am I being perceived?' is the question that is uppermost in my mind during almost every waking moment." Her response is the epitome of shy narcissism.

In truth, a conversation is not an evaluation. This social worker is the only person watching for mistakes and evaluating her every move; she believes she is on trial every time she opens her mouth in an uncertain situation.

You too may feel that you're constantly being evaluated. This thought process is due to a phenomenon called objective self-awareness, a trick the mind plays when you feel self-conscious. Objective self-awareness takes you out of the moment and out of yourself.

Here's how it works. If I'm conversing with a good friend and become thirsty, I'll reach for my glass, take a sip of water, and replace the glass without much thought. But if I'm talking to a bank loan officer whom I believe is scrutinizing me, I will become self-conscious. In fact, if I feel she is watching me intently, I will become intensely self-conscious.

Now, when I'm thirsty, I will think, "I'm reaching for the glass, and I'm trying to do it gracefully so I won't spill all over the pile of papers on the desk. Okay, I've got the glass in my hand. Now I'm raising it to my lips. I'm doing my best to keep my hand still; I don't want her to think I'm nervous about applying for this loan." I am so self-conscious, I actually step outside of myself and observe my actions. I am objectively self-aware. Indeed, I'm not my usual self because I'm so absorbed in what I'm doing and how I'm performing.

Usually objects or situations that trigger objective self-awareness—a mirror, a video camera, a visit to a loan officer, or a public-speaking engagement—provoke and sometimes even exaggerate your dominant response—silence and inhibition being the most common among those who are shy.

When you feel someone is watching you, you will have a more exaggerated inhibited response because of your acute self-consciousness. Eventually, you may feel that you're being scrutinized and evaluated whenever you're out in public. Sometimes the mere presence of another person can bring on objective self-awareness, making you even more acutely inhibited.

In order to counteract excessive self-evaluation, it is helpful to rethink your dominant response and get back into the moment. Here are some ways to accomplish this:

Reflect on your current response. Do you become entangled in objective self-awareness? Does that lead to your becoming inhibited? Must this be your only dominant response? You have other options that are more active and direct (remind yourself, for instance, that you are slow to warm up in new situations).

Relabel your dominant response. Think of it as your first response rather than your only one. What happens next? Can you use your warm-up period to gather information and attend to cues in the environment? You might look around the room to observe who is standing alone or at the edge of a group. Once you identify potential conversation partners, try approaching them.

Find your strengths and go to them. Determine which qualities are your best. When you're feeling self-evaluative, rely on these, whether it's being helpful, remaining calm during a crisis, or smiling brightly.

Understand the role of accentuation and exaggeration. From my stint as a radio host, I know that a slight pause can seem like an eternity when you're trying to speak well. But this agony is subjective and highly exaggerated. Lulls, tied tongues, and stammers aren't as apparent to others as they are to you. It doesn't sound as bad as it feels.

Practice. Repetition helps you become more comfortable in evaluative situations that bring on objective self-awareness. Talk into a tape recorder or in front of a mirror or video camera to get used to feeling watched and evaluated. It may be embarrassing at first, but you will relax as time goes on.

Focus on something else in the environment. This can help you take the pressure off yourself and bring you back into the moment. You might ask a question or give a compliment. Or do something familiar that will bring you a bit of comfort, talk about a current news story.

In Parts III and IV, I will show how you can alleviate self-consciousness in specific situations.

Add a Dash of Negativity

A gardener in his late thirties wrote to me, "I tend to feel anxious and ill at ease around others, especially those who incite my shyness. This is because I'm constantly worried about embarrassing myself, which in turn is due to being overly concerned with the opinions others have of me. (I tend to believe those opinions are skewed toward the unfavorable.)"

Being evaluated (even if it's you who is doing the judging) may not be so terrible, in and of itself. Like a reasonable dose of anxiety, self-evaluation does keep you alert. It becomes a problem, however, when like this gardener, you *always evaluate yourself negatively.*

You may set yourself up for this misperception by narcissistically focusing on yourself, your fleeting thoughts and fears, your need for approval and acceptance, and your constant search for perfection. All people have these emotions, but you may experience them intensely when, rather than paying attention to the other person during pauses in the conversation, you concentrate only on yourself and your inner voice. Your fears and need for approval can escalate during these isolated silences.

As a high school student in Massachusetts wrote to me, "When I'm listening to someone talk in a one-on-one conversation, I'm usually more worried about what they're thinking about me than what they're saying." The truth is, however, this young woman does not have much to fear, and neither do you. Others are simply too busy, disinterested, or self-absorbed to notice what you do throughout the day. You do not live under a microscope.

Now, this may sound harsh, but it's certainly not as harsh as what you may tell yourself. Shyness researcher Jonathan Cheek observed, "Shy people are their own worst critics." You may anticipate that you will fail, fail to act, and then beat yourself up for failing. You may remain silent, petrified of saying something foolish. You may tell yourself that others are bound to reject you, so you retreat into a narrow comfort zone. Or, paradoxically, you may avoid risks for fear of success. That would force you to reexamine the myths you have come to believe, and even your identity.

In truth, you don't have to give credence to these negative thoughts just because they enter your head. Thoughts are not facts, and if they're generated during the altered state of objective self-awareness, then they're exceedingly unreliable. When you're highly aroused and under duress, as you would be if objectively self-aware, there is a great deal going on in your mind, and this is precisely when you're most prone to faulty thinking and errors in judgment.

Moreover, your negative thoughts have specific patterns that can lead you to disparaging conclusions about yourself. For instance, you may overemphasize the significance of your role in social situations. When you do that, you unfairly bear the burden for social mistakes. For example, you may automatically assume a lull in the conversation is due to the "fact" that you're boring, failing to recognize that perhaps the other person is boring or maybe just collecting his thoughts.

Claiming Responsibility for Failure

Paul is shy, but he mustered the courage to go to a party. There he met Mary Beth, an insurance agent whom he found attractive. Since Paul was recovering from an ulcer, he engaged Mary Beth in a conversation about the difficulties he had with his HMO. He recounted, in vivid and candid detail, all of his symptoms and his trials and tribulations with the insurer. He asked Mary Beth if she could advise him on how to handle the situation.

Mary Beth seemed sympathetic to Paul's woes, and he thought the conversation was going swimmingly. He was happy, in fact, until Mary Beth abruptly and inexplicably excused herself and headed to the other side of the room where the bar and buffet table were located. Paul stood alone in front of the stereo speakers, bewildered. He didn't approach Mary Beth to continue the conversation, say good-bye, or ask for her phone number. Rather, he left early and dejectedly.

When Paul ran into Mary Beth the following week at their local Chinese take-out, he pretended not to see her and hurried out with his shrimp lo mein, his eyes glued to the floor.

Attributions help us render life more predictable, orderly, secure, and reasonable by explaining seemingly random events. Shy or not, we all make them, usually when we lack sufficient information to know exactly what caused an incident.

Unfortunately, shy people often jump to certain predictable conclusions, usually looking inward to blame themselves for failures, while at the same time disregarding other plausible causes. Here's what Paul thought about his interaction with Mary Beth: "She left because I was boring her. I have a problem with women. I always turn people off. Mary Beth is just like the rest."

Typically, he took full responsibility for the rupture.

In general, we attribute events to three types of causes, and use these rationales, in various combinations, to explain any occurrence, be it a car crash, forest fire, strange lights blinking in the northern sky, or even a social snub.

1. *Internal or external.* A circumstance can occur due to something within your realm of responsibility (internal) or something outside of it (external). You can hold yourself responsible by making an internal attribution

("She left because I was boring her"), or you can cite an external factor ("She stopped talking to me because we were in front of the speakers, and the music was too loud").

2. *Stable or unstable.* The cause may be something permanent ("I have a problem with women") or temporary that can change easily ("I'm not feeling well tonight, so my conversational skills are off").

3. *Specific or global.* The cause is something that occurs in every situation ("I always turn people off") or something particular about a situation ("Mary Beth is hard to get along with, but that doesn't mean I'm unattractive to other women").

Naturally, anyone in Paul's position would want to explain Mary Beth's slight, but he chose reasons that denigrated him and his sense of self. If you want to be confident about your attributions, you must consider every possible outcome. Let's look at a wider range of potential explanations for the social failure:

Internal attributions: Either Paul was a boring guy or Mary Beth was rude.

External attributions: Possibly the music was too loud or Mary Beth wanted to sit down.

Stable attributions: Maybe Mary Beth vowed never to talk about insurance when she's not on company time, or Paul has a problem with women.

Unstable attributions: Perhaps Mary Beth was hungry and wanted to eat, or Paul was having an off night.

Global attributions: Paul always turns people off, or conceivably Mary Beth has no social skills—never had them, never will.

Specific attributions: Mary Beth could have had a headache

and been in a bad mood that night. Or Paul grossed her out by talking about his ulcer.

Perhaps it was some combination of these causes. Nobody, except Mary Beth, knew what was going on in her mind, and since Paul hadn't mustered the courage to ask her or even talk to her again, he was unable to check out the truth and correct his thinking.

However, had Paul not blamed himself for her departure but rather got up the nerve to speak to Mary Beth at the Chinese restaurant and ask about why she had taken off so quickly, she might have replied, "I'm really glad to see you and I'm happy you asked. You know, while we were talking, I suddenly saw my old roommate, Melissa, out of the corner of my eye. It looked like she was getting ready to leave, and I hadn't talked to her in ages. I just had to say hello. But when I got back to where we were standing, you were gone. I asked around, and people told me you left without saying good-bye. I guess I did leave you pretty abruptly; I hope I didn't hurt your feelings. In fact, I was disappointed that I didn't get a chance to give you my phone number."

In his current mind-set, however, Paul was incapable of discovering the truth about Mary Beth's intentions. Instead, he believed the worst about himself, and he suffered deeply from that belief.

The Pessimistic Attributional Style

Like Paul, you may blame yourself for whatever goes wrong in your social life by relying on internal, stable, and global attributions. "Something is wrong with me," you may reason. "It has always been that way; it affects everything I do." (Rather than, "This is a lousy party; sometimes I'm happy at parties and sometimes I'm not; just because I haven't met anyone tonight doesn't mean that I'm an unlikeable person.")

It matters little what the situation is—a brief pause in a

conversation, no dance partners at a singles mixer, or a rough start with a new client—you hold yourself responsible for every difficulty. In fact, you may be unable to fathom how others could be responsible for mistakes.

What's worse, when you do have successes, you take no responsibility for or pleasure from them. You attribute a great conversation to external, unstable, and specific causes—luck, an extroverted conversational partner, loose lips from alcohol, or a good mood. You never take credit for your successes. Indeed, I have found that shy people take too much responsibility for the bad times and none at all for the good.

This doomsday mentality is known as a *pessimistic attributional style*, and it effectively destroys self-confidence. It is impossible to be self-assured when you believe that you, and only you, cause foul-ups.

What's worse, this mind-set affects current as well as future social problems. Because internal, stable, and global attributions apply to all situations, past, present, and future, it's unlikely that Paul will find reasons to change his behavior. He will think, "Mary Beth didn't want to hear what I had to say because I'm boring. Why bother talking to her or anyone else? I'm just going to get the same response—rejection. It's hopeless."

Not surprisingly, shy people share this bleak view of life with those who are depressed. After all, why keep trying when you're doomed to fail? Why go out in public if you're only going to have a good time when the planets are aligned a certain way? Why bother meeting people when, ultimately, you only cause yourself and others misery?

It's important to determine whether you have a pessimistic attributional style in order to take some corrective action. The following questionnaire will help you analyze how you attribute favorable and unfavorable events in your life.

Shyness Attributional Questionnaire

For each of the situations below, make the following three ratings by circling the number that best represents your answer under each column:

External/Internal: On a scale from 1 to 7, with 1 representing "totally due to other people or circumstances" and 7 being "totally due to me," how would you assess the cause of the situation?

Unstable/Stable: On a scale from 1 to 7, with 1 representing the statement "The cause will never be present again" and 7 representing "The cause will always be present," how would you assess the cause of the situation?

Specific/Global: On a scale from 1 to 7, with 1 representing "just this particular situation" and 7 representing "all situations in my life," how would you assess the cause of the situation?

External/Internal	Unstable/Stable	Specific/Global	Total

1. Someone walks away from you at a party.
1 2 3 4 5 6 7   1 2 3 4 5 6 7   1 2 3 4 5 6 7   ____

2. You tell a joke and people laugh.
1 2 3 4 5 6 7   1 2 3 4 5 6 7   1 2 3 4 5 6 7   ____

3. You spill a plate of food at a restaurant.
1 2 3 4 5 6 7   1 2 3 4 5 6 7   1 2 3 4 5 6 7   ____

4. Someone gives you a compliment.
1 2 3 4 5 6 7   1 2 3 4 5 6 7   1 2 3 4 5 6 7   ____

5. You fail to contribute to a group conversation.

    1 2 3 4 5 6 7   1 2 3 4 5 6 7   1 2 3 4 5 6 7   ____

6. You are invited to a party.

    1 2 3 4 5 6 7   1 2 3 4 5 6 7   1 2 3 4 5 6 7   ____

7. You are asked a question to which you don't have the answer.

    1 2 3 4 5 6 7   1 2 3 4 5 6 7   1 2 3 4 5 6 7   ____

8. Someone invites you to dance.

    1 2 3 4 5 6 7   1 2 3 4 5 6 7   1 2 3 4 5 6 7   ____

9. You forget someone's name ten minutes after being introduced.

    1 2 3 4 5 6 7   1 2 3 4 5 6 7   1 2 3 4 5 6 7   ____

10. You answer a question that was raised in a group discussion.

    1 2 3 4 5 6 7   1 2 3 4 5 6 7   1 2 3 4 5 6 7   ____

     Unfavorable Outcome Score:_____
     Favorable Outcome Score:_____

Scoring: For each question, add your ratings of the three dimensions and write the sum in the "Total" column. The higher the score, the more likely you are to assume personal responsibility for the outcome. Next, combine the totals for items 1, 3, 5, 7, and 9; this number is your Unfavorable Outcome Score. Now combine the scores for items 2, 4, 6, 8, and 10; this is your Favorable Outcome Score.

Compare these two scores. Did you hold yourself more responsible for unfavorable outcomes than favorable ones? If so, you may be subject to a pessimistic attributional style. I'll provide strategies for how to rethink your attributional style later in this chapter and in Parts III and IV.

Why Embrace the Doomsday Mentality?

While you may not consciously wish to adopt a pessimistic attributional style, there are several reasons why you may do so.

The narcissistic paradox may play a role. You may be so intent on observing and checking your own behavior (objective self-awareness again) that you fail to notice how the other person is contributing to the botched encounter.

Paul, for example, was so absorbed in his own insecurities that he did not attend to any of Mary Beth's gestures and signs. He missed that she was glancing toward the bar with anxious excitement before she left. It never occurred to him that perhaps she was rude enough to end a conversation without providing a reason. Paul may have had nothing to do with Mary Beth's behavior, yet he fully blamed himself for it.

This excessive self-focus can prevent you from reading between the lines. So much of the meaning of any conversation comes from what *isn't* expressed verbally—body language, nonverbal cues and gestures, subtle shifts in conversational tone and eye contact, lulls, people entering and leaving conversational groups—that when you concentrate only on your own performance, these nuances escape you. Indeed, others may be speaking this "second language" quite eloquently, but if you don't heed their reactions, you won't catch on. No wonder their behavior can seem random and inexplicable.

Moreover, when you do notice cues and receive feedback from your partner, you may interpret these, including compliments, negatively. Even if Mary Beth had said to Paul, "I really enjoyed talking to you about your HMO troubles, but I've got to see my old roommate before she leaves," he still might have taken her comment to mean, "You really bore me, and the roommate is just an excuse to leave you and talk to more interesting people." You can never win if you blame yourself for everything that goes wrong while simultaneously ignoring or dismissing positive feedback.

Why would you be so hard on yourself? The continual reinforcement of negativity may fit into a despairing self-image. I have found that people with low self-esteem have difficulty accepting new information (such as compliments) about themselves because that would force them to alter their self-image. (See Chapter 7.) Consequently, they become stuck in a safe and familiar albeit painful myth about themselves that they are unworthy of praise. The truth is, the more compliments you take in, the easier it becomes to accept them.

Finally, I have found that shy people dwell on their "failures" and blow them out of proportion. Paul actually spoke with many people at the party, but he forgot their laughter, warm responses, and appreciation, and only remembered the low point of the evening—Mary Beth's departure. Like Paul, you may quickly overlook your successful encounters and continually rehash failures.

Mulling over your blunders is helpful when you analyze what went wrong and change your behavior. But if you dwell on your mistakes and have a pessimistic attributional style to boot, you will only learn that you are a failure in social situations. You may further inhibit yourself in order to decrease your chances of making a mistake in the future. Consequently, you never allow yourself to take risks, try something new, and enjoy success.

Other Attributional Styles

Now that you realize how and why you are thinking about yourself so negatively, you may wish to seek out other thought patterns. For some situations, I recommend using patterns of attribution designed to enhance your sense of self. You may feel that these attributional alternatives are self-serving, but if you're accustomed to heaping blame upon yourself, they allow you to assume more control over your successes, maintain a higher level of self-esteem, and shrug off less-than-perfect behavior. They may give you a more balanced view of your situation.

But be realistic. Learn to recognize what you can and cannot control. This comes from feedback, experience, attempting new behaviors, and the problem-solving process I'm providing in this book. It also comes with the understanding that you will be anxious, that change takes time, and that you need to be persistent.

Practice external/unstable/specific attributions when things are going poorly. You may have become accustomed to reasoning only in an internal, stable, global manner. Try this new way of thinking when the situation is going poorly: "This is a lousy party; sometimes I'm happy at parties and sometimes I'm not; just because I haven't met anyone tonight doesn't mean that I'm an unlikeable person." Or: "Speaking in front of an audience is a difficult task; sometimes I'm good at it and sometimes I'm not; just because I didn't do as well as I wanted today doesn't mean I can't do better in the future."

Practice internal/stable/global attribution when things are going well. Likewise, take some credit when a social situation is going your way. "I'm having a great time tonight, and it must be because I am so gracious. It has always been that way; it enhances everything I do." Or: "I am an effective public speaker. I know how to do this. My speaking skills will help me in all my future engagements."

Blame the other and absolve yourself. Many nonshy people assess mistakes as follows: "When someone else errs, I hold him responsible by assigning internal attribution. But when I err, it's due to the passing circumstances of that situation, an external attribution. For example, when Claudia misses a witty retort, I may think, 'Wow—Claudia is sort of slow.' But when I can't conjure one, I think, 'Hey—Claudia caught me off-guard with that comment.'"

The trick is to balance the responsibility for your behavior with a sense that you are not *always* to blame when social situations sour. Perhaps the other person has contributed as well. With a balance, it's possible to make a more realistic assessment of your role. If you temporarily withhold judgment, it's easier to discern when you are truly to blame and when you're not. You sidestep the arousal, anxiety, and stress, see the situation more clearly, and learn from the error.

Remind yourself, "Everyone else feels this way." It's easy to rationalize less-than-perfect behavior when you believe that the rest of humanity is in the same boat. If you feel nervous when making a big presentation in front of the boss or when introduced to an attractive person of the opposite sex, it may help to remember that almost everyone feels anxious in these high-stakes situations.

Remind yourself, "I'm so special." When you are shy, you may believe that you have it worse than everyone else around you, whether or not this is so. For instance, you may be convinced that you are the *only* shy person at a party, when clearly you cannot be. Try altering this attitude by thinking that you have it better than others—your shyness makes you empathetic, sensitive, sincere, thoughtful. You add to the lives of others.

These attributional alternatives are best taken in small doses. They may not be effective permanent lifestyle choices, but they can help raise self-esteem by allowing you to take credit for success while relieving you of the constant burden of failure.

Checking Out Attributions

We rely on attributions when we are unsure of the reason behind an event. Paul, for instance, blamed himself when things seemed to go poorly with Mary Beth. Confronting her later was too threatening, given his negative self-talk and fragile self-esteem.

There are other ways, however, to evaluate attributions and correct your thinking even if you feel unable to ask the individual directly. Here is another instance in which the Four *I*'s—identification, information, incorporation, and implementation—can be useful. If an interaction isn't going well,

Paul needs to identify the problem first. Did Mary Beth leave because he was boring? Was she a rude person? Brainstorming alternative scenarios and testing them out in various situations helps in the information-gathering process. For instance, at the Chinese take-out, Paul might have thought:

- "Maybe it was those darn stereo speakers. Will Mary Beth talk to me longer now that we're in this restaurant and there's no loud noise?"

- "I could ask her if she's in a hurry. If she's not and she still leaves, then I have reason to believe she wants to avoid me."

- "Maybe she doesn't like talking about business when she's off. Will she talk to me longer if I lay off the insurance problems? In fact, maybe no one likes to discuss business after hours. Do they walk away when I bring up the subject? Maybe I should avoid talking about work at social gatherings."

- "Maybe it's not me; maybe it's her. What did other people at the party say about Mary Beth? Is she standoffish? Is she a jerk?"

By testing out alternative attributions, Paul identifies the difficulty and establishes a wider comfort zone. In attempting to solve the problem of what caused Mary Beth to leave, he is turning into a sleuth rather than dwelling on his responsibility for the problem.

As a result of his investigations, Paul could decide that he was not to blame. He might incorporate the knowledge that he is a good conversationalist into his sense of self and go on to have even more contact with others.

Unfair Comparisons

We all compare ourselves to others. Social comparison helps us determine how to act, what to discuss, where to stand—in short, how to integrate into society. Comparisons are especially helpful when you are in new or uncertain situations, such as a fancy dinner party with intricate table settings. You observe which fork the host is using to eat his salad and follow suit. There's absolutely nothing wrong with that.

I have found, however, that shy people often compare themselves unfavorably to others and as a result constantly feel inferior. When you focus on people at the center of attention—the speaker on the podium, the life of the party, or the celebrity at the premiere—rather than audience members or other quiet people lost in the crowd, you can't help but think of yourself as deficient.

You may be more inclined to engage in comparison than others because you are highly distressed and unsure in social situations. Indeed, social comparison may become a salient and important mental activity; you find yourself continually measuring yourself against others.

A female college student suffered deeply from such comparisons. She wrote:

> As I see people around me surrounded by their groups of friends, I feel almost abnormal as I do not have a group of close friends. This leads to an almost constant feeling that I am missing out on life, as I am not able to share these experiences. This is especially apparent as I see groups of people at public places (i.e., a bar) enjoying each other's company, laughing and having a good time. I am constantly very self-conscious and worried about others passing judgment on me.

Social comparison also helps you to determine whether you belong at a gathering, and this can affect your identity, self-confidence, and self-esteem. For example, if you're confused about how to handle the array of silverware at a dinner party, and upon looking around the table discover that everyone else seems to be comfortable with it, you may conclude that your social expertise is inadequate, and that you don't belong with these people—they're too sophisticated for you. You're likely to feel bad about yourself and anything you might have to say to your dinner partners.

When you are feeling shy, you may also negatively compare yourself to other people, especially those who seem talkative, charming, and relaxed. And since you don't measure up, you may feel that you don't belong because you are inferior. Your self-confidence and self-esteem suffer.

The overwhelming negativity of the shy mind is once more to blame. You will feel less socially accomplished if you only notice the most outgoing people in every crowd and fail to pick out those who are more reticent or awkward. Once caught in the grip of an unfair comparison, you may be unable to carry on an appropriate conversation with another. Even compliments will sound like criticisms to your shy ears.

Fortunately, you don't have to jump to conclusions or decide that you are less than equal to your companions. Here are three guidelines for making accurate social comparisons:

1. *Decide which qualities are worth comparing.* Since comparisons ultimately affect self-esteem, compare only aspects of your personality that matter to you. For example, trendy clothes hold little appeal to me. I wear what I like. At a gathering, I don't observe others' apparel and ruminate, "I'm less acceptable than they are because I'm not dressed in the latest style." I do notice their clothing, but I don't belittle myself for being unfashionable; I'm not out to impress anyone in that sphere.

Similarly, you may place a great deal of emphasis, perhaps even too much, on being able to talk to new people. But is this skill really desirable? Does being able to chat with a stranger make you a better person? It's wise to compare yourself only on those qualities that affect your sense of self, such as individuals who are of some interest or importance to you. If being great at small talk with everyone is important to you, then compare. But if other factors—personal integrity, compassion, being a dedicated spouse and parent—are more meaningful, then forget about the glib. There is no reason to let them ruin your life and make you feel miserable.

2. *Compare yourself to people who are more like you than unlike you.* Even though I've hosted a radio call-in show for a number of years, I never liken myself to great interviewers I admire, such as Oprah Winfrey, Larry King, and Terry Gross. I just try to keep up with my cohost, who has as much skill and experience as I do.

Shy people often compare themselves to the most outgoing person in the room or to glamorous celebrities who seem worldly enough to handle any social situation. It's only normal in this media-saturated society to think, "This actress has a witty comeback for every insult. Why can't I do that?" or "That celebrity is welcome in any nightclub. What's wrong with me? Why don't people treat me that way?"

What's "wrong" is that normal people neither follow scripts nor have the aura of fame that draws others in and makes them want to associate with us. The rich and famous have unfair advantages.

Like me, you will find it more helpful to compare yourself to "the right people." If you're lacking in small-talk skills, push those talk-show hosts out of your mind. Not only are they paid to chat, but they also rely on well-rehearsed jokes (and a gaggle of comedy writers). Rather than looking to the most gregarious people at a gathering in order to establish your self-worth, find those who are more reticent and who probably feel awkward during the first part of the event. Like you, they may come out of their shells as the party progresses.

Compare yourself with people who seem to experience the same emotions you do to determine where you stand. In fact, if you take a hard look, you will find others who are shyer, more nervous, and more tongue-tied than you are. And when you find them, introduce yourself. They will be grateful for your courtesy.

If you must watch more socially successful individuals, do so with an eye to learning what makes them so good at what they do. I listen to and read everything I can about Oprah, Larry, and Terry in order to ascertain their secrets and incorporate them into my conversations with callers to my radio shows. I'm not comparing myself to them; I'm learning from them.

You can learn from those who seem to speak effortlessly by observing how they perform. How do they engage others? Do they tell jokes? Do they share stories about their lives? Do they respond to others' spoken and unspoken needs? Rather than feeling bad about your own inadequacies, try to learn from these contacts.

3. *Remember that comparisons are culturally biased.* Americans tend to value outgoing, vivacious, bold, confident revelers over quiet, introspective conversationalists. Unfortunately, this biases us against shy people. But why buy into this prejudice? If almost half the population is shy, why isn't our society more accepting of this silent-but-sizable minority?

Besides, cultural values are quite arbitrary. For instance, Asian cultures view silence as a sign of power and strength, while in America, the same silence means that you have nothing to contribute. (I'll explain these cultural biases in Chapter 15.) So even if you feel as if you don't fit into our fast-paced, technologically driven, competitive culture, stop worrying. There's nothing wrong with you.

Using Social Skills to Solve Social Problems

Imagine being acutely self-conscious. Add the sense that you can only fail and will never succeed. Next, blend in feeling inferior to everyone you encounter and the notion that you don't belong. That's a pretty lethal mix. Now try to solve a difficult puzzle with all of these negative thoughts stewing in your mind. It can't be done—at least not well.

But that's exactly what happens when you try to deal with a difficult social problem like navigating a networking meeting, speaking up during a conference, or asking someone for a date. Shy thoughts can cloud your thinking so completely that you can't figure out how to deal with the task at hand. Problems may seem overwhelming, and you may find yourself unable to divide them into manageable pieces. You may become caught in a labyrinth of shy myths from which you cannot escape.

You need strategies—what are commonly known as social skills—to help you in situations like forgetting a new acquaintance's name or making a graceful exit from a conversation. Here are some of the most common social problems and how you can solve them:

Forgetting names. Everyone worries about forgetting a name as soon as it's uttered. It helps to introduce yourself first because that puts you in control of the introduction. If you're unable to do so, be sure to repeat the other person's name and comment on it. "Nice to meet you, Rosanna," you could say. "My best friend's name was Rosanna, when I was in grade school."

Making small talk. Much small talk has to do with finding a topic about which two strangers can easily converse. It's best to skip empty clichés about the weather and find a subject the two of you have in common—your companion's presence. Compliment or at least notice his tie, a piece of jewelry, a lapel pin, a watch, a book or videotape he may be holding, an hors d'oeuvre he's eating—anything. Take an interest in your companion, and you'll never again have to say, "Nice weather we're having today, huh?" (See Chapter 12.)

Getting the brush-off. This happens frequently at work. You gather the courage to approach your supervisor about some concerns, but she doesn't have time for you. The solution is easy: just ask if this is a good time to talk. If it isn't, set up an appointment that's mutually convenient. (See Chapter 14.)

If you're brushed off at a party, don't take it personally. It may have nothing to do with you. Even if this person rejects you, others may not. Rejection stands out like a red spot on a white sweater; it's inconsistent with what normally happens. That's why it hurts so much.

Seek out other information and alternative attributions. "I've had other conversations, and those went well. Why did I get rejected? Is it something about me? Am I dominating the conversation? Am I avoiding eye contact?" Test new behaviors to discern what went wrong. (In Chapter 12, I will cover how to include rejection in your comfort zone and how to make conversation and small talk.)

Circulating. Crowds may overwhelm you, but every group is composed of individuals. The trick, then, is to use your warm-up period to identify a few who seem as if they are alone (standing by the door, next to the buffet table, at the edge of a group and trying to break into a conversation) and talk to them. If it's a business crowd, research who would be the best contacts for you. Strategically targeting a handful of people increases your chance of success. You need not talk to everyone.

Ending a conversation tactfully. You may have trouble exiting an interaction because you're such a polite, patient listener. Talkative people can take advantage of your silence by dominating the conversation, but don't worry about interrupting the monologue. Politely say, "I really enjoyed speaking with you, but there are other people I must greet. Can we talk again later?" You'll make a good impression and escape the conversation gracefully.

A Last Word About Shyness of the Mind

Shy thoughts follow a progression. If the body is aroused and tense, you focus attention inwardly. Concentrating exclusively on your own reactions (the narcissistic paradox) leads you down the primrose path of self-criticism, objective self-awareness, and pessimistic attributions. That gives rise to further arousal, which induces even more discomfort and uncertainty. You make unrealistic comparisons and begin to believe, as my correspondents do, that you will never succeed. As a result, you withdraw.

In this chapter I have provided effective tools for interrupting this sequence at every level. When you remove the attention from yourself and break the narcissistic paradox, you are better able to attend to others. Consequently, you make more balanced attributions (which absolve you of guilt, blame, and self-criticism) and more realistic comparisons. This reduces your arousal level, which, in turn, lessens your distress. Now you are in a position to make better decisions about more effective behaviors, as do the successfully shy.

You can attack the problem of shyness holistically in your mind; what you think really does affect how you feel and what you do. In Chapter 7 we will explore how what you think also determines who you are.

Shyness of the Self

Loretta wrote to me, "I despise feeling inferior to others, and I despise feeling as if people will find out something awful about me if I expose myself to them. I know that I am a good person with no terrible dark secret to hide, yet I battle with the feeling of hiding myself from others."

This is a powerful sentiment, powerful enough to keep Loretta from actualizing her self. Her "dark secret" is that she has allowed the negative aspects of shyness to dictate her identity.

Shyness can pervade your actions, thoughts, emotions, even how you identify yourself. Because it can influence so many facets of your life and prompt you to think about yourself and your behavior so emotionally, it reaches into your very core. Often shy people don't think of themselves as "having" shyness or being "good at" shyness—they "are" shy. Shyness can appropriate your self.

The Self

The self is the essence of who you are, the qualities that render you unique. It ties together all of your experience. Eminent psychologist Gordon Allport called the self "some kind of core in our being." It integrates your internal experiences and expresses them as your identity, which includes how you see yourself—your *personal identity*—and how you appear in relation to others—your *social identity*. These two aspects of the self are analagous to a diary entry versus a letter to a friend.

Journal entries—comprising your personal identity—are full of contradictions, self-analysis, and brutal honesty. When you write in a journal, you are only concerned with understanding yourself and your experiences. You may not care how you depict yourself—your journal is for your eyes only.

In a letter, you are conscious of how others perceive you. Most likely, you will express yourself in a more studied manner. You try to make sense of your experience. You tell stories chronologically. Perhaps you hide your inner doubts and contradictory feelings. This is your social identity.

Neither of these methods of expression is better. You, the writer, are the same, but the way you express yourself is tailored to the purpose of the communication. So it is with the self. It holds together your personal identity as well as your social identity—how you are to yourself and to others.

Shyness and the Self

Shyness is what shy people do, think, and say, how they identify and evaluate themselves. Shyness of the self depends on how you perceive all the facets of your shyness. It actuates how you express and analyze yourself—your personal identity—as well as how you behave when you're with others—your social identity. You might say that shyness of the self edits the manuscript of your life. Its influence can be benign as long as you retain some control over it.

Shyness becomes a problem, however, when you let it take over. Then it stops editing and begins censoring. You detect evidence of its heavy hand when you perceive yourself as "a shy person" who has overwhelming problems, a person who can't express himself around others. It can silence you, make you avoid challenges and growth, force you to concede defeat before the battle begins, and generally render you other than who you want to be. Others may stay away because you have given them no reason to approach. Eventually, the censor becomes the self; it is in charge.

When you label yourself a shy person, you create a self-fulfilling prophecy. Because you think of yourself as shy, you must comport yourself shyly. Shyness becomes your defining characteristic, sometimes even the organizing principle of your identity. It determines all of your actions, inactions, and reactions.

Here is how one woman described her shy self: "I experience self-abuse in the form of hating myself, disgusted with the way I'm acting. I rage at myself and others: 'Why can't I just be more confident?' 'Why don't others *encourage* me positively to be more confident?' In my professional life, I miss out on participating in group discussions. I feel uncertain and stupid. I force myself to appear relaxed and outgoing, but inside I'm just crawling."

And another wrote, "Shyness has created problems in all areas of my life—personal, social, and professional. I went through high school and college without a single date. Marriage was not meant for me, or so I thought. . . . My professional life, or lack of it, has been most severely hampered by lack of confidence."

Actually, shyness in and of itself is harmless. Many charming and positive traits such as modesty and cooperativeness accompany it. But you may ignore its benefits because of your *metacognitions*, your thoughts about your shy thoughts. When these are negative, they negatively influence how you perceive the world, your worth, and your identity.

Although you may spend a great deal of time thinking about yourself, you still feel lost. I have discovered that many shy people are self-conscious and self-critical but lack insight into their problems. They are afraid to experiment with roles and expectations because they are convinced they'll fail. They can be highly emotional and anxious but lack coping skills. And since they neither confide in friends nor share their problems, they feel isolated, frustrated, and believe their lot is worse than everyone else's.

If you identify with this doomsday mentality, you too may feel unable to discern how to help yourself, where you fit in, or what you truly like, dislike, want, and need. Your goal should not be to eradicate shyness altogether, however, but rather to understand how it can influence your life in every way. Shyness doesn't just keep you apart from others—*it makes you despise what you do and who you are.* In this chapter, we will work on eliminating these negative consequences— not necessarily the shyness itself.

Soul-searching and making peace with your true self is an essential part of coping with shyness. One of the most important steps you can take is to separate how you feel about your shyness from how you feel about yourself in general. If you fail to shine at a social gathering, you may think that you're inadequate in all cases, at all times. You may place too much emphasis on how you interact with others and not enough on the areas in you life in which you are successful. But this doesn't have to be. In this chapter, I will help you to find some balance.

Shyness of the self can exist in almost all aspects of daily life. You need to recognize and demystify it, not root it out and exorcise it.

Getting a Better Grip on the Shy Self

You can take your cues on how to build your sense of self from some of the most distinguished psychologists who theorized about self-esteem. In 1890 William James, the founder of psychology in America, wrote that self-esteem involves two factors: personal success (what you do well) and personal pretensions (what you hope to do well). When these two factors coincide, self-esteem grows because you can achieve your goals.

Carl Rogers's thinking followed a similar vein. He differentiated the real self from the ideal self. In his model, the real self is composed of your characteristic features—your strengths and limitations, likes and dislikes, physical appearance and emotional depths, to name a few. The ideal self is the person you would like to be. When you think "I should have . . . ," you are merely invoking what you believe your ideal self would do.

There is usually a discrepancy between the ideal self and the real self. If your reaction to the difference is positive (you did better than you ever thought you could), then your self-esteem rises. If your reaction is negative (you did worse than you thought you should), then self-esteem declines. Self-esteem is the evaluative dimension of the self.

Just like attributions, self-esteem can be global or specific. Global self-esteem relates to how you evaluate yourself in general terms. When you declare, "I'm a good person" or "I'm a loser," you are articulating global self-esteem. Specific self-esteem describes your evaluation of particular attributes—your talent on the playing field or in the boardroom.

I have found that when shy people take stock of their real selves, they cite qualities such as being a good spouse, a caring parent, a dedicated worker, a committed environmentalist, and a shy person. When they conjure up their ideal selves, they list those same qualities, save the last. They substitute "outgoing," "gregarious," or "a great conversationalist" for shyness. When they compare their two selves, the ideal self seems better than the real. Consequently, their self-esteem declines.

Increasing Your Self-Esteem

Self-esteem can be altered. The key is to trade self-criticism for self-awareness.

Must you regard yourself negatively just because you're shy? Absolutely not. You can have high self-esteem and still be your shy self. You can build a sturdy foundation composed of realistic expectations, clear self-awareness, and the courage to take risks. Start by reconsidering your perspective about your self.

In Your Shy Life Journal

1. Take inventory of your self: List at least ten qualities that you believe contribute to your real self. Mention your strengths and your weaknesses. Be honest. No one but you will see these results. In a separate column, list the attributes of your ideal self. Do you find discrepancies?

2. Reconsider your ideal self. Have you listed "being outgoing" (or a similar attribute) as part of your ideal self? Write about why you value this trait. Would you have more friends? You might, but would they be better friends than those you have now, or would they be mere acquaintances? You can feel better about being shy by bringing your ideal self closer to reality. What would a more realistic ideal self look like?

3. Reconsider the discrepancy between your ideal self and your real self. Don't assume that a discrepancy is bad. After all, wouldn't life be boring if we were all perfect? You need not regret "mistakes," but you should learn from them. They make life an adventure. If your ideal self would have bought a cup of coffee for that intriguing stranger, but your real self didn't because you were too shy, then you haven't failed. You've merely identified a lesson to be learned. Describe the lessons engendered by discrepancies between your real and ideal selves.

4. Reconsider the meaning of self-esteem. Describe aspects of your global and specific self-esteem. What is your global self-esteem? What are the various traits that comprise your specific self-esteem? Are you a good lawyer? A sympathetic friend? A generous grandparent? An ace tennis player? A terrible housekeeper? A slow-to-warm-up party-goer? The more specific you are, the more self-aware you will be.

When you think about yourself in terms of specific attributes, you will realize that shyness is only one aspect of your personality, not your sole identity. When asked to list the specific and global attributes of their self-esteem, most shy people list many traits and activities at which they are successful; they find a few areas that need help; and they usually note that they are terrible at making small talk with strangers at parties.

For instance, a college professor wrote to me:

> Despite my social shyness, I teach animatedly and volubly, answer questions well and quick-wittedly, and have no problem at all with intimate conversation with good friends. I'm sexually expressive, inventive, and uninhibited. But on the relatively unusual occasions when I do shine at a gathering, I then feel extremely self-conscious and seek as quickly as possible to deflect attention from myself. It's a no-win situation. Any social success makes me feel sad and annoyed at past anxiety and lost opportunities!

Once you have taken a broader view of your identity, you may realize that shyness is only a small aspect of your life. You aren't shy all the time, and there are many areas in your life that work well. You should not identify and censure yourself because of one issue—the shyness.

Shy people often generalize their failure in one area to their whole sense of self; they seem unable to maintain the discreteness of specific faults. As one unhappily shy person wrote to me, "I take any failure of interaction at a party, conference, et cetera as (a) yet another symptom of my total inability to deal properly with the world and (b) something that will make people think I'm a worthless person."

One way to rein in negative feelings is to adjust unrealistic expectations. Instead of wishing that you could talk to anyone anywhere, substitute a more attainable goal such as introducing yourself confidently to one new acquaintance. Rather than wishing you could be a flawless public speaker, strive to become a speaker who is easily understood and shows genuine interest in his subject. Bringing the ideal self closer to reality will help you reduce your frustration and perceived failure and increase your sense of control and mastery.

Does Shyness Equal Low Self-Esteem?

One of my correspondents, an events coordinator in her midforties, wrote, "I think shyness relates to self-esteem. If you have high self-esteem, you don't mind taking the risk. That's what it's all about—you're shy because you're afraid of being rejected. If you have high self-esteem, then you tell yourself, 'It's just his loss.'"

Many people hold this belief, but I am not convinced. Shyness does not automatically preordain you to low self-esteem. Researchers have found that it is only moderately correlated with these negative feelings. That is, you can be extremely shy with low self-esteem (the stereotypical shy person), extremely shy with high self-esteem, or not shy at all with either high or low self-esteem. You can feel good about yourself when you think of your talents as a worker, spouse, friend, or gourmet cook. You may think of yourself negatively when you consider how you act socially, but that doesn't necessarily mean that you have global low self-esteem.

The assumption rampant in society that shyness equals low self-esteem tells me that shy people believe their self-esteem is lower than those who are not shy. Low self-esteem provides a ready explanation of why they are not getting involved with others. They don't feel worthy.

People often ask me whether shyness causes low self-esteem or, conversely, if low self-esteem causes shyness. This is a moot point. Shyness involves the whole self, while self-esteem involves only one portion of one aspect of the self. This small portion sheds little light on the holistic nature of shyness.

While I agree that it is important to understand how self-esteem and shyness intertwine, I do not believe that self-esteem is the most critical issue related to shyness.

You cannot determine a linear causation for shyness. A plus B does not necessarily equal C. To grasp the origin of your shy self you must combine your unique experiences with your individual personality, the interaction and dynamics of your self with the environment, and, ultimately, a greater awareness of the human condition.

The Importance of Being Shy

Even if you are able to dissect your global sense of self into its specific dimensions, being shy with new people—just one fragment of your personality—can still haunt you. Like the university professor, you may recognize that you are talented, intelligent, caring, and compassionate, but because you are shy you pay little attention to these positive attributes. You become mired in what I call the "importance of being shy."

Here is how one woman explained the duality of her situation: "On a one-to-one basis I'm fine, but stick me in a group and my brain is mush. I have avoided getting into relationships due to shyness. If I feel threatened in any way, I will push the guy away or somehow get out of the relationship. Professionally, shyness has not affected me. I am very confident in my abilities and will not hesitate to speak up, stand up for myself, or apply for a promotion. I have had success in all of my employment experiences." Although this woman seems to succeed in other spheres, the fact that she is shy dominates her identity.

Perhaps being shy—or not shy—has become the most important factor in your life. Indeed, another perception of self-esteem comes from psychologist Roy Baumeister at Case Western Reserve University. He views it as a collection of specific attributes that vary in relation to how meaningful they are to each of us. We strive to be good at the attributes we have designated as the most significant, and our success or failure impacts our self-esteem.

If you value extroversion so intensely, no other qualities will surpass it. Shyness will overshadow your every positive characteristic. As one correspondent wrote, "Shyness has crippled me. Shyness is the epitome of all the fears and the possibilities of things going wrong. It is completely useless. It has misled other people as to my true self, my good qualities, my skills and abilities, and especially my potential. . . . It has kept me away from my goals and the people that I want to reach." Although she claims that shyness has kept *others* away from her good qualities, it has also kept *her* from appreciating them to their fullest.

Why does shyness gain such primacy? When you are shy, you may make social mistakes, such as refusing an invitation to dance because you believe everyone is scrutinizing you (when, in truth, they are only paying attention to themselves). When you focus on such mistakes, they automatically loom disproportionately large. Certainly, they seem a lot bigger and more serious than anything you do right.

It is human nature to focus on your own frailties and ignore faults in others. Most likely, when you are feeling shy you overlook the social awkwardness of others. Similarly, you may take for granted what you do well because it seems so easy. A shy pianist, for instance, may discount her talent. She was born with a musical ear and undervalues the rarity of this gift, since she has never had to struggle with it. On the other hand, loquacity has always been out of reach, so it becomes her Holy Grail.

Finally, as Roy Baumeister points out, once you believe something is important to you, no matter what it is, your success at it will affect your sense of self and your identity. Conversely, if it's unimportant to you, failure will have little impact on your sense of self. For instance, I am a relatively mediocre golfer. In fact, you could say I'm terrible at the sport. Fortunately, I do not stake my sense of self on my golf performance. Jack Nicklaus and Tiger Woods—people who live and breathe golf—would be devastated playing at my level. They risk their reputations and their fortunes on their scores. Golf is the most important factor in their lives.

So it is with shyness. If you decide that being outgoing is *the most important issue in your life*, then you will feel heartsick with each social setback. But you don't have to. Many quiet people are happy with their lot. They know there is more to a satisfying existence than being the life of the party. As one shy woman wrote to me, "I feel in many ways my shyness attracted my husband to me. He told me my naiveté intrigued him and he believed I was being coquettish. As he came to know me better, he fell in love with a person whom he found refreshing."

And another woman shared, "Shyness is not *so* bad. At worst, it's an inconvenience. Everyone's life has some form of persistent inconvenience. At best, shyness has some positive aspects: modesty, empathy, sensitivity are traits many shy people have. The truth is, many loud, self-absorbed people should be a little bit shyer!"

When you diminish the importance of being shy to your sense of self, it will release the hold it has on you. To help you ascertain how much weight you place on being shy, try the following quiz.

The Real-Self/Ideal-Self Quiz

Below each column, circle the number that best describes you.

Real-Self Rating: For each of the personal qualities listed below, determine on a scale from 1 (not like me) to 7 (very much like me) the extent to which you possess this personal quality.

Ideal-Self Rating: For each of the personal qualities listed below, determine on a scale from 1 (my ideal self does not possess this quality) to 7 (my ideal self possesses this quality) how your ideal self rates.

Difference: For each item, subtract your Real-Self score from your Ideal-Self score. Record the difference.

Importance: On a scale from 1 (not at all important) to 7 (very important), determine how significant this quality is to your sense of self.

Total: Multiply the difference score by the importance score, and enter that number to find your total.

<u>Real-Self Rating</u>	<u>Ideal-Self Rating</u>	<u>Difference</u>	<u>Importance</u>	<u>Total</u>
1. Being a good driver				
1 2 3 4 5 6 7	1 2 3 4 5 6 7	_____	1 2 3 4 5 6 7	____
2. Being trustworthy				
1 2 3 4 5 6 7	1 2 3 4 5 6 7	_____	1 2 3 4 5 6 7	____
3. Being a good worker				
1 2 3 4 5 6 7	1 2 3 4 5 6 7	_____	1 2 3 4 5 6 7	____
4. Being calm around people				
1 2 3 4 5 6 7	1 2 3 4 5 6 7	_____	1 2 3 4 5 6 7	____
5. Being honest				
1 2 3 4 5 6 7	1 2 3 4 5 6 7	_____	1 2 3 4 5 6 7	____
6. Being a good conversationalist				
1 2 3 4 5 6 7	1 2 3 4 5 6 7	_____	1 2 3 4 5 6 7	____

7. Being myself with new people

1 2 3 4 5 6 7   1 2 3 4 5 6 7   _____   1 2 3 4 5 6 7   ____

8. Being a good listener

1 2 3 4 5 6 7   1 2 3 4 5 6 7   _____   1 2 3 4 5 6 7   ____

9. Being a good dancer

1 2 3 4 5 6 7   1 2 3 4 5 6 7   _____   1 2 3 4 5 6 7   ____

10. Being self-aware

1 2 3 4 5 6 7   1 2 3 4 5 6 7   _____   1 2 3 4 5 6 7   ____

11. Being a good confidant

1 2 3 4 5 6 7   1 2 3 4 5 6 7   _____   1 2 3 4 5 6 7   ____

12. Being spontaneous

1 2 3 4 5 6 7   1 2 3 4 5 6 7   _____   1 2 3 4 5 6 7   ____

13. Being self-assured

1 2 3 4 5 6 7   1 2 3 4 5 6 7   _____   1 2 3 4 5 6 7   ____

The Difference score indicates the degree of overlap between your real self and your ideal self. The greater the score, the more discrepancy there is within your sense of self.

The Importance score reflects the degree of significance you place on that personal quality as it relates to your sense of self. The higher the number, the more meaningful that quality is to how you think of yourself.

The Total score indicates the importance of any discrepancy within your sense of self. The higher your score, the more divided your sense of self on those qualities listed in the quiz.

The traits I chose to include in this quiz may have little relevance to your own sense of self. To make this exercise more meaningful for you, try the personalized version of the Real-Self/Ideal-Self Quiz.

If you are like most of the people who have taken these quizzes in my seminars, you'll find that you possess many important and desirable personal qualities that you may overlook because you are too busy examining the relatively few qualities you lack but would like to acquire. It's admirable to want to improve your sense of self, but put your attributes into perspective. Don't forget the many fine traits you do have. Becoming aware of all of your strengths makes examining your perceived weaknesses easier.

In Your Shy Life Journal

The Personalized Real-Self/Ideal-Self Quiz

Go back to the Shy Life Journal exercise at the beginning of this chapter. On a new journal page, list all of the attributes you generated for your personal inventory. At the top of the paper, create the "Real Self," "Ideal Self," "Difference," "Importance," and "Total" headings. Use the same rating and scoring system as above.

Putting Self-Esteem into Action

How you feel about the discrepancy between your ideal self and your real self can come only as the result of your actions—doing better or worse than anticipated in a given situation. You can catalog and affirm your good qualities, but that won't change your identity, at least not in the real world. If you want to raise your self-esteem, you must challenge yourself by participating in activities that once intimidated and discouraged you.

A formerly shy teenage girl wrote to me, "Joining the high

school forensics team has helped me to feel comfortable in front of people and with myself in general. You meet many different people and get a chance to talk in a low-pressure atmosphere. Another thing was my summer job. I worked as a cashier in a food stand. Just talking with different customers every day showed me how easy it is to start conversations. I feel I am only 10 percent as shy as I was five years ago."

To raise your self-esteem, you must conduct your life more like someone who has high self-esteem. While those lucky people seem to lead a charmed life, they don't. They work at it. But first let's look at the characteristics of people with low self-esteem.

Characteristics of People with Low Self-Esteem

I have found that those with low self-esteem have a relatively rigid sense of self. They see themselves one-dimensionally and rarely explore other aspects of their identities. For instance, if you have low self-esteem and decide that you are incapable of making small talk, you may never try to prove yourself wrong; you are simply unable to envision yourself as gregarious. Therefore, you may stay away from situations that provoke small talk. Why put forth the effort if you're only bound to fail, you may reason. This is a sure sign of a narrow comfort zone, further reinforcing negative feelings about yourself.

People with low self-esteem can also take unrealistic risks, choosing activities that are either too difficult or too easy. As a result, they never feel successful. When you opt for an activity that is too difficult, you wager your whole self-esteem on the impossible; failure is predictable. For instance, if you believe that you are poor at introducing yourself or creating spontaneous and witty repartee and you still go to a large party filled with influential strangers, discomfort is guaranteed. Moreover, this unrealistic risk reinforces your rigid sense of self as a failure at small talk.

Alternatively, you may take on problems that are relatively easy to solve such as attending a business reception but only talking to coworkers whom you know well. You cannot expand your comfort zone in such a low-risk situation. Your hollow victory will do little to enhance your sense of accomplishment. It's easy to discount a success that has no meaning.

I have found that people with low self-esteem are quite cognizant of what they cannot do but have little insight into what they can do and rarely attempt new challenges. The old adage still rings true: *You'll never know until you try.*

People with low self-esteem are unhappy. They seem to fail whenever they try something new, they are only good at what everyone else seems to do well, and they uncover few positive attributes when searching their souls. It becomes a self-perpetuating cycle. Soon they confine themselves within their narrow comfort zones. They feel frustrated and choose the wrong activities when they do venture out. This only causes more frustration and a deeper retreat into their private world.

Characteristics of People with High Self-Esteem

People with high self-esteem have a relatively flexible sense of their identities. Although, like everyone else, they also experience frustration, failure, and occasional bad days, they handle these challenges more constructively than those with low self-esteem. They know that certain characteristics make them unique. They also appreciate that they have some talents. They are capable of taking action and incorporating new information about themselves.

Imagine Sally, a person with poor small-talk skills but high self-esteem. She may reason that she's not good at big parties crowded with strangers, but that may be tolerable since she is successful in many other areas of her life. Instead of going to these parties, she spends time with close friends. When a buddy introduces her to someone unfamiliar, she finds that after the initial awkwardness of the warm-up period she can communicate relatively easily.

In fact, after this encounter, it slowly dawns on Sally that she is good at talking to strangers. This seems odd to her, because she has never thought of herself that way. But, because her sense of self is flexible, she can incorporate the new information and regard herself as a person capable of making small talk under certain circumstances.

Sally's success gave her a small but tangible sense of accomplishment. Moreover, she didn't disallow her achievement by claiming that her new behavior meant little since the new acquaintance was a friend of a friend. He was a stranger, she had a nice conversation with him, and she felt good about it.

People with high self-esteem also experience failure, but they handle their losses gracefully by asking for feedback that helps them in the future. Constructive criticism is essential. Instead of thinking, "That was awful. I'll never try it again," with proper feedback and constructive criticism, you can think, "I know where I went wrong, and I won't make that mistake again."

Feedback helps you become more self-aware, not more self-critical. In fact, I've found that often when people with high self-esteem are successful they beg for even more constructive criticism and poke around their tender spots until a negative trait arises. I believe that's because they're unhappy with easy success—they want to know how they can improve in the future. Survival isn't enough; they want to thrive. And they can only do so by incorporating information that will expand their comfort zones, self-awareness, and view of themselves. They want to understand themselves and their world so that they can feel in control and master their fears.

Let's consider Sally again. Believing she is bad at small talk, she puts herself into situations that allow her to converse comfortably. She doesn't hide from the world, but she measures her exposure to strangers. She doesn't berate herself because of it. She understands her weaknesses and breaks the problem into manageable pieces that she can handle successfully. And for all her effort, she finds that she can do what she once thought was impossible—make a new friend.

Emulating People with High Self-Esteem

Sally is living a successfully shy life. She is shy, yet she maintains high self-esteem. This is not just a stroke of luck. And it doesn't just happen to people who only experience social success. In fact, just like the rest of us, successfully shy people often endure self-doubt, trepidation, and frustration. But unlike those with low self-esteem, they learn from their mistakes and sustain an optimistic vision of themselves and their futures. Here's how you can do it, too:

- Set your own standards. Don't let others bully you into situations that you know just aren't right for you. Instead, please yourself by doing what you love.

- Accent the positive—and take responsibility for it. It's human nature to overlook success when it comes easily. If things go well for you, realize how you contributed to the success and take pride in your wise actions.

- Control your negative self-talk. The shy mind can make it difficult to quiet negative self-talk, but you can do it. Give yourself the benefit of the doubt.

- Set realistic standards of success. Keep in mind that a party consists of all types of people, not just the gregarious individuals who must always be "on." Besides, being the life of the party may not be all it's reputed to be. Often extroverts feel burdened by their self-imposed duty to ensure that others are having a good time. Recognize that simply showing up at a party is better than not going at all.

- Challenge your ideal self. Are you sure you want to be a full-blown extrovert? Are celebrities happier than everyone else? It's doubtful. There's a price to be paid for fame—pressure to seem perfect at all times. Think twice about your fantasized ideal self.

- Examine your real self. Enhance self-awareness by understanding what you can do as well as what you can't. Accept your strengths and limitations, and realize that they contribute to who you are but are not the sole determinant of who you can become.

- Recognize that you're a work in progress. Instead of thinking of yourself as a shy person, change labels and become a person who's learning how not to be shy in certain situations.

- Depend on good role models. Spend time with people who have a healthy level of self-esteem. Ask them how they deal with failure, self-doubt, and perfectionism. Adopt their viewpoint and associate with them whenever possible.

- Take control. Take moderate risks so that you can experience meaningful successes. Make a plan of action. Remember, your situation may worsen before it improves. Have patience during your warm-up period.

- Accept new information about yourself. Try novel activities, and ask for and incorporate feedback. Learn from your mistakes and your triumphs.

- Foster outside interests. If you're engaged in an activity you enjoy, you will not only feel more confident in general, but you will also be less bothered by your shyness.

As a wise forty-year-old in Michigan wrote to me, "Perhaps the way to overcome shyness is to do something one really loves, and little by little the shyness will be diminished by the act itself, rather than be overcome by oneself. Sometimes I feel we spend too much time worrying about how we look, how we feel."

Daniel took this last piece of advice and profited from it. For years he had hated the fact that he became nervous when approaching women he found attractive. He decided to look for a new way. He temporarily suspended dating to reassess himself and his behavior.

First, he took stock to determine his flaws. That was easy; he was poor at approaching new women. He then reviewed where he excelled and what made him truly happy. This took a little time because he hadn't thought of himself in those terms, but soon he came up with a list. He was a good accountant and sailor; he was patient, polite, and kind; he was at least average-looking; he respected women; he had a dry sense of humor that people enjoyed once they got used to it; he was a great cook. He recognized that he was good at most of the pastimes he enjoyed and needed help only in one area—meeting women.

How could he use his assets to cancel out that big deficit? Daniel recalled that he was always happy when he was on a boat, taming the wind, waves, and sails. He decided that if he spent more time sailing, he'd become a better sailor and enjoy himself. Gathering his courage, he called a fishing-supply store. The proprietor rattled off a list of sailing groups that met at the local beach.

Daniel joined one of the clubs even though he felt awkward asking questions over the phone. He was nervous the first time the group met, but he knew a lot more about sailing than most of the others, and soon he relaxed. When female members approached him for help, he was able to explain some of the intricacies of knot tying. Daniel and his fellow sailors started meeting even when they weren't scheduled. He got to know more women and, because the sailing enlivened and distracted him, his nervousness evaporated. He knew that they liked him and admired his skills. He felt as if he were a different person, even though he was never more fully himself.

A Last Word About Shyness of the Self

Personality theorist Alfred Adler believed that our "style of life" encompasses personal and environmental factors that influence our desire to strive to be the best people we can through self-enhancement. He stressed what he called *social interest*: helping yourself through giving to others. That's exactly what Daniel did. He desired to become a better sailor and more relaxed suitor, and he did so not only by spending more time on the water, but also by teaching his fellow club members.

Adler claimed that well-adjusted people create a style of life that allows them to unify all aspects of their lives, take risks, and tackle problems head-on as Daniel did. Maladjusted individuals, on the other hand, feel inferior, show little social interest, think in a simplistic manner, and hold a self-defeating outlook on life. They blame others for their difficulties and flaws. Rather than creating a healthy style of life, they live "as if" reality were different ("as if" intimate relationships were unimportant, "as if" they could achieve a personal, professional, or social goal without withstanding some risk).

If you become immobilized by self-defeating attitudes of personal inferiority, you may find yourself in this same difficult position. The myths of the shy life may cause you to believe that you can't overcome your shyness, that you would be better liked if you were more gregarious, that you're less worthy than others, that you have nothing to offer your community. You may fall victim to the fundamental myth that people can only be happy if they're outgoing.

But in truth, you can be happy, even if you are shy, by controlling your shy feelings and thoughts. You can be happy by incorporating shyness into your life decisions so that you make appropriate choices. You can be happy by mustering the courage, insight, and heart to face life's challenges.

Shyness only becomes a problem when you incorporate shy myths into your very being—myths that tell you that you will never succeed, that there is no sense in trying, that you are a failure. The successfully shy embrace their shy selves and incorporate shyness into all aspects of their lives. Their self-awareness allows them to chart a life course with clarity and honesty.

Examining the influence of the body, mind, and self helps us understand the essence of shyness because it reveals the hidden forces that you battle every day, in a variety of situations. These experiences are the most difficult to control, rationalize, and overcome. They are the forces that most profoundly affect your identity, your self-esteem, your style of life, and your soul.

Throughout the rest of this book, I will show you how shyness of the body, mind, and self influences you throughout your life.

Shyness Through the Life Cycle

We experience a personality trait as important as shyness in different ways at various points throughout our lives. As babies, we cannot rightly be said to be shy, but we may have been born with a brain that is highly reactive to novelty. As young children, we must learn to make friends and play with others in the sometimes chaotic school environment. As adolescents, we may feel stigmatized by our shyness and seek ways to hide it. As adults, we struggle for strategies to connect with others—friends, lovers, coworkers—and assuage our loneliness.

But although different issues arise at each of these life stages, the same underlying principles apply; in dealing with shyness of the body, mind, and self we grapple with our slow-to-warm-up tendencies, the approach/avoidance conflict, and restrictive comfort zones.

In Part III, I will explain the underlying dynamics of shyness throughout the life cycle and offer tips for making beneficial choices about these issues.

Are We Born Shy?

Betty described her baby granddaughter to me:

> If Kelly were at my house and you walked in—no matter how much fun we were having—she would just stop and crawl over to where her mom and dad were sitting. When she was a year old, if anyone would go to her or talk to her, she would break out in tears. On her first birthday, the whole family was at her house. She was playing and was just fine. Then we sat her down in her high chair to have cake. Everyone gathered around to sing "Happy Birthday," and she looked at us with an expression like, "What are you doing to me?" She went from a happy little girl to one in tears in seconds!
>
> Even now, when we first come into her house, she doesn't run up to us and give us a kiss. It takes five or ten minutes before you can approach her, and then she's loving.

Kelly's responses are consistent with those of other infants and young children who react intensely to novelty. We might even surmise that she came into the world with what is known as an *inhibited temperament*.

Temperament and Personality

All of us are born with a temperament, our innate biological predisposition to act in certain ways. Your temperament can lay the groundwork for whether you will become a violinist or a basketball star, a mathematician or a painter.

One aspect of temperament—inhibition or the lack thereof —is a function of the brain's responsiveness to stimulation. Scientists have discovered that differences in this reactivity appear even before birth. About 20 percent of all babies are born with an inhibited temperament and, like Kelly, seem highly sensitive. They may kick vigorously or cry when you present them with a new toy or an unfamiliar face. Forty percent are relatively uninhibited. These hardier souls remain calmer in the face of a novelty.

Temperament is only one aspect of personality. The latter develops over time and consists of a combination of factors: biology (temperament), environment (family, culture), experience (education, expectations), and psychology (motivation, self-esteem). Estimates have placed the influence of temperament on personality from 25 to 50 percent. *Shyness is a personality trait, not a temperament.*

As a child's personality develops, an inhibited temperament can turn into a shy personality with the influence of environment, psychology, and other factors. Interestingly, however, not all children born with inhibited temperaments go on to become shy adults. And clearly some uninhibited babies do become shy—otherwise shyness would affect a smaller segment of the population than 50 percent. Biology is not destiny.

So why study inhibition? Because it helps us understand the biological processes of shyness in the brain. Inhibition is a purely visceral, exaggerated reaction to novelty and perceived threat. The brains of inhibited babies like Kelly respond much like the brains of shy adults, only without the attendant cognitive and psychological baggage we explored in the previous two chapters.

Still, the biological roots of shyness remain something of a mystery. We cannot say with certainty that babies are born shy, since there is no scientific evidence to affirm it. Besides, shyness, being a personality trait, is much more complex than it appears on the surface and therefore is not easily traced to specific structures or reactions within the brain; rather it may encompass many structures and a variety of reactions at once.

Shyness researchers are engaged in some exciting investigations that have delved deeply into the brain's responses to stress. In addition, they have traced genetic links among generations of shy and not-so-shy family members, established the usefulness of medication to help shy people cope with their physiological experience, and tracked the evolution of timidity through various species.

These scientists help us understand whether some people are born with a predisposition to becoming shy as well as whether there is a shy body type or a shy gene. And perhaps more important, they help us conceptualize, at the molecular level, what the body does during shy episodes.

The Shy Brain

Shyness can be linked to nearly all the structures of the brain—from the spinal cord and brain stem, which provide for reflexes and the bodily functions necessary to our existence; to the limbic system in the midbrain, which makes quick decisions based on instinctual responses; to the cerebral cortex, the higher brain, which plans strategies, determines specific and long-term goals, weighs alternatives, acquires specialized knowledge, ensures that all parts are functioning, and makes the ultimate decisions about the future.

The reflex to avoid something frightening or recoil from danger (flinching from a lit match, for example) is located in the brain stem, and the instinct to avoid (our aversion to rats, for instance) is located in the midbrain, but the *decision* to avoid (walking around a ladder) comes from the higher brain, the human mind. Each mind is as unique as each shy person. It is difficult to predict how yours will influence your reflexes and instincts because the decision-making process is so complex.

Let's examine the role of each of these structures in more detail.

The Brain Stem

The brain stem is the oldest and most primitive part of the nervous system. Located at the nape of the neck, it is the direct extension of the spinal cord, the structure that brings information from throughout the body to the higher parts of the brain. It regulates our most primary, subconscious functions such as breathing, heartbeat, digestion—all the internal activities to which we are usually oblivious but can't live without. It also regulates reflexes such as blinking in a sandstorm or quickly withdrawing a finger from a pinprick.

The *reticular activating system* (RAS) is the part of the brain stem that alerts us to information in the environment. When a blaring car alarm awakens us, that's the RAS in action. The RAS may play a role in inhibited behavior. The late Hans J. Eysenck of London's Maudsley Hospital has argued that introverted people react to environmental stimulation differently from extroverts, and he pointed to differences in the RAS as the cause. You might think of its influence as volume control. If you have a more highly attuned RAS, your sensitivity to environmental stimulation will be magnified. Everyday sounds become more intense and harder to ignore because your RAS is receiving more audio input than others do. Background noise is not as disconcerting to people with a less sensitive RAS; it doesn't seem to interfere with their activities.

This sensory overload may explain why many shy people complain of discomfort at large gatherings or loud bars. Verify this phenomenon for yourself. If you're uneasy in your surroundings, note the background noise. Is the music too loud? Is a boisterous conversation annoying you? Do traffic, car alarms, and noise pollution drive you crazy? Perhaps it is your sensitive RAS at work.

The Limbic System: The Midbrain

Just above the brain stem, deep inside the brain, resides the limbic system. This group of structures regulates feeding, fleeing, fighting, and sexual reproduction—our instinctual responses. In many ways the limbic system is the primary biological mechanism of shyness. These are its components:

- The hypothalamus. The "regulator" ensures that your internal state is up to the challenge by managing the hormones and other bodily functions you require during stressful encounters.

- The hippocampus. The "database" stores and retrieves memories and emotions.

- The amygdala. The "central switchboard" is crucial for relaying nerve signals related to emotions and stress. It notes threats in the environment and decides whether the body should flee or fight. It both associates a specific stimulus with the emotion of fear and decides how your body will respond.

- The bed nucleus of the stria terminalis (BNST). The "wild card" is a little-understood structure that mediates anxiety rather than fear.

Your limbic system may associate certain stimuli—notably strangers, authority figures, or members of the opposite sex—with fearful reactions. Here's how it works when you have found yourself in a situation that might provoke a stress reaction. Imagine a colleague has invited you to meet some of her friends at a restaurant after work. Your dominant response might be fear because this is a strange and new situation. Your amygdala will send a signal to either the hippocampus or the hypothalamus that you should prepare to defend yourself or run away.

These signals will first trigger your hypothalamus and your autonomic nervous system, which will make you more alert.

As you approach the rendezvous, you think more quickly, sweat profusely, and your pulse races. In fact, your whole body prepares to deal with the alarming situation in the ways I have described earlier.

Now imagine that you have arrived at the restaurant. As your colleague introduces you, the group barely looks up to acknowledge your presence, and then continues on as if you were not even there. Their hostility threatens you; it hurts your feelings and undermines your personal identity. You have two choices: you could protect yourself by becoming aggressive and telling them off, or you could withdraw and avoid future contact. Most likely you choose the latter.

But the incident does not end here. You store the memory of its pain within your hippocampus. Indeed, you retain the image of the specific people who were rude as well as the general environment in which you met them: a restaurant, after work, in the presence of your coworker.

The next time you encounter that colleague or her friends, the hippocampus will bring forth the memory of the past injury and will signal the amygdala that a threat is coming your way. The amygdala will, in turn, alert you to protect yourself from the potential harm these people could inflict. It will act upon the current and previous information, and your heart may begin to race once more. If you have only unsuccessful encounters with these people, you will probably always be afraid of them.

But the limbic system won't merely affect your relations with this group; it will impact your response to the environment too. That's because it stores general, contextual information along with the specific memories. If a different coworker invites you out or if you must meet unfamiliar clients in a restaurant, the hippocampus will match new information about the current restaurant with your memories of the previous one (you were hurt there).

Because you anticipate feeling injured again, the hippocampus will send fear-laden information to the amygdala, which signals the rest of your system that danger is lurking. This may produce a stress reaction, and you might feel uncomfortable, even if there is nothing to fear. (Of course, repeated pleasant experiences would help to weaken this reaction.)

Unless you also collect happy memories when eating out, with every future repetition of this situation your amygdala will receive negative signals from the hippocampus. Eventually, you will either hate going to restaurants (an aggressive response) or avoid going (a defensive one). Shy people usually take the defensive approach and withdraw from these situations to avoid future embarrassment and emotional pain.

Everyone has negative reactions to social injuries, but not all people retreat. Why do shy people? Perhaps their limbic system creates withdrawal signals more often or more intensely than those of others. Let's take a closer look at the limbic system to understand if it operates in a unique way in people who are shy.

The Hypothalamus: The Regulator

You might think of the hypothalamus as a sensitive thermostat: it makes us experience hunger when we should eat and causes us to sweat when we need to cool down. In new, uncertain, or frightening situations it helps us to become alert, aroused, and prepared by triggering the autonomic nervous system, the part of the body that stimulates the sweat, tears, digestive juices, and hormones of stress reactions. These are the very sensations you experience when you have a shy episode, so it seems logical that the hypothalamus plays a role.

Do shy people have a faulty or overactive hypothalamus? No one knows for sure, but it is likely that their hypothalamus works a lot. Jerome Kagan of Harvard University found high levels of cortisol and epinephrine, stress hormones released when novelty or threat activates the hypothalamus, in very inhibited children. So while we don't know if the hypothalamus is "shy," we do know that some inhibited children feel highly alert in uncertain situations; the hypothalamus works intensely to prepare them for battle.

The Hippocampus: The Database

The biological process of withdrawal is universal, but the situations that provoke withdrawal vary with each of us. Some shy individuals can find almost everyone threatening, whereas others are intimidated only by authority figures, or large groups, or attractive members of the opposite sex. Why we fear what we do may, in part, be related to emotional memories stored deep within the hippocampus.

The hippocampus stockpiles and retrieves memories. It helps us create continuity in our daily lives because it is constantly matching new experiences with old ones. It remembers not only specific information such as a classroom embarrassment in the second grade, but contextual information as well: the emotional tenor in the room and the feelings you experienced before, during, and after the incident. In a new situation, it asks, *Is this something I've done before?* but also *How did I feel when this happened to me? Where was I, and what was my sense of the surroundings?*

Thus the hippocampus remembers details and the emotions that accompany them. It does all of this quickly and subconsciously, so thirty years after the embarrassment, you may not even recognize why you hate speaking in front of a group.

During a shy episode, the hippocampus equates old memories of bad experiences in the specific sense (being jeered at when you answered a question incorrectly) and the context of that memory (being singled out and ridiculed while among peers). Through this process of contextual conditioning, you may come to associate certain general environments—business meetings, client presentations, group discussions to which you are expected to contribute—with unpleasant feelings. In fact, you may begin to experience a stress reaction in anticipation of the feared event—even before you enter the room where the meeting is to take place.

Because the hippocampus compares new information with our memories, this process cannot operate until we're six to nine months old. Before then, infants show no fear of strangers; they have insufficient information with which to make comparisons. Parents, baby-sitters, or the couple at an adjacent restaurant table can all play peek-a-boo with a tiny baby. She doesn't withdraw in fear until her brain has matured.

Jerome Kagan has a differing view about the role of the hippocampus in inhibited children. He theorizes that it may not be retrieving *any memories at all*. Kagan believes that the inhibited children he studies have an overactive hippocampus, which makes them feel that with each new encounter they are virtually starting from scratch. Because they don't know how to behave in this constantly changing environment, they never feel comfortable. They withdraw in order to cope.

He notes that while the common reaction among animals to an unfamiliar environmental element is to strike out at it, he has never observed an inhibited child do so. Much like Kelly, such a youngster is likely to freeze when something new comes her way in an attempt to avoid the unfamiliar.

The Amygdala: The Switchboard

The amygdala is the puzzle piece that brings us closest to understanding the physiology of inhibition. In fact, when scientists tamper with it in experiments with animals, timid behavior stops altogether. It has been speculated that chronically inhibited people have a more excitable amygdala, which perceives more threat in the environment.

In many ways the amygdala is the decisive commander. This is where the perception of the current threat begins and where we make the initial approach/avoidance decision. Memories of past experiences coming from the hippocampus help the amygdala evaluate whatever is currently arousing it. If it determines that the stimulus is threatening, it sends a message to the hypothalamus to create a stress reaction. It also sends messages to an area of the brain regulating movement and the mouth. (This is where the sudden inability to speak and the feeling of being frozen originate.)

The amygdala does so by signaling two structures within it, one leading to approach, the other to avoidance. Because there are several neural pathways within the amygdala, it may seem as if it can choose equally and freely between its options after reviewing all of the information and deliberating rationally. But the amygdala is not so equitable. While we don't know the precise mechanism in humans, some researchers have studied what occurs in cats, and it seems that the amygdala favors either an approach or an avoidance pathway.

In some of the most fascinating work done in this area, Robert Adamec at the University of Newfoundland classified groups of cats as "inhibited" or "uninhibited" based on how they interacted with mice, other cats, and humans. The inhibited cats were reluctant to explore new territory and to attack mice. And when they did pounce, they seemed to avoid direct confrontation. They stalked from behind the mouse or from the side. They were more defensive and vigilant than bolder cats. Noise upset them, too. The uninhibited cats were easy with others, roamed freely, and attacked mice straight on, often with gusto.

Adamec found that the cat amygdala would signal either a portion of the hypothalamus or a portion of the hippocampus. Triggering the hypothalamus stimulated apprehensive behavior like crouching or cowering in a corner. But when the signals went to the hippocampus, it created aggressive reactions such as attacking behavior.

Not surprisingly, the inhibited cats seemed to have a more sensitive pathway to the hypothalamus. Consequently, the amygdala transmitted more signals to it than to the hippocampus. Conversely, the bold cats received more attack messages directed at the hippocampus.

We are not yet certain how these findings apply to humans, but if they do, we could say that inhibited people have more sensitive amygdalas than those who are uninhibited. Consequently, they would detect more threats in the environment (every stranger would be a potential enemy) and respond by avoiding the danger. But what would happen next? Would they stay away?

I have my doubts. Even though the amygdala has an impact on your initial reaction, it does not affect behavior that is planned, rational, and powerful enough to override the dominant response. This comes from your free will, your intelligence, and the universal desire to be with others. So even if it is ultimately proven that inhibited people do have a more sensitive amygdala, it doesn't mean that they will automatically be shy.

In my opinion, a less aggressive amygdala may benefit society. Jerome Kagan analyzed a number of animal-based amygdala studies and found the size of the structure significant. The portion involved in defensive, withdrawing behavior is relatively bigger in highly evolved mammals like primates than in less intelligent ones such as rats. It appears that the more advanced a being, the more likely its amygdala will signal withdrawal. Kagan surmised that as we evolve we become less inclined to blindly attack when threatened. We are more apt to pull back and reason a solution to an uncertain situation.

Kagan also analyzed studies of domesticated horses, pigs, and dogs and concluded that the tamed animals have smaller limbic systems. He inferred that the "attack" portion of the amygdala is smaller in the tamed animals than in the wilder ones. If the amygdala makes us attack less often, perhaps it makes us more civilized and better suited to live in groups.

The Bed Nucleus of the Stria Terminalis: The Wild Card

I have been describing shyness as a response to the fear of a distinct stressor in the environment. But "fear" may not capture how you truly feel about your social encounters. For most shy people, the emotion is less specific, more diffuse. It is anxiety. As I explained earlier, anxiety creeps upon you more slowly and has a vague focus. And although it is less intense than fear, it takes longer to dissipate.

This is when the wild card is played. Anxious reactions are thought to emerge from the activity of the bed nucleus of the stria terminalis (BNST). This little-understood structure of the limbic system sends information to the hypothalamus and the brain stem—the same structures implicated in fear reactions that are associated with the amygdala. The BNST receives emotional memories from the hippocampus, too.

Michael Davis at Yale University found that the BNST processes the contextual information from the amygdala and hippocampus and sends it on to the rest of the body. There, it emerges as a low-level, long-lasting uneasiness, a hypersense that something bad is afoot. Anxiety, plain and simple.

We're unsure how the BNST operates. Let's say that the idea of going to a party provokes anxiety. This anxiety involves the interaction of the hippocampus, which provides you with information about a place; the amygdala, which tells you this place is dangerous; and the BNST, which combines this information and sends it to the hypothalamus and brain stem to produce the prolonged sense of arousal. Perhaps BNST is more active in inhibited, shy, or highly anxious people, or maybe it is triggered occasionally in those who are situationally shy. But we do know that the BNST may heighten social anxiety.

Controlling the Limbic System

Knowing how the limbic system works gives you insight into conquering shy symptoms. It helps you understand how and where you create the decision to retreat, why you retrieve unpleasant (or few) memories, and what instigates stress reactions. It determines whether you should approach something pleasurable or avoid what you find threatening. Our growing understanding of the function of the BNST also helps us conceptualize why some people feel more anxious than others do when pondering social interactions.

The inhibited limbic system differs from the uninhibited in the degree to which it reacts to perceived threat and stress. Think of the limbic system as a thermostat with different settings that automatically adjust according to the climate. The inhibited body's thermostat is more sensitive and kicks in a bit sooner than others' do. But you can adjust your thermostat by taking action. Much like insulating a house, which modulates a real thermostat's activation, you can "insulate" yourself by becoming more aware of the process that creates shyness, the conditions in which it arises, and how you can alleviate shy reactions.

If you believe you were born with an overactive or biased amygdala, this does not mean that you should resign yourself to a life of silent, passive withdrawal. You can change the action of your amygdala, and maybe even the structure of your brain's responses, by altering your perceptions.

A study by Deane H. Shapiro and his colleagues at the University of California at Irvine found that the amygdala is involved during bizarre, disturbing dreams in which the dreamer has no control over the danger (say, when he is being chased by a pack of rabid dogs and can neither scream nor run). Conversely, the amygdala is inactive in dreams in which the dreamer maintains control and can escape an awful situation (the dogs are howling and yelping, but the dreamer can fly above them and save himself). The researchers pointed out that the perception of control is critical. If you accept that you have control, you feel more tranquil, and your amygdala is quiescent.

Based on this finding, I believe that when you realize you can control your environment and your reactions, you will still your sensitive or biased amygdala and feel calmer in habitually anxiety-provoking situations. You do this by following the suggestions I've provided throughout *Shyness*. For example, if you find yourself being self-critical, you might reassess the evidence and reframe (see Chapter 6), or if a first date feels threatening because you don't know how to act, rehearsal and reconnaissance can be helpful (see Chapter 13).

Not all shy people have overreactive limbic systems from birth; many simply repeat the same timid behavior frequently enough to reinforce more "fearful" brain pathways. Robert Adamec found in his work with rats that when he stimulated or "kindled" one part of the rats' amygdala, their timid behavior became more intense; when he kindled another part, this behavior stopped. Similarly, the more you retreat in social situations, the more you may stimulate or strengthen the withdrawal circuit in your amygdala. If, on the other hand, you fortify your approach behavior, you can alter your brain to reinforce the neural "attack" connections. You can do this by anticipating when you will feel shy and threatened; perceiving how and where you have control over your social situations; and planning and executing strategies that will help alleviate your discomfort.

You don't have to act on primitive urges to withdraw just because you feel driven to do so. You can become more rational, confident, and successfully shy by reconsidering your habitual shy behavior. The exercises and suggestions I provide should help you. You can use your anxiety to propel you toward a future unfettered by irrational, deep-seated fears of other people. By learning how to appropriately respond to your anxiety—not necessarily eliminating it—you can thrive and become more self-assured.

The Higher Brain

While the brain stem and the limbic system process threatening information and create responses on a primitive, instinctual level, the higher brain—the structures that reason, produce speech, and analyze complex information—may be involved in shy reactions, too. It stands to reason that if shyness provokes a conscious choice to withdraw, then the part of the brain making such deliberate decisions would be implicated.

The higher brain, or cerebral cortex, is a thin sheet of neurons, about the size, shape, and thickness of a crumpled page of newspaper, covering the midbrain like a glove. It is the most recent evolutionary addition to the brain and quite literally makes us human. It governs complex cognitive processes such as speaking, reasoning, and resolving conflicting information.

The frontal lobes, the front portion of the cortex, are located behind the forehead. They oversee activity through planning, control, logic, and reasoning. They receive information from the limbic and the nervous systems and make decisions about experiences, or they direct us to seek out additional information and rethink matters so that we can reach better decisions. They are responsible for the interpreting of emotions—defining physiological arousal as excitement or fear.

Is there a shy area in the cerebral cortex? Not really. Shyness and inhibition have not been detected in the more highly evolved areas of the human brain. But these structures may be involved in creating the emotions and thoughts connected with shyness and generating strategies that create the shy mind-set and shy behaviors.

While the instinct to withdraw is located in the limbic system—brain structures that our species shares with rats, cats, and monkeys—the cognitive processes involved in shyness, such as the narcissistic paradox, unrealistic social comparisons, self-evaluation and self-consciousness, pessimism, negative attributions, and poor self-esteem, are located in the higher brain. Only humans have this highly developed structure and these thoughts, which is why only humans can be shy.

Using the Higher Brain to Counteract Instinct

Shyness of the mind and self most likely originate in the higher brain, but we can also use the higher brain to overcome shy reactions. To grasp its role, we need to understand our instincts.

All organisms instinctively approach what is pleasurable—an inviting morsel of food—and withdraw from what they find threatening—a fire raging out of control. But higher brains in humans make conscious decisions about what actions we should take, despite those instincts. Our varying reactions can create a conflict between the perception of threat or pleasure and what we should do about it. Indeed, the human instinct to approach or withdraw is more accurately labeled a physical dominant response, which we can override with conscious thought.

For example, when a dog spies something pleasurable, say, a thick, juicy steak, he will devour it without a care. When we see that steak, we too salivate, but we also worry about its cholesterol content, the ethical implications of eating meat, or our growing waistlines. We listen to our body's response, consider the implications, mull options, and make the decision. No steak tonight! This is our higher brain in action.

We determine how to deal with threat in much the same way. As a consequence, although our instincts tell us to automatically escape danger, our minds sometimes dictate otherwise. When a cat finds itself in a burning house, it will flee to the nearest exit as quickly as possible. Our dominant response is also to run for the door. It is an instinctive reaction to withdraw from physical danger. But the mind participates as well; it wonders whether we can rescue the family photo album in the second-floor bedroom. Acting upon this thought could lead us into greater danger. And a firefighter makes the conscious decision to enter the burning structure to save others. For better or worse, we don't always follow our instincts to approach pleasure and withdraw from danger.

This same instinctive process is evident in the symptoms associated with shyness. Here the threat comes from an unfamiliar or frightening social situation rather than a physical menace. As we have seen, the dominant response of the shy body is to become intensely aroused and to withdraw into the safety of silence.

By the same token, however, we can use the higher brain to override or reprogram our dominant response. The key is to render these feelings and memories conscious and bring the rational mind into play. Just as we may make the decision to forgo a delicious piece of meat, thereby acting against our approach instinct, so can we use the higher mind to prevail over our instinct to withdraw.

This reprogramming may help prevent the production of shy symptoms and related anxiety. You can take steps toward rewiring your brain by applying new thought processes to your social interactions. You can calm the amygdala by changing your perception of its control over your body, mind, and self during social interactions.

The Lateralization Enigma

The sides or hemispheres of the frontal lobes have specialized properties. This is called lateralization. The right side is generally more creative and emotional, while the left is more rational, logical, and verbal. However, a growing body of research indicates that both sides are involved in creating emotions, but they generate different ones. Specifically, the right side seems to be responsible for emotions such as fear and anxiety, while the left side governs joy and laughter. So it seems logical that the right hemisphere should be more involved in shyness.

To see if the right hemisphere predominates in inhibited reactions, researchers tested inhibited and uninhibited babies through age four. Babies and young children make ideal subjects because, since their cerebral cortex is underdeveloped, they operate on their instincts. They don't have a lot of experiences to weigh, nor do they rationally select a course of action or an emotional response. They just try to do whatever makes them feel better. The tests showed that inhibited children through age four do indeed show signs of more activity in the right hemisphere. And, not surprisingly, uninhibited youngsters had more reactivity in the left hemisphere, which generates positive, approaching emotions.

Louis A. Schmidt and Nathan Fox at the University of Maryland tested adults to determine if this brain lateralization was still apparent later in life. They asked their subjects whether they were shy (inhibited when interacting with others, a behavioral trait) or "sociable" (tending to seek out the company of others, a psychological trait). They added physiological traits to the mix, measuring heart rate and the activity of the vagus nerve (which affects heart rate and the autonomic nervous system).

Schmidt and Fox predicted that shy adults would have more active right hemispheres and sociable adults would show more activity in the left sides, but their results were inconclusive. In fact, they found that no real difference exists in the left and right hemispheres of shy and sociable adults. They did, however, find that shy adults have a higher and more stable heart rate than sociable adults.

What can we make of this? We cannot conclude that you will "outgrow" the brain activities that make you shy. If this were so, there would be no shy adults. But we can say that shyness is extremely complex. Once your fully integrated brain develops the intellectual capacity to create shyness of the body, mind, and self, it becomes difficult to measure and identify specific brain processes.

While we can track the limbic system's more primitive reactions, as far as the whole brain is concerned, the truly human personality trait of shyness remains enigmatic. In fact, we may never fully comprehend the intricacies of the adult shy brain because a seemingly infinite array of connections, reactions, and responses take place there.

Is There a Shy Gene?

How does the inhibited temperament originate? If the amygdala is more sensitive or more likely to favor a withdrawal pathway, how was this bias created? Do we learn to react in a certain ways, are our nervous systems damaged because of an early trauma, or were these traits passed on genetically? Is there a shy gene? If there is no genetic cause of shyness, can it still be inborn?

In their quest to uncover the biological basis of shyness and answer these questions, researchers have discovered many interesting and surprising physical characteristics that seem to accompany this personality trait.

One intriguing finding indicates that highly reactive or inhibited children tend to have narrower faces than their more outgoing peers. How does the shape of one's face relate to shyness? According to this research, a narrow face can render breathing slightly more difficult. Distress or threat could further impede respiration. A person with a narrow face might try to avoid distress and its attendant breathing problems; interestingly, many shy people excuse themselves from crowded rooms with the statement that they "need to get some air." Perhaps this has to do with their physiognomy.

Similarly, an unrelated series of studies has shown that shy people are more apt to suffer from allergies or hay fever than the nonshy. They also have a keener sense of smell. These correlations could reflect highly reactive immune or nervous systems that are susceptible to impurities in the air. The connection between allergies and shyness can also be made on the behavioral level. If you don't feel well, you are less likely to be socially outgoing and adventurous. Panic symptoms such as shallow, unnatural breathing could play a role in this correlation as well.

Jerome Kagan and Harvard sociologist Stephen Gortmaker found preliminary evidence that shy people are more likely to be conceived during August and September. They speculate that because the hours of daylight are shrinking, the mother's body produces more melatonin, a hormone thought to regulate the pituitary gland and perhaps produce sleep. Since the mother has more of this hormone in her body, she will pass it on to the fetus, perhaps rendering it more highly reactive.

Shyness has also been associated with a thin body type and light eye color. Inhibited Caucasian children are more likely to be thin and have blue eyes, and uninhibited children of the same race are more likely to be plump and have brown eyes. Scientists have been baffled by the relationship of these traits. Some have speculated that thirty to forty thousand years ago, when Homo sapiens migrated from Africa to northern Europe, they needed some means to warm their bodies in the Ice Age climate. Their genes might have mutated to provide them with extra layers of fat or body hair. Instead, they developed a heightened level of physical arousal, which brings more blood to the surface of the skin, preventing the loss of body heat. This arousal would increase the body's level of norepinephrine, the neurotransmitter involved in stress reactions.

It seems that norepinephrine can impede the production of melanin in the eyes (the more melanin, the darker the eyes) and, through a reaction with other chemicals, the growth of the facial bones. And since inhibited children tend to have high levels of norepinephrine as well as more stress reactions, perhaps this is why they're more likely to have blue eyes and narrow faces.

Taken together, these differences indicate that some people must cope with a physiology that is more reactive than others'. Their limbic systems perceive threat more frequently and signal withdrawal more readily than approach; their hippocampus stores negative or few memories of past social interactions; their autonomic nervous system creates numerous stress reactions. Allergies, narrow breathing passages, and panic attacks bring on respiratory troubles during tense situations. These people may be "chronically" or "physically shy," since they must constantly adjust their surroundings to accommodate their physiological arousal. But are these differences inborn? Are we shy by nature or by nurture?

As with other questions related to shyness, the answers are equivocal. However, one of the best ways to understand whether inhibition is inherited is to analyze fraternal and identical twins who have these traits. A few recent twin studies have explored whether shared behavior, such as inhibition, comes from hereditary traits (nature) or how the children were raised (nurture).

Investigations of identical twins are particularly helpful because these youngsters have the same chromosomes, in contrast to fraternal twins, who share only half their chromosomes. If a trait is inherited, then pairs of identical twins will exhibit increased similar behavior when compared with pairs of fraternal twins. If environmental factors such as parental treatment or education influence a trait, then fraternal- and identical-twin pairs should experience the behavior roughly equally, since they share the same household, school, nutrition, and income level.

In 1994 a team of researchers at the University of Colorado

and the Pennsylvania State University tested for inhibition in fourteen-month-old identical and fraternal twins. They repeated the tests at twenty months. They found that genetic factors seemed to play a role in how infants approach or withdraw from stimulation. But they could not guarantee that these "inhibited" genes would be as influential when the twins matured.

As we grow, we develop intellectual abilities that can modify our inhibited tendencies. Moreover, we cope with increased verbal demands, the emergence of the sense of identity, the judgment of ourselves and others, and our adherence to the rules and standards set by others. Babies at fourteen and twenty months have no grasp of these intellectual functions or influences. Fortunately, this research team plans to continue testing these children as they grow to maturity. Perhaps their efforts will teach us more about the evolution of inhibition's genetic impact on shy behavior.

Other tests of twins at twelve, eighteen, twenty-four, and thirty months have also indicated a genetic influence on inhibition. However, a comparison of twelve studies on fearfulness/emotionality in twin children concluded that while a genetic factor is involved in creating these responses, environmental influences come into play as well.

The degree of inhibition is a factor, too. Lisabeth Fisher DiLalla, Jerome Kagan, and J. Steven Reznick found that extremely reactive, temperamentally inhibited children who are likely to have intense responses to novelty are more apt to have inherited their inhibited temperament. In contrast, youngsters who experience mildly aversive reactions to novelty seem to have acquired this response.

They also found that identical twins were more likely to have intense inhibition than fraternal twins do. But despite this evidence, they stated that environment (how parents or teachers treat the children) is also involved in the appearance of inhibition in childhood.

Perhaps studies of dairy cows and beef cattle can help explain how genes and environment interact to create an inhibited response. A team of American and Brazilian researchers found that dairy cows and beef cattle have differing reactions to an approaching human. Humans milk the dairy cows every day, so the cows allow people to approach, whereas beef cattle do not let people get anywhere near them. These traits seem to have been passed on through the generations.

But the researchers were lucky enough to find instances of dairy cows being raised as beef cattle and vice versa. This allowed them to investigate how the cattle's biological predisposition interacted with their environment.

Interestingly, they found that the cattle bred to be eaten but raised to produce milk were more approachable than those born and raised as beef cattle. However, the dairy cows raised as beef cattle were no less approachable than they would have been had they been raised as dairy cattle.

The researchers claimed that environment and handling do have an impact on cattle biologically predisposed to avoid human contact. And the same is probably true for people. Even if you are biologically predisposed to feel uncomfortable around "threatening" or new people, you can, over time, become accustomed to the contact. Don't limit yourself by your initial reaction. The longer you stare down your fears, the less likely they are to continue bothering you.

Are We Born Shy?

Temperament does not act alone to create shyness. Your biological makeup, along with your life experiences and how you interpret those experiences, help to create shyness.

Biology influences your body's reactivity. You have been born with the capacity to handle a certain level of threatening stimulation. But biology is just a starting point, an influence you can surrender to or control through determination and wisdom. Its power will manifest throughout your life but will be most obvious when you are young—before experience and intellect come into play.

If you were born with a highly reactive system, your inhibited temperament may have been instrumental during the first two years of life because you had neither the mental capacity nor the experience upon which to rely. Consequently, like Kelly, you might have clung to your parents, cried when you were separated, and fussed when strangers came near.

But after the age of two, biology ceases to be the most important factor. Environmental experiences come to the fore during the second year of childhood and beyond. How your parents and teachers treat you, the friendships you form, your relationship with your siblings, the classroom environment—all of these factors and the memories they evoke may instigate or extinguish shy behavior.

During adolescence the mind becomes the most potent force, and it will hold sway into adulthood. But it need not ordain a life of shyness. The shy adolescent, attempting to interpret his experiences as a highly reactive child, can begin to make appropriate choices that will calm his nervous system. He can select friends who support those choices by sparing him from overwhelmingly stimulating situations. He can build a strong identity based on his strengths and decide how he will use those strengths in the business and social world. Using his higher brain, he will be able to take charge of his life.

Almost half of the adult population claims to be shy, yet only 20 percent of babies are born inhibited. So, many of these adults must have acquired their shyness—through mental and emotional experiences and using their higher minds.

Just as parental care and experience influence temperamentally inhibited children, so are temperamentally *uninhibited* children shaped by these factors. But their shy minds interpret these circumstances and create shyness, scoring it into the brain's wiring with repetition and reinforcement.

Their shyness comes from without. The shy mind is critical to this course.

Some people are born with bodies that make them highly reactive, but this does not mean they will become shy. In the next chapter we will explore how these biological processes are important during childhood, before we acquire learned shyness or the experience and wisdom to combat it.

Shyness in Your Preschooler

"I remember feeling mortified if someone noticed me," explained Jenny, a filmmaker in New York.

> When I was very young, before kindergarten, I remember hanging on to the back of my mother's skirt and trying to keep her between me and anybody whom I didn't want to notice me while we were shopping or out in the world.
>
> I couldn't meet other children. The only kids I knew were my next-door neighbors. My parents tell me I wouldn't associate with anybody but my immediate family and the kids next door. I was terrified of my grandparents; I didn't even like to go to their house. With other relatives or family friends, I'd just hide in my room and hope that they'd leave me alone. I thought people could see through me—that burning sensation I still get occasionally—and I wanted to disappear through a hole in the floor. I'd even hide behind the furniture.

Jenny had bright red hair, which everyone noticed, commented upon, and wanted to touch. She hated the unwelcome attention. In addition, she had many allergies at birth. "I had to drink soy milk," she explained, "and I had a lot of skin allergies when I was growing up. I could only wear cotton. I hated going to church because I had to wear nylon tights, and they'd make my legs break out."

Jenny's parents were sensitive to her plight and found ways to make her feel more comfortable. "My mom took me to my first day of kindergarten," she explained. "She talked to the teacher in advance. We spent about fifteen minutes in the classroom, and then she took me home. Each day, we stayed a little longer, and by the end of the first week, she left me there. My mom eased me into school."

Once Jenny became accustomed to her environment, she did well. She was often the teacher's pet because she worked hard. She developed a close best friend who shared everything with her and became queen of the playground due to her natural athleticism. "Physical release has helped me overcome my shyness. In fact, starting in the third grade, my parents involved me in organized sports, and I played competitive softball and basketball. The structure of the game made it easy to get along with other kids because I didn't have to talk one-on-one."

Jenny is grateful that her parents helped her gain confidence by encouraging her to explore her strengths. "They recognized that my shyness or my sensitivity in general was a real problem, and they always tried to be supportive and guide me gently into things that would help me open up. Whenever they found an activity that worked, they would encourage me by coming to all of my games and making whatever sacrifices they had to."

Over the years, Jenny's shyness has lessened to such a degree that she no longer considers herself shy. "I've overcome the paralysis and the inability to talk to people," she said. "Now I can put my shyness in context and realize that I'm not always responsible for mistakes, and I'm never going to be perfect."

I'm always delighted to hear stories like Jenny's. Although she had a few challenges, she has become successfully shy. She didn't make her way out by fighting or retreating. Rather, she grew to understand that she had certain traits that might obstruct her path. Her parents helped tremendously. They acknowledged her shyness but didn't excuse her from taking part in the everyday experiences of childhood. I believe, and I'm sure Jenny would agree, they did the right thing.

But not all shy children have parents and teachers who are sensitive to their needs. These children may endure childhoods filled with fear, insecurity, and discomfort. They may be overlooked, misunderstood, or bullied by parents, siblings, friends, and teachers. These children can retreat into their shyness because they don't know how to make sense of it and, unlike Jenny, no one has shown them a way out.

With the help of sensitive, patient, and devoted parents and teachers, shy preschoolers can grow to be successfully shy. Shyness in early childhood can be a burden, but with the proper guidance it need not be a life sentence.

Temperament Redux

Temperament is often mistaken for destiny because it develops in utero, away from the direct effects of birth, environment, parental behavior, nutrition, or culture. But temperament is malleable. As I explained in the previous chapter, being born with a certain temperament does not fix a child's fate. Characteristics apparent early in life can become more or less salient as the child grows into adulthood; personal experience and intellectual analysis modify them.

A temperamentally uninhibited child, for example, who has been picked on at day care or teased by older siblings, may learn to distrust others. This child acquired his fearfulness from experience. Similarly, although a baby may be born with an inhibited temperament—the predisposition to react more readily and vociferously when faced with threatening circumstances—she is not fated to act on these impulses in adulthood. Her mind and self-concept can counteract and control them. She need not be shy.

Three theoretical views of inhibited temperament in young children help us make sense of their withdrawal. You might think of these perspectives as a way to appreciate the precursors of shyness, not shyness itself.

The Highly Reactive Temperament

Since we know that stress reactions are at the heart of the physical symptoms of shyness, Harvard University researcher

Jerome Kagan and his colleagues set out to measure these reactions in very young babies placed in new situations. They
wanted to determine if some babies produce more frequent
or intense stress reactions than others.

Kagan measured the infants' general responses to a variety
of stimuli. He played two tapes to them, one with recorded
sentences and one with a female voice uttering disjointed syl-
lables; he waved cotton swabs dipped in diluted alcohol under their noses; he dangled colorful mobiles in front of their
faces and popped a balloon behind their heads. He then measured their heart rates, pupil dilation, and hormone levels, as
well as crying, kicking, and arching of the back—all markers
of arousal—to ascertain whether these children were experiencing stress.

In about 35 percent of the children he tested, Kagan had
mixed results. Some stimuli stressed these youngsters, whereas
others did not. Another 40 percent of the babies showed relatively little arousal to any of the stimuli. They would notice the
stimulation but seemed less fazed by it. Kagan labeled these
calm children "low-reactive" or "uninhibited."

The last 20 percent had extreme reactions to stimulation.
They kicked, fussed, and cried. Their muscles tensed; their
hearts raced. In fact, when Kagan examined their prenatal medical records, he found that their heart rates were high before
birth, too. All in all, these fussy children had extreme stress reactions in new situations. He called them "high-reactive" or "inhibited" because their responses were so dramatic and so frequent.

Interestingly, quiet, complacent babies whom we often assume to be shy are actually low-reactives. They are less likely
to become shy when they get older. The babies who kick,
grab their mothers, and cry have the biological predisposition
to become shy later in life.

Kagan found that in adolescence the high-reactives experienced the same internal physical responses they had had as

babies, although obviously they didn't kick and scream anymore. However, all in all, the differences between the three groups—high, middle, and low—weren't as clearly delineated as during infancy. Some uninhibited or middle-level babies had become shy teens. Some inhibited and middle-level babies had become extroverted teens. Some didn't modify their childhood behavior at all.

It becomes clear from Kagan's research that as a child grows and develops, his inborn temperament can no longer predict his behavior. Beginning around age three, a child moves from the safety of home into day care, the playground, or preschool. As a consequence of becoming more involved with others, he starts to make social comparisons, and he becomes aware of his limitations.

Soon the other elements that comprise personality—experience, psychology, and culture—become more critical and the influence of temperament shrinks. The emerging ascendance of personality corresponds with a preschooler's increasing mental development—the workings of the higher brain. Children who are inhibited at birth may or may not develop strategies and coping mechanisms to help them deal with their initial intense reactions to new or threatening situations. Based on their experience and reasoning, they may or may not become shy.

The Slow-to-Warm-Up Temperament

While Kagan's experiments explain inhibition as an initial reaction, researchers Stella Chess and Alexander Thomas at the New York Medical Center in Manhattan investigated what happens to children after they react to novelty. Observing the children shortly after birth and following them for several years thereafter, they found that all of them handle unfamiliarity by either accepting it, acting against it, or taking a long time to acclimate to it. Shy people typically use the last strategy. Indeed, I've been emphasizing this slow-to-warm-up theory because I believe it applies to most aspects of your adjustment to what is outside your comfort zone.

The slow-to-warm-up tendency appears in about 15 percent of the children that Chess and Thomas studied. These kids encounter difficulty dealing with *anything* new: clothes, foods, teachers, schools, or day care settings. They even have problems with new demands, such as toilet training or dressing themselves.

With patience and persistence, slow-to-warm-up children can become accustomed to their new situation. Just as shy adults claim that they become relaxed and gregarious with people who know them well, slow-to-warm-up children lose their inhibitions once they feel more comfortable.

The Wait-and-Hover Temperament

The wait-and-hover temperament explains what occurs when inhibited children want to initiate contact with other youngsters. Jens Asendorpf, a researcher at the Max Planck Institute for Psychological Research in Germany, observed children from three to six years old in their natural play settings and realized that not all shy children are alike. Rather, there are three types of temperamentally inhibited youngsters, each with differing motivations and strategies for joining others at play:

1. The unsociable child. Happy alone, the unsociable child neither fears other youngsters nor wants to join in their play. She has little motivation to approach them, since she has little interest in them.

2. The avoidant child. Aggressive and disruptive, the avoidant child joins other youngsters when he can make a mess of things. It's his way of adapting, even if it's maladaptive. Still, his peers are unhappy around him and often ostracize him.

3. The shy child. The shy child is unhappy alone but has no wish to disrupt others' play. She waits and hovers, lingering at the fringes of the action, watching the other children. She feels anxious because she wants to approach but lacks a strategy that would integrate her into the group (a typical approach/avoidance conflict). Instead, she watches passively, hoping the others will notice and invite her to join them.

Rather than focusing on silence, the trait most often associated with shyness, these theories of inhibited temperament in children identify three factors—ease at becoming stressed, inability to acclimate to a new environment, and conflicted desire to approach other children—that precede silence.

When we highlight what goes on under the skin, we see that shyness is not merely a communication problem. Rather, it is a phenomenon of the body, mind, and self that affects experiences in a complicated manner. In this and the next two chapters, I will provide suggestions for how to help prevent your temperamentally inhibited child from becoming shy.

Unfortunately, children with highly reactive, slow-to-warm-up, and/or wait-and-hover temperaments can become lost in the family shuffle because another child may be loud and demanding. That can make the inhibited child seem "quiet" and "easy" by comparison. You may also overlook a withdrawn child because you simply don't know how to recognize temperamental inhibition in young children.

Before you can intervene, you must be able to identify whether your youngster is inhibited. Following are the most common characteristics of temperamentally inhibited children:

- Crying, kicking, or fussing when in unfamiliar territory or with unfamiliar people

- Dislike of loud noises and chaotic environments

- Easy arousability by others

- Strong reactions to impurities in the air, such as dust, and certain foods or fibers in clothing

- Hating changes in routine, even if it's just wearing a shirt for the first time or trying a new food

- Preference for being alone, engaged in activities they know they enjoy

- Clinging to parents when in an unfamiliar setting or confronted with new people

- Strong and negative reaction to being separated from parents or familiar people

- Hanging back and watching other children play

- Reluctance to initiate contact with other children

Bear in mind, however, that it's important to avoid making assumptions about your child's mind and self before these aspects of her personality develop. Refrain from labeling your preschooler shy based on these characteristics of inhibition. Rather, become aware of how her body reacts to new situations. Understand her and make her feel loved and secure.

Helping a Temperamentally Inhibited Child

You may believe that if your youngster is temperamentally inhibited, you need not encourage him to socialize because he's happiest when left alone or when safely ensconced within the confines of the family. Your reticent child dislikes being separated from you—at day care, at preschool, or on the playground—so you keep him close by. When he cries out of discomfort or fear, you naturally soothe him with the assurance that he can skip whatever disquiets him. You may label this child shy and expect him to act that way.

Despite your good intentions, this can be a serious mistake. Based on my experience, temperamentally inhibited youngsters who are labeled, coddled, and told that they don't have to do what others do have a slim chance of becoming successfully shy. These youngsters will believe that their fears are bigger than your expectations. When they feel tense and frightened, they may cry, give up, and run back to safety. Unfortunately, you reinforce their withdrawing behavior by telling them that this is okay.

One woman who responded to my shyness survey wrote, "My mother always allowed me to quit any situation in which I was not comfortable," which she feels helped reinforce her shyness. Another wrote, "When parents and grandparents are worried and anxious, and convinced almost anything is going to end in disaster, some of the attitude rubs off. Young children don't have the experience to recognize that catastrophizing is a distortion of reality. The world can look like a place filled with danger and hostility when there is so much pressure to be careful. Even good intentions to shelter children from problems can leave them unable to cope with ordinary things."

No child, no matter how inhibited, lives in a plastic bubble. There are certain developmental tasks that all children must face and master, whether it's playing with friends, functioning at preschool, understanding their feelings, learning to ride a bike, or taking appropriate risks. Children cannot accomplish these goals if you don't encourage them.

A temperamentally inhibited, slow-to-warm-up, wait-and-hover child will naturally stay away from new situations. But try not to reinforce his bashfulness by giving in to all his fears.

Teach him how to conquer his fears and become successfully shy at a young age. Here are some strategies:

Be mindful of the slow warm-up period. Your shy child will most likely react negatively to new experiences, so don't force her into noisy or chaotic environments. Rather, ease her into situations that you believe she may reject, and take it one step at a time. Explain and be patient.

Set an example for your child. If you back away from social commitments, your child will sense your anxiety. By your actions, show him that others are friendly and can be trusted. Entertain in your home, and maintain friendships with extended family and friends. Involve your child in your errands, socializing, and community events.

Don't overprotect your child. Don't let her feel that she can't do something because she is "shy." Make sure that she has opportunities to interact with other children.

Communicate with your child. Tell him about your own experiences, and let him learn from your mistakes. Explain the benefits of friendship, help him understand his feelings, prepare him for upcoming events, and together choose appropriate activities for his temperament.

Prepare your child. Give her advance notice if your family routines are about to change. Help her anticipate what to expect. Talk about upcoming events—from car pools to birthday parties—so she won't feel surprised.

Prepare others. If it takes a few extra minutes for your child to get used to other adults, explain to them that he is sensitive and requires a little more time to warm up. Ask for their patience in gaining his trust.

Don't label your child or assume she has a serious emotional or developmental problem. At a young age, she will react to her natural tendency to be frightened by the new or unusual. There's nothing wrong with that. Help her understand how to get over her fears and doubts. Labeling creates self-fulfilling prophecies.

Love your child for who he is, not who you want him to be. Children don't fail; they only fail to meet their parents' unrealistic expectations. Try to understand your child's experiences from his point of view, and talk through his troubles.

Overall, temperamentally inhibited children need to expand their comfort zones slowly by developing trust in themselves, their playmates, and the widening world. Rather than isolating and protecting them, love and encourage them.

All in the Family

In addition to temperament, experiences within the family have a profound impact on the development of your child's personality traits, including shyness. The family is his first social environment; it teaches him how to cope with relationships. What he learns there will be reproduced in adulthood.

Siblings

A Pennsylvania college student explained to me why she believed she was shy. "I have a brother who is three years older than me," she wrote, "and as long as I can remember, he dominated the conversations where I was present, whether it be with our parents, relatives, or friends. Because he did all the talking, I never had to. I could just fade into the background. To this day it continues."

Siblings are our first peers. How we interact with them often affects how we deal with others later in life. It may be a cliché, but it's still true that older siblings seem to be overly responsible and mature, middle children want to be noticed as individuals, and youngest, the "babies of the family," can shirk responsibility because their parents are permissive with them.

Intense sibling rivalries often affect how people see themselves and the world. A cartoonist wrote, "I don't know if I am genetically predisposed to being shy, but I do know that, while growing up, I always felt like I was second best to my six-years-older sister. I was nothing, and my opinions didn't matter to anybody. Maybe that wasn't the case in reality, but I always felt like it."

But according to Harvard University researchers Diane Arcus and Cathleen McCartney, even if they didn't experience full-blown sibling rivalry or stereotyping because of their place in the family, children are influenced by how they relate to their brothers and sisters and can develop shyness as a result. Sometimes this influence starts as soon as the baby comes home from the hospital.

Imagine that Karen was just born to the Nelsons. When they introduced her to her two-year-old brother, Jonathan, he took a long look. He knew that he was himself, he knew that he was different from Karen, and he knew that he now had a rival for his parents' affection. He needed a way to get their attention, so he spilled his milk, threw tantrums, and was generally hostile toward his sister. The Nelsons responded immediately. But although they became angry and punished Jonathan, he felt he had won the battle; he had successfully diverted their attention from this interloper.

Little Karen became lost in the shuffle. The Nelsons did not neglect their new baby by any means, but as she gained awareness, she became cognizant of her older brother's demands. She learned that his loud behavior was his way to get noticed. Because she was temperamentally inhibited, however, she didn't act out, too. The commotion created by Jonathan's deliberate "naughtiness" made Karen irritable, but she knew she was no match for him.

This dynamic can sow the seeds of future shyness. Karen will have learned that her role is to be quiet, compliant, passive, and "good"—everything Jonathan isn't. The Nelsons may unconsciously encourage her meekness because it's so much easier to handle than their son's acting out. Karen will undoubtedly read their unspoken message and keep her concerns, frustrations, and complicated feelings to herself.

As she grows toward a shy adulthood, she may constantly wonder whether she's making a fuss, creating trouble, or blundering. She may be drawn to the more vocal people at gatherings and may compare herself negatively and harshly. She may expect to be ignored despite her talents and insights and may fail to reach out to others. Although she may be more comfortable as a wallflower, inside she may wish to be more like Jonathan.

Sibling rivalry can be tough on younger children, especially those who are temperamentally inhibited. This may be why younger children in a family are more likely to be shy.

Giving birth to children less than two years apart can intensify sibling rivalry and shyness. Children born close together tend to be more alike. When they compare themselves with their siblings, older siblings may increase their misbehavior or regress to a more babylike state (soiling their pants, for instance, after having been toilet-trained, or reverting to thumb-sucking) in order to gain their parents' attention. This quest for the spotlight could lead to the development of shyness in the less dominant child.

In addition, if a new baby appears in the home when the older child is just developing his sense of self and self-consciousness, the infant could temporarily displace the older child, causing jealousy and regressive behavior. This doesn't mean that he will encounter developmental problems or even become shy later. It's simply a way of adjusting to changes in the environment.

According to Arcus and McCartney, parents have a window of opportunity to minimize sibling rivalry and regressive behavior. A new baby can come into the family with very little disruption when the older child is between thirty-six and fifty-four months old. Perhaps by then the older sibling's sense of self is relatively autonomous from his parents. He can handle a new baby in the house without feeling too insecure or displaced.

If you are unable to space your children's births, be aware of how an older sibling's misbehavior can affect a younger child. Make sure that each of your offspring receives enough love, affection, and individual attention.

The Mother's Role

Shy youngsters, in particular, depend on their mothers for emotional support; they want to feel safe and loved in a world that seems frightening and threatening. When they are separated from their mothers, they become irritable and confused, sometimes even frantic. They trust few people outside the immediate family. Mother is their protector and defender.

As a mother, you do not "create" shy children, nor are you to blame if your youngsters grow up to be shy. You simply need to be aware of your child's temperament when making decisions about discipline style, caregiving, and guidance.

Overprotecting or "hothousing" can be a destructive strategy for shy children. Sheltered, timid children will never learn to achieve developmental milestones such as sharing, playing with others, or taking direction from adults if you constantly excuse them from doing so because they are shy. It's only natural to give these children extra attention, but you should not give in to *unreasonable* demands, no matter how cute, coy, or upset they are.

Many mothers overprotect their shy youngsters because they are—or were—shy themselves. In fact, shy children are more likely to have shy mothers, perhaps due to a genetic link or caregiving style. As one woman wrote to me, "My mother's fear of people has definitely influenced my life." If you are shy, you may see yourself reflected in your child and make special allowances for his fears. Or your interactions with other adults may be limited, so your child doesn't experience a broad range of people and subsequently leads a relatively quiet, isolated life.

However, I have spoken with a number of shy mothers

who go out of their way to spare their children the pain of shyness by encouraging them to speak up, fight their own battles, and value friendships with many other children. A shy mother of two in Ohio said, "My kids aren't shy, and I'm really glad because I didn't want them to have to go through the same stuff I've gone through. They're quite talkative and independent. I didn't want them to be like me. I always encouraged them to do things on their own and speak up for themselves." And an acutely shy social worker told me, "When I have children I plan to work hard at encouraging their interactions with others." These women are to be commended. Not only are they helping their kids, but they're helping themselves as well by being socially active.

Several studies have examined how mothers have encouraged their temperamentally shy children to become successfully shy. These mothers help their children understand that sometimes they will feel uncomfortable and insecure but that they are expected to accomplish certain tasks, such as staying in preschool for a full day or sharing toys with others. They guide their children out of shyness by expecting them to take the same risks that bolder children take, despite their initial hesitation.

If you sense your child's apprehension in approaching a potential playmate, it's helpful to talk through the whys and hows of the encounter. Instead of backing away from the threat, help your child plan for it. This requires patience on your part, because your shy youngster may warm slowly to new situations, but you will be rewarded in the end. Your child will incorporate these lessons throughout his life. Here's how you can guide your child toward being successfully shy:

Teach him to tolerate frustration. Highly reactive babies tend to fuss when separated from their mothers. Their cries seem shrill and urgent to caring adult ears. Naturally, you will want to rush to soothe your baby, but you need not. When you allow your inhibited infant to cry for a short time instead of picking him up as soon as he starts fussing, you are not neglecting him, but rather helping him become accustomed to dealing with internal arousal. You are teaching him that discomfort is temporary, normal, and a condition that you can't always attend to immediately.

Eventually your child will learn how to soothe himself and will accept mild discomfort as a normal, not-too-bothersome fact of life. When he's older he won't be bewildered by anxiety-provoking situations, because he has managed them before.

Develop a firm and consistent style of discipline. A study of shy college students found that many were adversely affected by inconsistent discipline. When they were younger, they couldn't tell which of their actions would be punished and which were acceptable. According to these students, their confusion inhibited their speech and behavior.

Shy children are naturally inclined to second-guess their actions. To create a feeling of safety in their lives, it's best to establish stable guidelines and expectations for behavior coupled with consistent follow-through.

Be careful about criticism. Temperamentally inhibited children are more likely to internalize criticism because they're aroused, self-conscious, and fearful. When disciplining your child, draw a distinction between a "bad child" and "bad behavior." Let your youngster know that while you don't appreciate the Magic Marker drawing on the walls, you love her nonetheless. Not surprisingly, this is the best way to discipline children while encouraging healthy self-esteem.

Overall, reassure your child that you love her while gently nudging her out of the nest and into the broader world outside.

The Father's Role

Most dads teach their youngsters about power and self-expression through their style of play. They toss their kids into the air, give piggyback rides, scare and chase them, wrestle with them, or hold them tightly until they cry "uncle."

Your child learns many life lessons from this rowdiness. First, he sees that you and adults in general are stronger and more powerful than he is. He also must tolerate a certain level of frustration in a world that is rough, tough, and scary. He carefully watches your moods and nonverbal cues, your face and body language, to predict what will happen next. He also learns to clearly communicate his emotions by giggling, crying, struggling, asking you to stop, or wandering away from the uncomfortable situation. This forces him to listen to his emotions, which may signal that the roughhousing is getting out of hand.

In short, through play, you train your children to hold their own in the world by teaching them to tolerate frustration, solve problems, and interpret and communicate emotions.

Highly reactive children may be poorly equipped to handle the rough-and-tumble play that many fathers prefer. Sadly, this can create a rupture in the relationship, especially with boys. An inhibited child may be too frightened to develop a close emotional connection with his dad. And because this child dislikes rough games, he may fail to learn the lessons he needs to acquire about how to get along in the "rough" world.

Similarly, a father may reject his inhibited child in favor of an extroverted offspring because he doesn't know how to play with the quieter one. After a few too many tears, he may believe that he's not good with children (or with that child) and withdraw. You should avoid this eventuality at all costs.

If you are the father of a shy, highly reactive child, recognize his relatively low tolerance for stimulation. Some of the games you like to play may simply be too much for him. Not that you should stop roughhousing—it does teach your child valuable lessons. Rather, tone down the play and perhaps find other, quieter, but equally challenging activities that your child will enjoy.

Clinical psychologist Mitch Golant suggests noncompetitive play, in which "you emphasize your child's effort, not necessarily the result. Stress diminishes when you dwell on the process (how your child approaches a situation) of play rather than the goal. In noncompetitive play, there are no winners or losers, only people cooperating, getting closer, and having fun." Activities such as reading with your child, storytelling, playing with puppets or clay, and drawing have the added benefit of enhancing your child's creativity, which may augment his ability to make friends.

You can also take on some of the more feminine aspects of parenting—being sensitive, nurturing, and understanding—in order to relate to your child in an emotionally intimate manner. If you are shy, make an effort to play rough-and-tumble games with your children to do your part in the delicate balance of family life.

The Impact of Divorce

Divorce is hard on children in general and can be especially difficult for a shy child, who reacts more to change, is more sensitive, and has less social support than his outgoing siblings. Even when the breakup is relatively painless for the spouses, it is a trauma that can bring about shyness in temperamentally uninhibited children or make an inhibited child withdraw even further.

Indeed, withdrawal is merely one sign of adjustment to the new situation. To cope with their confusion about divorce, young children may also become depressed, blame themselves, develop intense fears, create reconciliation fantasies, and even become aggressive and hostile. If you divorce, keep in mind that your children will be profoundly affected by the loss. Be sure that both of you are communicating with them clearly, compassionately, and honestly.

If you do not have custody of your children, it's important to remain in the picture. Your shy child especially will need emotional stability and your reassurance that he is not to blame for the divorce. On the other hand, it's easy to feel guilty and give in to a child's withdrawal or spoil him, but constant support and communication are more constructive approaches.

You should also watch for the isolation your child may feel during periodic visits with you. Shy children can feel acutely lonely when separated from their custodial parent, friends, and neighborhood for extended periods. If your child is spending an extended time with you, it might be helpful to introduce him to your friends' children but also stay with him during playtime so he won't feel abandoned.

You might also spend time engaged in mundane activities—shopping, running errands, washing the car. At those times, you may have wide-ranging conversations and build a strong relationship despite the separation.

If you are a custodial parent who must work, be sure that your shy child isn't isolated at home with a baby-sitter or grandparent. A day care center or preschool will help your youngster socialize. It's also helpful to join a group for single parents and keep in contact with neighborhood families to receive the emotional support you need. A few families can gather at one house with the children and baby-sitters in one room and the parents in another. All members will then enjoy the benefits of being with a peer group, reducing their stress, and enjoying active social lives.

Overall, the key is to make sure that your shy child doesn't suffer emotionally or socially because of your breakup. Make sure that both of you are involved in child rearing. You both need to be attentive and loving because you both provide valuable lessons. All children who lose contact with one parent will feel the loss acutely.

Day Care: An Extension of Home

People often ask me if shy children can benefit from day care or if they need the extra security and individual attention that only a parent can provide. For many families, this is a moot point. A stay-at-home parent is not an option. Besides, if the center is good, a child, even a shy child, will be just fine.

In fact, I believe day care benefits shy children because it places them in a group of peers with whom they can interact, acquire social skills, and expand their comfort zone. They learn to negotiate, solve problems, share, cooperate, and play in groups—skills that don't come naturally to shy youngsters but that are vital to their future adjustment.

Seek out a center in which the caregivers are warm, patient, and experienced in handling shy children. A setting that is stimulating but not chaotic is best. Ask for a schedule of activities so that you know what your child will be doing each day. Shy children need diverse activities and experiences, with a good balance between personal and group interaction. If you see a television, don't even consider sending your child to that center. Chances are, the staff will be using the TV as an electronic baby-sitter, and that removes opportunities for socialization and intellectual development.

Once you select an appropriate facility, work with the staff to ensure that your child is comfortable and receiving the proper attention. Alert the caregivers to the fact that she adapts slowly to new activities, people, or places, so they don't misinterpret her natural reticence and believe she is afflicted with a more serious condition.

Like Jenny's wise parents, you might ease your toddler into her placement by starting slowly. First tell her that she is going to day care, and prepare her as much as possible for what to expect. Reassure her that the teacher will call if she needs you. Let her stay for a short time at first and gradually extend the duration until she can handle a full day. If she's old enough, you can talk to her about her fears and how she can cope with them. Observe her reactions.

Shy children eventually come around and enjoy themselves at day care but may need more help at the beginning. There's no need to feel guilty about placing your shy children at a center. Appreciate its social aspects and encourage her to make friends and become self-sufficient.

Time Alone Can Be Helpful or Harmful

While I have encouraged you to help your child become accustomed to spending time with others, solitary play, which many shy youngsters prefer, can also be valuable. It allows your preschooler to relax, to think through her experiences, and to develop creativity.

But spending time alone is useful only up to a point, and only if it is accomplished in a certain manner. Kenneth Rubin at the University of Waterloo analyzed the nonsocial play of four-year-olds and found that it falls into several categories. He concluded that there is no need to be overly concerned if your child likes to play alone. Rather, you should notice how she is playing and encourage her to spend time wisely.

Parallel Constructive Play

Parallel constructive play occurs when children engage in a constructive activity like building a block tower or solving a puzzle. They play next to each other but not with each other. This kind of play builds good problem-solving ability and helps with social adjustment. Other children approach "parallel players" for help with their own projects. Parallel constructive play can turn your child into an "expert" while it builds self-confidence and self-reliance.

You can encourage parallel constructive play by providing indirect support. If, for example, your child is building a block tower that keeps falling down, rather than rebuilding it for him, make suggestions like, "What would happen if you tried bigger blocks on bottom and smaller ones on top?" In this way, you are helping him to solve a problem without accomplishing the task for him. This allows him to experience

frustration, become comfortable with it, overcome it, and finally gain a sense of accomplishment.

Solitary Constructive Play

This "introverted play" occurs when children play well by
themselves without being in proximity to other youngsters.
In fact, they do so well alone, others don't try to join them,
thinking that they probably prefer to be left by themselves.
This benign play is fine in the short run but can cause problems if your child never engages in parallel play. Other children don't think badly of constructive, independent loners,
but they have no chance to get to know the child who plays
alone, and friendships can't develop.

Solitary Functional Play

This occurs when your child repeats a movement continuously with or without a toy. He may step on a chair over and
over again, spin in circles, or bang his toy truck on the floor
repeatedly.

When children engage in this type of play, they are not
thinking about anything in particular. Most likely, others will
not approach them to play, and they will lose opportunities to
socialize. Indeed, children who spend a lot of time playing in
this manner may have difficulty solving problems and may
encounter emotional and social developmental lags because
they don't experience novelty or expand their comfort zone.
They never learn alternative play strategies, nor do they interact with other children.

If you find your child engaged in this solitary functional
play, ask him why he is banging his truck. If he is the only
child at home, offer alternatives and gently encourage him to
participate in new activities like fantasy play with other
youngsters. Together you can look for leaves or birds or play
on the swing. Try a variety of experiences that will expand his
comfort zone.

Fantasy Play

It's normal and helpful for preschoolers to act out imaginary roles and hypothetical scenarios, as long as they play this way *together*. But children who are lost in fantasy by themselves may have problems adjusting to real-life social play. Teachers find that children who spend a lot of time in fantasy play alone are socially maladjusted and take a long time to solve interpersonal problems. They interact poorly with their peers and have relatively low status within their classroom; they are lost in their own world and can't relate to or show empathy toward others.

You and your child's caregivers should be alert to this type of behavior and should make sure that she doesn't become lost in the clouds by herself. Encourage her to play with others at the playground, or invite others to the house. It might help for her to play with slightly younger children because she will be more cognitively and physically developed, and they may be easier for her to relate to. Besides, playing with younger children can reinforce her self-confidence if she is cast in the role of teacher. This will also make her more sympathetic to others' struggles and help her to become less self-involved.

Structure activities that require constructive and/or interactive play. Bring her back to reality and out of her own world.

Wait and Hover

Shy children want to get involved with others but have a hard time taking the risks necessary to make friends. Children who wait and hover tend to be mentally "younger" than their peers. They engage in fewer conversations and are less socially adjusted. Waiting and hovering is useful only as a temporary strategy. In Chapter 10, I will give you some tips on how to help your youngster outgrow it.

You need not worry if your preschooler likes to play alone. In fact, engaging in constructive parallel play enables children to become experts and to operate in their own comfort zones. You can introduce new activities to a child who likes to play alone. But be alert to a child who is lost within herself, and encourage her to fill her time constructively. Children need to stretch their minds when they're alone and should avoid passive activities such as television or computer games. Invite your preschooler to draw, dress up, solve puzzles, play games, build castles, create clay menageries, look at picture books—anything that occupies her imagination.

Goodness of Fit

A highly reactive child may feel overwhelmed at a chaotic, noisy birthday party. A slight, shy child may feel overrun at the playground when others become wild. These situations may not suit your quiet youngster.

The "goodness of fit" concept entails your child's search for conditions that are consistent with her temperament and eventually her personality. It means matching her environment with who she truly is. Like a rudimentary comfort zone, the goodness of fit constantly shifts as your youngster grows, investigates unexplored territory, and masters new tasks.

You can see goodness of fit in action on an instinctive level when a frightened toddler crawls back to the safety of his mother's lap after encountering a kitten. Even at this most fundamental level, the child is attempting to control his environment, his temperamental reactions, and the demands of the situation by finding a safe harbor. When he feels comforted and confident, he will venture forth again to explore what was once threatening.

Perhaps your shy toddler must spend time at a day care center because you work. Although she can handle the separation, she may not belong at this center. You don't have to battle every morning as you try to surmount her reluctance to go. Instead, try to adjust the fit so your daughter is more comfortable. Using the guidelines I've outlined above, seek a new center that more accurately matches her temperament. And don't push her faster than she can comfortably go.

If you watch, listen, and learn about your child's needs and work with all of the elements that comprise a good fit, you can help your child be successfully shy. Young children express their emotions when upset, but they don't yet have the cognitive ability to make decisions about how to remedy their situation. It is up to you as a parent to make adjustments and choices that encourage her to participate in activities that suit her.

Perhaps your shy five-year-old wants to play T-ball with the neighborhood kids. Tommy yearns to wear the uniform and be part of the team but fears he's not good enough and that his friends will laugh at him. You, too, believe that the experience will coax him out of his shell. How can you help him control some of the factors that bother him and encourage him to play?

If Tommy is calm, he will concentrate on his skills and play well. The goal of your intervention should be to increase his calmness by helping him become more ready to play. You can begin by sharing your own experiences with Little League. Describe your defeats as well as your triumphs so he understands that winning and losing are just part of the game. Practice throwing, catching, and batting to improve his skills and augment his confidence about his playing ability. Give him time to warm up to the sport by letting him sit on the bench for a few practices and games. Provide the opportunity to play, but don't push him if he's unready.

If, after all this effort, Tommy still feels apprehensive about playing T-ball, you might help him select a more appropriate sport the following year—perhaps swimming or gymnastics.

These lessons will continue throughout your child's life. Successfully shy people who understand goodness of fit have learned to control their environment. They may walk out of a loud, chaotic bar and choose to spend the evening at a quiet café instead, with no regrets. They may select a profession that suits their personality—becoming a professor of business rather than a Wall Street floor trader—so that they're not overwhelmed by the tumult inherent in certain occupations. They become successfully shy because they have learned at an early age that they can control their feelings, reactions, and fate by listening to their instincts.

10

Shyness in Middle Childhood

"When I was between four and eight years old," a woman in the armed services wrote to me, "I was painfully shy. My stomach would ache, and I always felt like I was on the verge of tears if any adult spoke to me or anyone tried to be my friend. Adults were easy to deal with; I simply avoided them. I would start fights and pick on other children to keep them away from me; almost all of my report cards said, 'Has trouble getting along with other children.'" Shyness in the middle years can indeed be painful.

You and your family members will have the first and most fundamental influence on your child's shyness. But this may wane as your youngster discovers other children in the neighborhood, at play centers, and at school. In fact, children naturally turn to playmates at the age of six or seven and enter what is called the latency period, during which they become sociable.

The latency period is a dress rehearsal for the roles children play as adults. Youngsters care for their dolls to practice parenting, play catch to mimic professional athletes, prepare tea parties to feel like hosts, and play war games to experience powerfulness. In the process, they learn valuable lessons about cooperation, sharing, friendship, leadership, and negotiation. Not only do they *want* to play with each other, but they *must* in order to grow.

The latency period can be the most critical in the development of shyness. Children need to learn social lessons during this time but cannot do so if they isolate themselves by watching television, playing computer games, or reading. They need to be with friends and to explore the world.

Not surprisingly, many shy children have trouble during latency because this is such an overwhelmingly social period. In fact, this is when most people claim they were first identified as shy. They balked at kindergarten, were reluctant to play with children, and were more withdrawn among peers than at home. A Connecticut woman wrote, "Even in kindergarten, I remember being one of the quietest kids in class and spending many play periods alone when I'd rather have been with the other kids."

If your child was born with a highly reactive nervous system, she may feel threatened and fearful around other children and prefer to play alone. If you don't encourage her to make friends or if she is isolated and lacks the opportunity, she can develop shyness during the latency period because she is not accumulating social experiences. My Connecticut correspondent, for example, believed her shyness came from being discouraged from participating in after-school activities. "It was less of a hassle for everyone if I just came straight home after school," she wrote. "My neighborhood was rather affluent, and many kids started taking private tennis, swimming, and dance lessons in early elementary school." She didn't, and believed the lack of social interaction hurt her.

Fortunately, just as shyness can set in during the latency period, it can also be minimized then. I've seen uncertain, fearful, or socially inept children quickly learn how to get over their fears with proper guidance. Throughout this chapter, I will show you how to help your child so that being in school or making friends does not frighten her.

The Challenge of Starting School

A successful real estate broker in New York shared, "My first encounter with panic was my mother leaving me alone my first day of kindergarten. I felt as if I had been left in prison. They even had bars on the windows." Her experience is common among shy children who naturally dislike changes in routine, people, or places. Many find the first day of school traumatic. They cry, cling, and make a run for the door as soon as they step into the classroom.

It's not just the fear of abandonment that bothers them. The school environment itself may seem rigid and threatening when compared with home. You may have instinctively or deliberately adapted your lives to fit your shy child's needs, but this individual attention is unfeasible in a class of twenty-five or thirty children, many of whom are gregarious. Following a schedule, taking orders from an adult, being surrounded by a group of boisterous children all day, and lengthy separation from you may all be daunting to her.

Your child may not understand her reactions, but she knows she doesn't like how she feels at school. Even thinking about it can bring on headaches, stomachaches, anxiety, and nightmares. In class, her self-consciousness and nervousness may prevent her from concentrating on her tasks. She may refrain from joining other children because it's difficult for her to adjust to their presence and activity. In fact, her teachers may believe she's immature or even less intelligent than the others because she refuses to try new activities.

One young man who wrote to me, a student in a technical college, recalled this happening to him. "As a young child just starting school, I noticed how all the other children were playing together in groups, but I wasn't a part of anyone or anything. When people tried to talk to me, I turned away, so they assumed that I was dumb and put me in remedial classes. From that time on, the shyness continued to make me into something I wasn't (or am not)."

He may not have been any more or less intelligent than his peers. Probably he was outside his old comfort zone and was slow to warm to his new circumstances. Unfortunately, the misinterpretation of his shy behavior left him feeling that he was never appreciated for who he was.

There is no need to panic or punish your shy child if he

hates school. Anxiety and withdrawal are his normal reactions to a new environment filled with many unfamiliar faces and activities. Rather than overreacting to your child's natural instincts, counteract them by anticipating the challenges he will encounter in the classroom. Here's how.

Prepare your child and her teacher for the first day. Meet the teacher before the school year starts, and explain that your child is slow to warm to new people and situations. It would be great if she could become acquainted with the teacher and explore the room before September. You might show her where the bathrooms are and where the kids hang their coats. If this is impossible, be sure you have walked the route to school and explained what will happen there and what her teacher will expect of her.

Communicate with your child. If she's having nightmares, stomachaches, and headaches because of school, don't dismiss these signs of stress. She does feel terrible but may not know why. Tell her that her fears are causing these reactions, and help her work through them. Explain that it's natural to feel uneasy about a new situation. Everyone gets butterflies, but this doesn't mean she is sick. (You can give examples from your own life, such as starting a new job or giving a speech.) More than likely, her symptoms come from her wanting to remain in the safety of home. Explain slowness in warming up so that she can understand. She'll feel better when she realizes that what she's going through is normal and will pass.

Use positive reinforcement. Focus on the fact that she went to school, even though she was uneasy. Build on successes.

Help her to branch out. If she's having problems with school, encourage her to take lessons and be with other children who are not her classmates so she develops friendships that are free of the school environment. When car-pooling, talk about school with the other children (to minimize its novelty).

Stay involved. Even though the first day passes quickly and your child may be able to tolerate a full day in the classroom, she may have other problems because of her self-consciousness. If she fears being called on in class, drill her at home on her school-work so she's prepared for the next day and can articulate what she has learned. This will augment her confidence and reduce self-consciousness.

The greater the continuity between school and home, the easier your child's transition will be. When possible, take an active role in the classroom experience. Spend some time as a volunteer. If you are unable to participate during the day, go to after-school meetings and programs. Serve refreshments, take tickets, attend holiday concerts. You will communicate the value of education to your child, and she will feel heartened by your presence.

It's also important to try to remain nearby and available while your child is doing homework. By reading your own newspaper or book, you show that you're involved in intellectual pursuit. Periodically ask how she's doing. Let her know that you're willing to help if she needs it.

Stay involved in continuing conversations with the teacher. If you can't get away during the day, call for feedback or write letters of inquiry. Ask what you can do at home. Pay attention to the classroom environment. If it is chaotic, your child may have difficulty learning and adjusting. The goodness-of-fit principle applies here, too. (See Chapter 9.) If you can identify a more appropriate environment, it may be wise to move her.

Give her a longer warm-up period. Try to take her to school early each morning to be alone with her teacher and build rapport. She can then warm up to each child individually as they arrive, making it less likely that a room full of classmates will overwhelm her.

Bear in mind that your shy child may backslide at the beginning of each school year. Remind her of the prior year's experience: she was frightened at first but eventually lost her inhibitions. She can do the same this year! Keep her from dwelling on her fears by focusing on her successes. "Last year you were afraid; it took you a while to adjust; and then you did really well." Go over the strategies that were successful last year. "Remember I called Ms. Lindsay, and she explained the homework. Chances are this year we can call Mr. Patterson if you have trouble and he'll help, too." Show your child that you have the confidence in her ability to adjust. Rather than focusing on her fears, explain the slow-to-warm-up phenomenon, the approach/avoidance conflict, and the comfort zones.

However, unless the problem is severe or your child has other developmental issues, I do not recommend holding her back. She should not be penalized for adapting slowly, because in truth, she is merely acting on her instincts. Repeating a grade may damage her self-esteem.

I would also like to caution against home schooling as a way to alleviate shyness and anxiety. Unless you have major philosophical disputes with the local schools, home schooling can adversely affect your shy child. The long periods of isolation will only reinforce her dependency and fear of other youngsters. Because your child must be with other children during the latency period, home schooling may delay her social-skills development by shrinking her comfort zone. It teaches her that avoiding challenges brings its own rewards. Unfortunately, this reward is increased shyness.

If you do decide to home-school your shy child, be sure she has plenty of social involvement with children outside the family.

The Growing Impact of Shyness in Latency

During the first few years of elementary school, young children seem oblivious to the fact that some of their peers are more reticent, but their attitudes change as they get older. Gradually, almost inevitably, the more dominant children begin to shun, reject, and bully their shyer classmates. Sadly, those who are naturally less vocal and assertive and who do not benefit from a network of supportive friends can suffer for it.

Although they may emerge from their cocoons when among new children who don't label them, children tend to become stuck in their shyness with those who are familiar. If classmates believe a child is shy, no matter how much he wants to make overtures, he may be unable to break out and create a new persona.

This bias against shy children soon takes its toll. As early as the fourth or fifth grade, they realize bashfulness and anxiety are problems for them. In fact, surveys of shy fifth-graders show they have lower self-esteem than their more gregarious classmates.

Withdrawn boys, in particular, suffer. They hold negative views of themselves, feel lonely, and believe that they lack social skills. These boys, who are also convinced that they're less athletic than their peers, seem to have difficulty participating in all-important sports activities, and they blame themselves for their perceived inadequacies.

It's important to be aware of how the perception of shyness shifts as your child matures. It isn't enough to tell your stigmatized child, "Sometimes kids are cruel" or "Popularity doesn't matter." Unfortunately, it does. Even young children are keenly aware of who's "in" and who's not, who's cool and who's a "geek." It hurts to be friendless. And it hurts even more to be unable to gather the courage to make friends, especially when you risk being taunted, teased, or manipulated by a potential playmate.

Your shy child may be rejected if you do not step in early. But wise parents who can communicate honestly about how to make and keep friends and capture the excitement of childhood can alleviate feelings of isolation, inadequacy, and self-doubt.

Taking a Small Risk: Making Friends

Just like in adulthood, making a friend in childhood means taking a risk. Indeed, to a shy child, being able to share a box of crayons or join a group of children working on a puzzle can be a big gamble. He may have to relinquish an activity that feels comfortable to him or initiate contact with others. That means someone may be entering his comfort zone or taking him out of his.

There are three ways that kids take this risk: by cooperating, disrupting, or waiting.

Imagine a second-grade classroom filled with children who each have a lump of clay. Four classmates pool their resources and start building a castle cooperatively at one table. Andy, Tracy, and Corey stand off to the side watching their friends.

While he squeezes the clay in his hands, Andy observes the group's activity. The kids laugh and argue about how tall and wide the castle should be and where the moat should go. One of them tries to build a tower, another the base, and the other two flatten out the walls and poke holes in them to make windows. They grab some blue construction paper to make a moat.

Andy pats his clay flat and moves closer to the table. "You need a drawbridge," he says from a few steps away. "You can use my piece." He offers his handiwork. The group stops momentarily and looks at the nearly completed castle and then back at Andy. They laugh because it's true; they made windows but no means for the king and queen to get in or out. They poke a big hole in one wall of the castle, and Andy attaches his piece to the bottom. It reaches the shore. Everybody cheers. Andy is now part of the group, and they start adding a forest around the castle.

Tracy, watching from the side, has been edging a bit closer while rolling her clay into a ball. She decides that she wants to join the group, so she runs toward the table and raises the ball of clay above her head. Smashing it into a side of the castle, she shouts, "I'm invading you!" as the wall collapses. The other children scream angrily while Tracy laughs and grabs pieces of the foundation. She tries to sit down with them, but her classmates push her away. She is unwelcome in their kingdom. She runs to a corner of the room and rummages through a stack of books. Tracy enjoyed her assault, but no one else did.

Corey has watched the progression of play from a few feet away. He holds his clay while the group rebuilds the castle. Corey thinks that maybe it would be stronger if he added his piece to the foundation. He waits for one of the children to mention fortifying the walls, but nobody talks about it.

He flattens his piece of clay and whispers to nobody in particular, "You can use my piece." No one hears. He steps toward the children, just a little bit, but they are nearly finished. Corey thinks that they won't need his clay anymore. His classmates talk excitedly as they put the finishing touches on the castle and forest while Corey goes to an empty table and starts working on a vase for his teacher.

Andy, Tracy, and Corey all wanted to join their classmates at the table, and they knew they had to take a risk to work on the castle. Even though they all started by watching, waiting, and mimicking the others, they each handled the challenge differently.

Andy cooperated. He waited, watched, and used his time alone to discern how he could be of help to the other children. Eventually, he thought of the drawbridge. He figured that if he could show his classmates that he could be trusted and add to their castle, they would let him join them. He was right. Not surprisingly, Andy is well-liked in this class.

Tracy disrupted. First she waited and watched, too. She decided that if she were more powerful than the other children, they couldn't refuse her. Her strategy backfired, and her classmates shunned her.

Corey waited and watched. And watched and waited. He

hoped that if the other children saw him off to the side, they would invite him to join them, but that never happened because they were engrossed in their play. He tried talking to them, but that didn't work either, since he merely whispered under his breath. When a person thinks out loud in that way, and no one hears what he says, there's no consequence, and so he initiates contact with minimal risk of rejection. Besides, Corey was so self-focused, he might have believed he was speaking louder than he actually was.

Soon he lost the opportunity to make his move. This happens to Corey often, which is why his peers neglect him and label him shy.

We could surmise several reasons for Corey's restraint. Perhaps the physical characteristics of the clay made him uncomfortable; he needed time to get used to its squishiness. It could also be that Corey is slow to warm to new situations and needed extra time to become accustomed to the seating arrangement and task. But because children have short attention spans, his classmates moved on to a new activity just when he was ready to join them.

If Corey were a highly reactive child, he may have been too aroused by the threat that the kids posed. They had rejected Tracy, and this frightened him. But if he were reacting to the threat, he would not be thinking clearly about how to approach the others. Or perhaps Corey was hindered because, having spent limited time around children his age, he simply did not know how they operate. It's almost impossible to learn social skills by osmosis.

Millions of children behave exactly like Corey does. Despite the countless hours they spend watching others in the classroom and on the playground, they can't seem to identify how the popular children join an ongoing activity. Shy children can become excellent friends, but they don't know how to make the initial connections that establish friendships. Indeed, to a shy youngster, having a new friend can seem magical; the mechanism is hidden from him. Consequently, he waits for others to notice him, invite him to play, and show him that they want and appreciate him.

How You Can Help

Children like Corey need gentle explanation and positive reinforcement to help them become part of the crowd. If your child is spending most of his time ambivalently waiting, watching, and hovering near a group in play, he need not suffer on the sidelines.

Your role is vital. As one woman wrote to me, "I've always been kind of introverted and secluded. When I was a kid, I played by myself a lot, and nobody pushed me into doing anything more social. There was no 'Why don't you join a club?' or 'Why don't you take some lessons?' They basically just shoved me in front of the TV."

There are many ways to help your shy child become successfully shy.

Teach your child how popular children make friends. Popular children focus on others. Show your child how to watch the play in progress, deduce how he can be of help, and make his helpfulness known to the other kids. Point out opportunities for offering assistance or sharing.

Modeling is critical. Life offers plenty of opportunities to teach your child how to be helpful. For example, when you and your child are in the produce section of the grocery store and the shopper next to you is weighing fruit, tear off a plastic bag and offer it to her. The more you can relate what you're doing to your child's life, the better.

Encourage him to take the next step gradually. For instance, if in the same market a baby drops her teddy bear, encourage your child to retrieve the lost toy and return it to the mother. This increases his altruistic risk-taking behavior in a safe environment. It's easier for him to take this gradual approach than to just jump into a boisterous group of kids on the playground.

Teach him how to share. Children can share toys without much sacrifice. When your youngster is the recipient of a friendly overture, teach him how to thank his friends.

Talk to other parents and their children at the playground. This will help your child become part of total interaction. Begin the conversation, then bring your child in. You might say, "My son likes to play with trucks too, right, Billy? Why don't you show your new dump truck to this little boy?" Then gradually step away and let Billy move into the interaction. This helps to create confidence within your child's comfort zone.

Modeling is always effective. Let your child observe you sharing your own possessions.

Show her how the rewards are greater than the risk. Emphasize the value of friendship and cooperation. Relate stories about how you got to know your friends, and explain to your child how she can learn from your experiences. Use old yearbooks and photos. It can be reassuring for her to know that you overcame the same problems she is facing. Remind her that becoming involved with others also helps the other children have fun.

Be sure he has opportunities to play with other children. Invite other youngsters to your house so that your child will be on his own turf and will feel more confident. Suggest a playmate who is slightly younger (and less intimidating) or naturally gregarious. Two shy children may not know how to play with each other. An outgoing playmate will provide more opportunities for social interactions. Encourage your child to reciprocate rather than shrink from opportunities for interaction. You might want to stay in the room for a while, to provide hints or direction that will spark play and help the youngsters find common ground. After getting into the swing of things, your child won't need you any longer.

Teach her about persistence. Help her to understand that if she stays in a situation long enough, she'll get used to it. When the play experience is over, remind her that she felt uneasy initially but hung in there and eventually enjoyed it. It's important for her to know that uncomfortable feelings pass. This will help her become accustomed to the initial discomfort and tolerate anxiety.

Read him books that portray healthy friendships. Ask the teacher, librarian, or bookstore owner to suggest books, or consult parenting magazines. As you read together, stop to talk about how the characters got to know each other, and allow your child to talk about how and why friendships are formed. Point out how the lessons being taught in the book relate to his life. Your active participation, rather than simply reading the story, will enhance his learning.

You can also attend the story circle at your library or bookstore with your child. You might even want to form a reading group with other parents and their shy children.

Reinforce burgeoning social skills. Your child may be unable to control the outcome of an interaction, but her attempts are worthy of praise. When she does make contact with other playmates, reward her efforts. Focus on her attempts and successes to build confidence. Remind her that playing with a new friend is like going to school. "You did that well, and you can do this, too." Talk about the comfort zone, slowness in warming up, and the approach/avoidance conflict in terms your child will understand.

Remember the old maxim: children learn from what we do, not what we say. Whenever you have an opportunity to invite friends to your home, help a stranger, or share your experiences, do so. Your child will become more comfortable with people when she sees you put your words into action.

A nurse in her early forties explained the consequences of neglecting to do this. "I was raised in an environment in which there was not a lot of social interaction," she wrote. "My parents were basically homebodies and didn't have any friends themselves. Self-expression was not encouraged." She believes this contributed to her shyness.

Strategies for School

School can be a snake pit for shy children who must pick their way through potentially embarrassing and anxiety-provoking situations. While we can't expect teachers to tailor their curriculum to fit the needs of a few students, they can make some broad changes in the classroom environment to render it more amenable to shy children.

"I had a lot of problems in school because of my shyness. I remember when I was in the first grade and the teacher called on us to read something. I started crying because I just didn't want to do it. I wasn't really sure why I felt like that; I just didn't want to talk in front of people. Now I can understand it, but at the time I didn't know what was going on. I just didn't want to be noticed by others."

"The first time I can remember feelings of social fear or shyness was in third or fourth grade, when I remember becoming uncomfortably aware of the sound of my own voice while reading aloud in class, and realized that I could see my heart pounding through my blouse. Previously, I had been an eager participant in class."

Shyness is not an emotional disorder, a learning disability, a sign of a larger and more serious problem, or a developmental glitch. Rather, it is a perception of threat that creates feelings of discomfort in about 20 percent of students. Shy children may not need extra counseling or remedial classes, and certainly they should not be left to their isolation. They simply need to be integrated into the classroom at a slower pace. Once they're comfortable, they'll do just fine.

Teachers can do this by integrating social-skills training into the general curriculum. That benefits everyone in the class. They should stress the importance of friendship, manners, cooperation, tolerance, and sharing. They can encourage their students to act out various social tasks, such as sharing or cooperating, and by leading them through the cycle of joining friends at play detailed earlier: watching, mimicking, and offering help. All children need to understand the importance of being a member of a larger community, and if they learn this lesson early, they will take it to heart.

Students who are placed in chaotic, rowdy, low-achieving environments are more likely to be shy, even if by nature they are temperamentally uninhibited. Youngsters can feel uncomfortable with the constant stimulation of a tumultuous setting. They may worry about being bullied and may fear the teacher, who may be more concerned about discipline than instruction. They may be afraid to speak up and draw attention to themselves. Consequently, they may retreat into silence and isolation to protect themselves. They may always be on guard, perceiving threats, unable to concentrate on their work.

While teachers should control classroom misbehavior, they shouldn't discourage their shy students' self-expression. In fact, they should help to draw them out. Take an activity as mundane as show-and-tell. Stereotypically it goes something like this: Laurie brings in a picture of a horse.

"What is that?" Mrs. Brown asks.

"A horse," Laurie replies quietly, and waits for another question. She is passive while in the spotlight and at the mercy of Mrs. Brown. She hates this and may dread future show-and-tell sessions because of the scrutiny. Shy children need more time to think on their feet.

A better strategy might be for teachers to guide their students through the discussion by sharing their own experiences. In fact, one study found that teachers who ask simple yes-or-no questions receive brief responses from their students, but those who volunteer personal information or make insightful comments while asking few direct questions are rewarded with more in-depth responses and increased participation.

For instance, if Laurie mutely presents the photo of the horse to the class, Mrs. Brown could prompt her with, "Wow, what a great horse. I used to ride horses all the time when I was your age. My parents used to take me to a farm that had stables."

Laurie could then reply, "I ride horses when I'm at my grandpa's farm. He took me riding last summer when I was there with my sister Rebecca. This is a picture of one of my grandpa's mares." Mrs. Brown and Laurie could then talk about the farm, what it was like sitting on top of such a large animal, or whether Rebecca liked to ride, too. They will be on a more equal footing when they find they have something in common. That could help their relationship in the future.

In this context, Laurie is not just responding to questions. She is also learning how to make conversation by offering information about herself and responding to her teacher's statements. Chances are that other children will pipe up with their own horse-related experiences during the interaction. Perhaps these conversations between Laurie and her classmates will spill over into the playground during recess.

Tips for Teachers

Many shy children fear their teachers, who are older, more powerful, and have the capacity to embarrass them. But teachers don't have to intimidate their shy students. They can help them become successfully shy students. Here's how:

Create a safe environment. When students have gotten out of hand, it's almost impossible to teach, to concentrate, and learn. Shy students do poorly when they're feeling intimidated by other students and can't predict what will happen in the classroom.

Understand the basic reactions of shy children. Be aware that they will most likely feel inhibited when introduced to new activities, settings, or individuals. Give them time to warm up to changes in curriculum or seating arrangements as well as the introduction of guests in your classroom.

Communicate with parents. They may be unaware that their

child is shy because he is comfortable in the safety of their home. Let parents know if their child seems fearful of other children.

Watch out for bullies. Shy children are often the target of bullies, so make sure that no one is treated unfairly just because they're less vocal than the others. Don't let a bully take advantage of a shy child who may have few allies to protect her.

Integrate social skills into the curriculum. This can be done by talking about how characters in a story became friends, asking and answering questions of others to get them used to spontaneous interactions ("Where are you going on Thanksgiving? What are you going to eat?"), crafts and cooperative games, group presentations, and explaining the value of friendships.

Use self-disclosure. If you know that some children are fearful of talking in class, tell them about your own experiences with anxiety. Then explain how you conquered your fears by facing them.

Design group activities. Students benefit from cooperative learning in groups of different sizes. Each group should contain children who have various levels of social skills so that the more reticent kids can follow the lead of their gregarious peers.

Notice and reinforce the strengths of your shy students. Let them speak up during their favorite subjects, and their self-esteem and self-confidence will rise as they shine.

Role-play. Let your students take on roles of historical figures, other teachers, relatives, characters from stories. Divide the class into groups who play out scenes while the other students watch. (Encourage shy people to be with nonshy, but be sensitive to the individual child. A really shy child should be grouped with one who is moderately shy but not extremely gregarious, or he may feel overrun.) Move quickly from one group to the next. The students will experience different cultures, different states—and they will get to be someone else. They can wear costumes, use voices. You can even include crafts like making hats.

Afterward, discuss the process and what your students learned. They might have been nervous at first, but soon have become enthusiastic. They might even suggest future topics. They see themselves in different activities with different people, and that helps to broaden their sense of self (they are able to stand before the class) and expand their comfort zones.

Encourage conversational skills. As mentioned earlier, ask open-ended questions. Don't let shy students live in fear of giving the "wrong" answer. They'll be more confident and talkative when they respond to a question that has no wrong answer.

A Last Word on Shy Children

Love your child unconditionally. Love her for who she is, not because she is as outgoing as you want her to be. Children, especially shy children, need parents who take an active, supportive interest in their lives, opinions, and feelings. Understand your child's special needs when confronting a new person, environment, or experience, and refrain from labeling her. Help her overcome her fears, and encourage her to think positively about herself.

Many parents want to change their shy child's natural behavior because they remember how painful it was to be timid, fearful, and sensitive. The suffering of an isolated childhood is difficult to erase. You may want your child to be popular, to have better and more socially successful experiences. But remember that it was not the feelings themselves, but rather being told you were wrong to feel anxious, afraid, or uncertain that caused much of your pain. Such conditional love can prevent a child from developing trust in her feelings and herself.

If your child establishes a secure sense of herself with your unconditional love and gentle guidance, she will be able to meet the challenges of shyness as she matures. She will use childhood lessons she has learned—how to approach another child, how to conquer physical arousal—in the more complex and intimate interactions she faces as an adolescent.

If your child can trust herself, her own power, and her instincts, she will be immune to the myths that undermine the lives of shy teens and adults. Instead, she will be successfully shy and won't know how to be anything else.

Shyness in Adolescence

"I was a terrible teenager," Kate admitted.

> My parents say that I was their hardest child to raise. I hung out with older people and generally did things I wasn't supposed to. You could say that I wasn't the cheerleader type. I didn't feel like I fit in. I'm from a small town that I thought was really boring, and I didn't want to be a good girl anymore, so I rebelled.
>
> Looking back now, I can see that I was shy, but I didn't know it. I did what I thought I was supposed to do—act tough, dress like a punk rocker, drink, stay out late—but underneath all of that I was extremely shy.

Nobody around Kate was aware of it. Neither she nor her friends or family recognized how unsure of herself she was. She had seemed such a confident, smart, outgoing, energetic child, but all of that changed when she started high school. "My parents only saw the good kid who was becoming a classic underachiever. Nobody labeled me shy—they just thought I was mixed-up, a typical teen. I wanted to grow up and show that I was an adult. I couldn't talk about my feelings or speak up in class and ask questions because I didn't want to show anyone that I didn't have all the answers."

Michelle recalls her high school experience, but it was much different from Kate's. "I was a shy 'good girl,'" she said of her teen years. In fact, Michelle believed that being so was helpful because she had excellent relationships with her teachers and school principal and wasn't tempted to drink or experiment with drugs.

She was a "good girl" during childhood too, although extremely shy. "I had friends in elementary school, but I was very quiet. I sat in the back of the classroom and tried to be invisible."

The larger, more complicated world of high school was a blessing and a curse. "Being a shy teenager was worse than being a regular teenager," she said. "But in some ways high school was a little bit easier than elementary school. It was bigger, so it was easy to get lost. I wasn't forced to be social or to do things that I hated."

Michelle found comfort when she blended into the crowd. She stuck with her friends and mostly hung out at the mall. She was taken aback when I asked her if she had dated during high school. "I didn't date at all," she confessed. "Imagine a guy approaching me or asking me out! I'd freeze! I wouldn't know what to say to him. And I wouldn't ask a guy out, either."

Michelle is in college now, pursuing a degree in psychology. "College is okay, but it's not great," she admitted. "I think it's harder to be shy here." But she is taking steps to become successfully shy. She participates in her smaller classes, has made friends in her dorm, and has joined a women's group.

The Enigma of Shyness in Adolescence

Based on outward appearances, Kate and Michelle couldn't be more dissimilar. Although Kate could have found a place for herself in high school, she rebelled against everything—parents, teachers, old friends, even herself and her innermost feelings. Michelle, on the other hand, seemed to have emerged from her teen years without severe trauma. She had friends, avoided antisocial behavior, and was true to her instincts.

But despite their seemingly different lives, attitudes, and levels of self-acceptance, they were both shy. How do two young women who seem so different share the same underlying personality trait?

Adolescence is a complex, contradictory time. But perhaps even more complex is shyness during adolescence. It manifests itself in many surprising, unpredictable, enigmatic ways when it impacts teens who are already caught in a tsunami of change.

Appearances can be deceiving. Shy adolescents like Michelle live ordinary lives. They are cautious about new challenges and stay out of trouble. Although they don't accumulate an array of experiences, they only deal with as much stimulation as they can handle. They have narrow comfort zones and do the best they can.

But many shy adolescents are hard to recognize. Like Kate, they become brazen, disrespect authority, and seem to have little problem expressing themselves and battling their demons. As one shy teen wrote to me, "These days, no one would even consider me shy. As a matter of fact, I'm the complete opposite. I go out of my way to be loud and draw attention to myself. Sometimes it can be as simple as speaking just a little too loudly, and at other times it's as dramatic as the time I flashed the U.S. Coast Guard while on a fishing trip!" How can this girl claim to be shy?

Just like the quiet shy teens, the rebelliously shy are doing the best they can during the most difficult period of their lives. These invisibly shy youngsters want desperately for others to regard them as grown-up but are not mentally or emotionally equipped to be adults. Their ambitions outrun their resources, since they cannot yet apply fully formed, mature abstract thought to their complicated lives.

But these teens won't admit their limitations. They cover their insecurities in rebellion, conformity, or scholarship. The prom queens, rebels, and geeks have much more in common under the skin than they would like to admit; they are all latching on to a secure prefabricated "identity" so they won't have to confront their true shy selves.

While shyness is ambiguous and sometimes so deeply

buried that it's hard to recognize, it still has a profound influence on many teenagers' lives.

Do Teenagers Outgrow Shyness?

Michelle was blunt about being misunderstood as a shy adolescent and young adult. "Everyone thinks that shyness is just in kids and not adults. It's really hard to convince people that you don't grow out of it. It's *real*."

In truth, only 20 percent of elementary-school children are shy, while 50 percent of teenagers are. In fact, many adults claim they acquired shyness, at least temporarily, during adolescence. If your youngster was shy in childhood, he may become even more so as a teenager, and if he was gregarious as a child, he may withdraw while he gets his bearings during adolescence.

Teenagers become shy because they're trying to make sense of the enormous physical, emotional, and social transitions they face. Not only do they have to deal with these changes, but they must also forge a more adult identity. Withdrawing from others helps alleviate pressure as they're caught between the conflicting comfort zones of childhood and adulthood. In the process of outgrowing their immature interests, they want adult responsibilities and privileges but may be ill-equipped emotionally or cognitively to handle them. They feel anxious, misunderstood, left out.

Moreover, adolescents are extremely self-conscious. And shy teens often lack a strong network of friends to help them through the turbulence. Often the friends they do have pressure them to get into trouble. According to Mary Pipher, author of *Reviving Ophelia*, adolescents may withdraw because they don't want to go along with the crowd and need to protect themselves by opting out of the social scene.

At a time when everything seems chaotic, the one element in life teens can control is themselves. They do that by retreating to safe comfort zones such as their bedrooms or familiar hangouts. All teens go through enormous changes, but special issues surround the shy ones' metamorphoses.

Adolescence Means Flux

Adolescents must deal with alarming physical changes inherent in the "adolescent growth spurt." Physical maturation begins at the extremities and moves toward the trunk, so feet and hands get larger first, then the arms and legs, and then the torso. Those who experience these changes feel awkward and self-conscious; they're not fully formed and want to hide their graceless bodies.

In addition, adolescents must deal with hormones. Sexuality, with all of its physiological changes, social pressures, and emotional confusion, begins to blossom. But to make the situation even more difficult, the genders grow at different rates, with girls maturing about two years earlier than boys. Eventually these disparities even out, but couples go through a mismatched phase for a while.

Emotionally and intellectually, adolescents are narcissists, plain and simple. They have difficulty shifting perspectives and gaining insight into another person's mind—a subtle and complex intellectual task—because they're so self-focused and self-conscious.

To help them make sense of themselves and their experiences, adolescents rely heavily on social comparison. But rather than weighing themselves against parents or siblings, as they did during childhood, they compare themselves with friends. They size up peers with a discriminating eye, decide where they stand, and conform. We've all seen groups of teens who look exactly alike. They dread standing out in a crowd.

Because they're so engaged in social comparison, adolescents are consumed with their friends and social cliques; they want more than anything to be accepted. These cliques have a profound effect on how adolescents see themselves and their peers. Being a member of a group eases uncertainty, but being a member of a highly valued group like a popular clique makes cohorts feel better about themselves.

But as we all know from sad experience, cliques can also be dreadful. Friends may act more like rivals, trying to bring one another down, and members are forbidden from associating with outsiders. If you can survive, you're cool; if you can't, too bad.

The desirability of belonging to a clique evolves over time. Early and middle adolescents, those in grades seven through ten, value them immensely and are willing to do anything to fit in. But belonging comes at a price: members must conform to rigid standards regarding what to wear, what to eat, where to hang out, with whom to associate. In late adolescence, as the power of the clique diminishes, teens become more reluctant to conform to group standards. They define themselves by being individuals, not just members of a group.

Not only do friendships become more important during adolescence, but they also become more intimate. Teens compare themselves on every level, so they painstakingly scrutinize themselves to make sure that they're experiencing the same emotions as their friends. Unfortunately, while teenagers may understand each other's problems, they may not have solutions. So even though friendships are more intimate than they were a few years back, they are still highly unreliable.

Not surprisingly, teens rebel against authority to push boundaries and test their resilience and independence. There is a reason for this. According to psychologist Erik Erikson, adolescents experience a period of role experimentation to find their own identity. This phase of rebellion and experimentation is an essential part of maturation.

Many of the problems in adolescence are related to finding an identity. People take shortcuts in this difficult quest by joining a gang, sleeping around, taking drugs, or becoming involved in antisocial behavior. Teens like Kate experiment with a "negative identity" before they can establish their true selves. The motivation for this can be rebellion against one's parents (to get back at them) rather than a true search for who one really is.

Adolescents come through a healthy identity crisis by making internal decisions, not in reaction to such external factors. For instance, the decision to reject peer pressure to take drugs emanates from a healthy sense of self, whereas the decision to take the drugs may evolve from a need to spite one's parents or to be accepted.

As teenagers slowly make their way into the adult world, those on the sidelines may not acquire the social skills they'll need. They may find it difficult to talk to adults, date, or deal with the usual teen jobs in fast-food or retail sales that require interaction with the public. They may be consumed with self-consciousness, social comparison, and conformity. Shy, socially awkward teens can feel "less than" others and may have a hard time expressing their true selves. Some claim that they suffer from low self-esteem because of their shyness. All of their classmates seem to be extroverted and happy, so they wonder what's wrong with them. The truth is, however, they are just slow to warm up to their new phase of life and believe that everyone else is adjusting more readily.

However, shy adolescents may have trouble forming a solid identity that will carry them into the future. People like Michelle often skirt the identity crisis because they're too inhibited to try new behaviors and perhaps fail. They don't rebel, could never imagine themselves acting out, and fail to prove to themselves that they're capable of what everyone else seems to be doing effortlessly. These shy teens may not acquire experiences that can lead to success and a robust view of themselves and their capabilities. They'd rather play it safe and withdraw into a narrow comfort zone made up of a handful of friends, emotions, and experiences.

This identity problem can carry into adulthood. This is why many shy people feel that they don't truly know or like themselves. They just know that they're shy and that they're missing out on life. But, more precisely, they've missed out on their chance during adolescence to gain experience without the responsibilities of adulthood.

Shy adolescents may also be more easily pressured into sexual activity. Shy girls, in particular, are more likely to use sex to feel accepted and dispel their loneliness, especially since they can take a more passive role. They don't have to be talkative or initiate activity. They are therefore more likely to be exploited and manipulated because they won't speak up. Young girls may establish their identity by hooking up with a boy.

Shy adolescent boys cope with more complicated issues. They have a harder time approaching girls and therefore are less likely to be able to express their sexual needs. Of course, this can be positive, since it helps to discourage sexual activity in adolescence, but when all of one's contemporaries are involved, it can make a shy boy feel insecure. In fact, since sexuality is a way of achieving a masculine identity, it can create additional pressure within a shy youth to become sexually active.

The following descriptions will help you assess adolescent shyness in your youngster. The more you recognize your child in these statements, the more likely it is that he is experiencing shyness beyond the normal discomforts of adolescence.

- They worry about sticking out because of what they do, say, or wear, so they don't express themselves fully with others.

- They spend a lot of time worrying about how popular they are and believe that they'll never be accepted by all of their classmates because they're not as outgoing or talkative.

- They feel awkward and don't know what to say to kids who aren't in their clique or to people who are different from them.

- They try to blend in with the crowd out of concern for how much others like them.

- They'd rather spend time in their room than be with others because that's predictable.

- When they feel uncomfortable, anxious, or uncertain, they don't let others know about it.

- They find it hard to talk to people to whom they're attracted.

- The thought of asking someone out—or even going on a date—terrifies them.

- They don't know what to do in social situations.

- They are afraid to try new behaviors.

- They think people don't understand them, so they don't talk much.

The Stigma of Adolescent Shyness

Young children seem to accept their shy classmates without much notice. They adapt well to a shy peer's reluctance to become involved in groups, and shyness seems not to affect her popularity among playmates. In fact, they may not recognize shyness because it is subtle and abstract. We may even expect shyness in young children because they're so dependent on others. It can be rewarded when a shy child receives extra attention and empathy from caregivers.

But as children mature and friendships and social status consume their lives, they begin recognizing shyness. They slowly stop forgiving this trait in their friends because they want to be daring, to gain attention, to become independent. They want to be seen as adults. Shy adolescents, who naturally adapt more slowly, can retard their bolder friends' progress. Consequently, their social status declines.

Inevitably teenagers realize that shyness is a social handicap. They observe not just what shy people do, but also how shy people make them feel. Being around shy peers renders adolescents uncomfortable. Therefore, others reject shy teens and their aggressive peers suddenly become more popular due to their seeming powerfulness and maturity.

Teenagers actively dislike shyness in their peers, and consequently, shy teens become especially prone to self-loathing and self-criticism.

How Shyness Hides

Because the consequences of shyness can be so devastating, many adolescents try to hide this personality trait by blending in with others. What's worse, you may not notice what's going on because you already expect your teen to be antisocial, awkward, or uncommunicative.

Teens create four "disappearing acts" that render them less noticeable and more comfortable with their shyness, uncertainty, and insecurity. After all, if they fit into a mold—any mold—they will feel safer because they belong somewhere.

The Shy Absentee

Many shy people with whom I have spoken have admitted to being frequently absent in high school. Consequently, they had a hard time completing their studies, not because they lacked intelligence, but because they couldn't deal with the social aspects of school. They skipped classes, avoided extracurricular activities, and tried their best to hide when forced to be with a group of peers.

This strategy only exacerbates social problems because shy absentees lose touch with potential friends and inhibit the development of their social skills. At a point in their lives when one should be expanding one's comfort zones, theirs shrink. Such withdrawal never works well in the long run.

Maggie, a student in New Jersey who was painfully shy as a teenager, told me how she hated being taunted by her classmates because she was overweight. "I missed class a lot because I just didn't want to be around other people. I've always had attendance problems. Or I wouldn't go to the cafeteria because I knew that everyone there would be looking at me. I'd want to sit on the edge of the room, but my friends would pick out a table in the middle, and I hated it."

Ultimately the teasing got to be too much, so she persuaded her parents to home-school her. "It was weird," Maggie said of her semester at home. "I got my wish because I didn't have to go to school and be with those kids, but being at home wasn't any fun. It was convenient because I didn't have to leave the house, and I didn't even have to get showered or dressed, but it was terrible because I didn't get to see people."

When Maggie returned to school for her exams, she realized that her tormentors were "quite pathetic." She refused to give them any power over her. She reenrolled in school permanently and more confidently. Facing her classmates changed Maggie's self-perceptions and helped her conquer her shyness. She's now an outspoken and successfully shy college student.

The Shy Conformist

Shy teens can also conform as a way to deal with social pressure. They can be part of a clique or find shelter in safe social networks like student government, sports teams, or clubs. These formal and informal groups can provide a comfort zone by setting up norms and standards that they must follow. Social comparison, naturally in the forefront of a shy person's mind, goes into overdrive in these status-conscious groups. Because shy teens are so good at comparison and want to fit in, they may follow the rigid, arbitrary social standards diligently.

Although groups do provide shy teenagers with social contacts, skills, and acceptable identities, they have drawbacks. They may not be based on true friendship, although camaraderie can develop while participating in a group. Nor are they permanent, which can be traumatic for a person who is uncomfortable making new friends. A suddenly abandoned shy adolescent can experience even more social anxiety and despair over her lower social status and difficulty reaching out to others than before her involvement. Losing a friend isn't easy for anyone, but it's especially difficult for a shy teenager who can rely heavily on one relationship for all of her social needs.

There is a great deal of pressure among adolescents to be popular and emulate those who seem to have it all. But social striving can cause internal pain. When a shy teenager looks beyond her old social circle toward a more fashionable one, she may find herself outside her comfort zone. She may be unfamiliar with new expectations, so she constantly assesses her actions, thoughts, and core self and conforms to be accepted. In the process, she may sacrifice her true self to the group identity. She may grow increasingly shy as she stifles self-expression and becomes a people-pleaser. Indeed, in her quest to be accepted, she may forget who she is, what she truly enjoys, and what qualities she brings to each friendship.

A shy conformist must learn to be herself with others. She can't do this if she's concentrating solely on fitting in. Encourage her to find a network of friends who accept her unconditionally for who she is, without strings, instead of trying to be popular or living up to some arbitrary standard of behavior. These are *true* friends, with whom she is free to be herself within her comfort zone.

The Shy Scholar

Some shy teens disappear by concentrating solely on academics and giving the impression that socializing is frivolous and beneath them. They may aspire to straight A's so they won't have to ask for help or be bothered with invitations and phone calls. Their academic success also makes them invulnerable to criticism; after all, who would criticize an ace student for excelling?

A college student wrote to me:

> Shyness, desperation, and loneliness accompanied the hormonal onslaught of my younger days. I was a "brain" and not a "jock," and so my social status was low with my peers. My only source of self-esteem for many years was academic success, and that wasn't enough to make me feel good about life. I was often (or mostly) introverted, and my friends tended to be as well. The social activities of my other peers have rarely been interests I've shared— dancing (I'm not very coordinated), drinking, and parties in general.

A study by Gary Traub at Florida State University found that shy college students had higher grade-point averages than their nonshy peers. Since high grades indicate success, Traub reasoned that these students probably found little reason to change. Superiority in school, however, can lead to social avoidance if students devote all of their time to studying.

High school students may do the same, if the one thing in their lives they do feel good about is their grades. Books and computers are their comfort zone, a stellar report card their reward. But there's no emotional risk and little social development in books and computers that would help the scholarly shy teen become more comfortable with her peers. She may confront adulthood with few close friends, inadequate social skills, and difficulties with intimacy.

The Shy Rebel

Shy teens like Kate disappear by masking their shyness in rebellion. They oppose social expectations as well as their true identity. Uneasy with insecurity and self-consciousness, they act out to conquer their fears and to show that they're "adults." They try to ignore their shyness and cover it up.

A high school senior in Louisiana wrote to me, "When I was fourteen I thought that if I acted like I didn't care what people thought it could help me overcome my shyness. I shaved my head, pierced my nose, my eyebrows, my lip, my tongue, and my ears seven times on each ear. As I got older my rebellion brought me more negative attention than positive."

Shy adolescents in social situations may believe they need a crutch like drinking or smoking to help them relax or to prove to others they're tough despite their quietness. One study found that shy adolescent boys were more likely to use drugs than their peers, perhaps to alleviate social discomfort and inhibitions. In another study, shy boys were found to smoke cigarettes more often than their less shy peers, to sort out their anxiety, social awkwardness, and distorted self-image.

While some rebellion is necessary during this time of life, your child can rebel and still remain true to himself if his rebellion is existential, not chemical or cosmetic. By observing, participating in, and evaluating a variety of lifestyles, he can explore himself and his values. He may try new friends and personas, but encourage him to ask himself if these alternatives express his true self and to be honest by rejecting actions that feel wrong to him. Help him to focus on what he loves.

In fact, shy teens may have an advantage over their more outgoing peers in exploring their inner self. They are more likely to be aware of their feelings and limitations as well as their assets. For example, instead of blindly following friends to a party that will involve drinking and taking drugs, they may feel anxious and insist on going home. If they are listening to their gut reactions, they will be cautious about such involvements.

The Impact of Shyness on Gender

Adolescence affects the genders differently. Shy teenage girls tell us that they're not too bothered by being shy, and that there are more shy girls than boys. On the other hand, shy boys tell us that they find shyness to be a real liability during adolescence. As a result, they feel bad about themselves and their shyness.

Gender identity affects how we think of ourselves and relate to others. It starts during early childhood and continues throughout our lifetimes. During adolescence, boys and girls try to live up to what they believe our culture expects from grown men and women. This goes far beyond dress styles, sexual activity, or career aspirations to a sense of self. Experimentation can be especially acute at this stage; teens are on a steep learning curve as they try to figure out who they are and how to be themselves.

Adolescent Girls

Shyness allows girls to submerge themselves within the traditional feminine role—that of a passive, submissive maiden who acquiesces. Conforming to the feminine stereotype is safe, acceptable, and predictable. In fact, society supports this retreat, which may explain why these girls believe shy behavior spares their self-esteem.

Unfortunately, this can cause shy girls to establish a false identity based on a role, rather than on their character and unique talents. They should be discovering who they are, what they do well, and what sparks their interest, but they won't consider all of their options if they choose to become passive and withdrawing.

Although they may not fully explore the external world, adolescent girls are able to form relationships that help them explore their inner selves. They create tightly knit friendships based on intimate knowledge of one another's hopes, fears, strengths, and insecurities. They help each other by sharing similar experiences to gain insight into a particular problem. They maintain relationships and soften criticism by using self-effacing phrases such as "I may be wrong, but . . ." and "Don't you think it would be a good idea if . . ."

The boundaries of girls' cliques are loose. They let others in and out and will accept a network in flux. While girls won't admit to back-stabbing, one-upping, or pressuring friends, we all know that these behaviors occur. When they date, girls still rely on girlfriends for emotional support rather than turning to their boyfriends.

Girls may say that they're untroubled by shyness because they feel comfortable within their intimate relationships and find that the traditional female role complements their withdrawing tendencies. They can talk easily to their best friends, get in touch with their emotions, and feel good about themselves. Society doesn't expect them to be argumentative or to conquer the world. As long as they maintain friendships, they believe they are okay.

Although shy girls may appear to be confident about their behavior and relationships, they are quite self-conscious. They may experience a high degree of *imaginary-audience phenomenon*, the feeling that the world is watching their every move. To cope with the scrutiny, they play to the crowd, perfect their physical appearance, and take criticism to heart. While this is a normal intellectual distortion that all adolescent girls experience, shy girls feel the heat of it acutely.

Based on the imaginary-audience phenomenon, shyness researcher Jonathan Cheek has argued that these girls have a higher level of "self-conscious" shyness, which is rooted in thoughts. Those who are self-consciously shy are extremely aware of what they're doing and thinking, are anxious, and control their behaviors. While self-consciousness may be normal during this phase of life, shy girls may be overwhelmed by it.

Consequently, concern with physical appearance can play a large role in girls' shyness. It buffers self-consciousness by allowing them to be confident about their looks. Unfortunately, our cultural expectations encourage girls' preoccupation with beauty. Unlike boys, they can modify their appearance by buying into the enormous cosmetics industry. We traditionally expect girls at this age to start wearing makeup and obsessing about hair and clothes. In effect, shy girls are just fitting in.

They can take this one step further by becoming preoccupied with their weight. Shy girls, in fact, have more body-image problems than their less shy peers. Perhaps because they're so focused on physical appearance, they only notice flaws. Some may develop anorexia or bulimia in an attempt to gain control over their lives. Others, like my correspondent, are driven away from peer interactions because of shame due to being overweight. A girl uncomfortable with her appearance may also be uncomfortable with self-expression.

Girls may develop self-conscious shyness due to the simple fact of biology: they undergo the adolescent growth spurt earlier than boys. Suddenly they must cope with maturing bodies, something their male counterparts aren't dealing with yet. However, while their bodies become more womanly, their emotions and thoughts are still childlike.

In order to avoid becoming involved in threatening situations like dating at an early age or going out with older men, girls may become more subdued and shy. Indeed, shyness can be a protective device; girls retreat into a narrow comfort zone because it makes them feel safe. Self-conscious shyness may be even more apparent among early-blooming girls. Not only must they deal with these changes at an earlier age, but they are also unable to turn to their friends for support.

In fact, these early-blooming girls tend to have more behavioral problems than their on-time peers do. Whatever coping style they used in childhood—withdrawal included—can become more predominant at the onset of an early puberty. They may experience internal problems—anxiety, self-consciousness, self-doubt, or low self-esteem—but will probably adjust once their friends catch up.

Ultimately, shy adolescent girls must become self-aware and self-assured. They need to sort out their thoughts about who they are today and what they want for the future. Each girl must take steps to find fulfillment in her life. Each must break out of her comfort zone by testing herself, her abilities, and her relationships.

Encourage your shy daughter to be herself. Tell her that it's normal to feel shy for a while, but she shouldn't let her shyness prevent her from making friends and exploring all of her potential.

Overall, shy girls need to remember that their identity is composed of more than just their looks and their shyness. They can discover their unique talents and gifts by becoming involved in their community. Their growing self-awareness will make them successfully shy.

Adolescent Boys

Boys can become shy because of perceived expectations that they take the lead. We anticipate them to slam-dunk, explore the final frontier, conquer uncharted worlds—and never betray themselves with self-doubt, conflicting feelings, or shyness. They should love sports, be sexually aggressive with girls (or at least initiate dates and physical intimacy), and sow their wild oats. They must decide on a career path that will lead to power and high salaries. In all of this, they should be untroubled by their emotions and their new place in society.

Men can be quiet, but only if they're the strong, silent type who inevitably come through in the clutch. Although the Marlboro Man is quiet, he certainly isn't shy.

Boys' friendships reflect the traditional male stereotype; they're concerned with hierarchy, status, and power. Their networks are rigid, and boys can be hostile toward peers who aren't in their group. In fact, they may even be hostile toward boys in their own crowd who are "weaker" than the others. They constantly vie for attention and dominance within the group, unconcerned with building intimate relationships or getting to know the other guys. They may hide their emotions from friends. When they want to talk about personal experiences, they turn to their girlfriends.

Above all, boys want to come out on top. They do so by taking action in the world—sports, academics, drugs, vandalism, fighting—not by talking. When they do talk, they try to prove their superiority by being more knowledgeable. (Think of sports statistics bandied about by the guys.) After they've proven themselves to the others, only the powerful boys will try to date girls. It's lonely at the bottom.

Even though boys are focused on their actions, they are self-conscious simply because they're teenagers. But unlike girls, who dwell on their physical selves due to the imaginary-audience phenomenon, boys are conscious of what they *do*. This distortion is called creating the *personal fable*. It makes adolescents feel unique, powerful, and misunderstood.

In these personal fables, the hero (the self) feels important and invulnerable. He risks himself as he acts out wild behavior—driving too fast, having unsafe intercourse, vandalizing property, taking exams without studying, and so on. The hero doesn't entertain thoughts of defeat because in these sagas, he's immortal and invulnerable. Adolescent boys feel misunderstood when adults warn them about the consequences of their behavior.

Rather than self-conscious shyness, adolescent boys deal with "active" shyness, which is rooted in what they do and how they feel about their actions. Society judges them on those terms. They may believe that they don't have the social skills necessary to integrate into society and that they are less athletic than their peers—all thumbs in the dining room and a fumbler on the football field. Their personal fables are not adventures, but the dark, moody dramas of a tortured hero.

Shy boys do not adjust easily to expectations regarding manhood. In the battle for dominance among their friends, they often come out on the bottom. Although they're expected to act rather than talk, their lack of self-confidence about their physical prowess inhibits their actions. Disinclined to live out the traditional macho stereotype, they withdraw. They become angry and frustrated by their difficulty in finding a place for themselves. Shy teenage boys are so intent on doing the right thing—being manly and dominant—they may lose sight of their true selves.

Negative body image is also detrimental to shy boys. They perceive their weaknesses in comparison to male friends. This phenomenon can start in elementary school. Unathletic boys often stay on the sidelines when their friends play sports and get into fights to try to top one another.

But just as we must not judge girls and women by their external appearance, so boys must not judge themselves harshly if they weren't built with dense muscle tone or physical agility or if they take little interest in sports.

And just as early-blooming girls feel acutely embarrassed because they're "off time" and noticeably different, late-blooming boys can be more self-conscious and susceptible to becoming shy. They may have an even harder time establishing dominance with their friends and can be the target of bullies. They may compare their strength and bodies to those of their maturing friends, feel inadequate, and stay away from the competition.

Many boys try to alleviate their shyness by smoking, drinking, or using drugs. They believe it helps them ease their anxiety and makes them seem hip. Even if they're thin and unathletic, they can top their peers by being the most stoned. This is a terrible solution because they rely on the substance to create their identity. And, sadly, they become shyer and chemically dependent as a result.

There are other long-term implications of a shy adolescence. Avshalom Caspi at the University of Wisconsin at Madison followed the lives of lifelong shy males and found that they got off to a rocky start in their early adult years. They were late in starting stable jobs, getting married, and having children. Their marriages tended to be troubled, and they generally floundered before they found their niche in life.

Caspi indicated that problems arise from the fact that these men were "off-time." They found little success at work because others expected them to be further along in their careers. They also lacked the support of same-age friends; the more outgoing men had already moved on to new challenges and couldn't relate to their shy friends who lagged behind and generally engaged in activities they should have already outgrown.

Shy adolescent boys have a rough time. They doubt themselves when most of us ignore that they have these feelings. While our society emphasizes the importance of girls' self-images, we often overlook the inner lives and self-esteem of boys. We expect them to be awkward at social gatherings, but we do nothing to help them develop social skills and a sense of competence and self-acceptance. We don't encourage shy boys to open up about their feelings to allow them to surface and be resolved. They don't even confide in their friends, who all seem to be adjusting to adolescence easily.

A word of advice regarding those thinking about joining a gang. Identity formation is difficult, and some may be tempted to circumvent the process by joining a gang. It's a quick route to instant acceptance at the cost of personal identity. Once in the group, you no longer make decisions based on your own needs but on the identity of the gang. This can be a dangerous situation.

Don't allow shyness to drag you down or society's myths to make you feel inferior. You have many opportunities to stand up for yourself, explore your world, and get to know who you are; when you understand the role of shyness in your life, you will be more apt to take advantage of them.

How Parents Can Help

You may become distraught if your formerly loving and bubbly child suddenly become sullen and uncommunicative. While you may try to help your teenager with his shyness, be forewarned that you have only an indirect influence now. Nevertheless, shy teens don't have to be traumatized by their experiences, conflicting emotions, and unfair expectations. Here's what you can do with the clout you do have:

Remain in the picture. Although your teenager will compare himself to his friends, stay involved and provide a better example for him to follow. Encourage him to speak out about the pressures he feels. Remind your shy son that silence isn't manly.

Maintain the lines of communication. Don't wait for a formal and uncomfortable "big talk." The more often and the earlier you have discussions with your teen, the better. Be persistent.

If your adolescent is rebelling, ask why, and discuss the meaning of rebellion. Perhaps he is trying to carve out his own identity. Reassure him that everyone goes through this phase. You might ask, "Are you rebelling against the fact that you're not popular, or you don't have enough freedom? Or are you searching for an identity?" Talk about the continued process of identity in your own life. You are still adding to your sense of identity, trying new classes, meeting new challenges at work, and so on.

If your child is isolating himself, explain the basic principles of shyness—especially the concept of the comfort zone—and how he can understand this trait more deeply.

Let him assume some responsibility for his life. The journey from childhood to adulthood is composed of small steps encompassing gradually increasing risk and responsibility. Your shy teens may withdraw from these challenges, so it's up to you to encourage him to pursue his interests, volunteer or work part-time, schedule his own appointments, and become actively involved in educational opportunities. Don't let him retreat into an isolated comfort zone.

Provide her with opportunities to be with others. Entertain at home, take her on vacation with you, or join a community group such as a mother-daughter book club with her. Make sure she associates with a variety of people so she can warm up slowly rather than avoid altogether.

Help him discover his talents. Discourage him from spending all of his time in passive activities like watching television. Uncover his strengths so that he can develop a positive identity, not just that of a socially awkward teen. Support him by attending math meets, swimming competitions, or piano recitals, and congratulate him on his achievements, no matter how small.

Moderate sexual activity. Adolescents with a strong personal identity may be less sexually active. Make sure to encourage your child to become involved in as many activities as her schedule permits—a part-time job, drama, sports. These not only keep her busy and socially involved, but also add to her sense of identity outside of being someone's girlfriend.

Encourage diversity. Many shy teens internalize their shy label at school but flourish when taken out of that limiting environment. Evening classes, a volunteer organization, or a part-time job will help your teen see himself in a new light. (Cutting the grass is fine, but it doesn't encourage interactions with people. He should work in places that help him develop social skills like restaurants or stores.) The experiences he gains will help him become more comfortable with people from all walks of life. He will make new friends, discover talents, and get used to spontaneous interactions, and he'll learn how to manage his time.

Remind him that he is not alone. He may imagine that others have it easier, but almost 50 percent of teenagers are shy and are experiencing the same upheavals he is. They may just hide it in different ways.

Encourage extracurricular activities. High school is a fishbowl. It can be difficult for a teen to try new activities when he feels constrained by others' gaze. If he is imaginative and curious, he can relieve the social pressure to conform by becoming involved in activities that have nothing to do with school. It may be easier to make friends in these groups because he will share a common interest. Invite him to volunteer at a food pantry, in a nursing home, or as a tutor. He will be less shy when he does what he loves and when he's unfettered by others' expectations.

Be patient. Don't allow your teen to go without rules, but realize that she may be slow to warm up to new challenges, including having adult conversations with you. If you haven't communicated when your child was young, she may resist your advances now. Persist.

Help her recognize the purpose of adolescence. Teens are supposed to make mistakes. This doesn't mean that they should be irresponsible, but they can experiment. Encourage your teen to try out different roles and interests to discover what's right for her. These experiences will help her not only today but later in life too when she must settle on a career path and create stable intimate relationships.

Help him resist peer pressure. Remind him that people who

pressure others to act in certain ways are immature, insecure, and have a weak identity. They manipulate others to feel better about themselves. Encourage him to listen to his instincts and choose friends wisely. He will be more self-aware and mature if he only does what feels right to him, no matter what others say.

Explain the role of drugs. They will not cure shyness, but merely worsen the situation. Help your teen find another way.

Help her find healthy role models and mentors. If you can't talk to your child about her feelings, help her seek a sympathetic teacher, coach, minister, physician, or job manager at her job to turn to her for help with wise decisions about her future.

Help her avoid self-consciousness. Remind your daughter that her anxiety and awkwardness are not as apparent as she may think. Her inner turbulence may feel painful simply because she focuses on it. Help her take an interest in others to take the focus off herself.

Encourage him to get moving! He may spend all of his time watching television, surfing the Net, or playing video games, but he needs real experiences to become a mature adult and develop a broad comfort zone. Encourage him to volunteer in the community, participate in religious groups, take a part-time job (ten to fifteen hours), or start a group of his own (have him approach a teacher or adviser to help him).

Encourage her to stay in touch with platonic male friends. This is the best way to learn how to relate to a man. Encourage your shy daughter to form a solid friendship with a male who isn't a boyfriend or a potential boyfriend, like her brothers, dad, or the son of your best friends.

Encourage him to stay in touch with platonic female friends. It may be a cliché, but it's still true that women are better talkers than men. They can discuss intimate matters without feeling strange, and they'll help your shy son understand women better so when he's ready to date he won't be surprised.

Encourage him to seek opportunities to use social skills. Suggest pretend dates (with people to whom he has no romantic attachment) to practice making conversation and datelike behavior while the pressure is off. He might try group dates and even help out when you entertain. Avoidance only makes him less confident about his social skills.

Encourage him to work for a woman manager or boss. Your shy son will be less likely to feel intimidated by women if he can take orders from one, especially if he's doing a good job. This will help him relate to women as people—not solely as potential dates.

Help them take inventory of their good qualities. Don't let your shy son buy into the boys-must-be-linebackers bias that pervades our culture or your shy daughter become obsessed about her weight or appearance. Value the fact that your child is a great mathematician, botanist, guitar player, or joke-teller. Reinforce their positive qualities.

Don't divorce your child. Children may not bounce back easily from divorce. If you are divorcing during your child's adolescence, don't let it adversely affect his view of relationships, trust, and communication. Talk to him and be willing to listen.

Love your child. If she knows that you love her unconditionally, the traumas of adolescence will only be a phase—not a lifelong stalemate.

All of these suggestions involve interacting and integrating your life with your adolescent's. Maintain a continued pattern of communication with your child. Work conversations into your daily life—at the dinner table, while running errands, or when cleaning the house. Adolescence is as much about parents as about teens.

You must lead by example. It's unwise to expect of your child what you're unwilling to do yourself. If you aren't involved with others, get involved. Expand your own comfort zone. You can't wait for your child to ask difficult questions; you must broach them first. By bringing up problems in advance, you are helping to inoculate him. Talk to him about the process of problem solving and alternative courses of action that he can take, using the Four *I*'s. Explain about the slow-to-warm-up tendency, comfort zones, and the approach-avoidance conflict.

The more he knows about the underlying dynamics of his personality, the more comfortable he will be with it. Be there for your child, early, often, persistently, and realistically.

A Last Word About Shyness in Adolescence

The developmental task of adolescence is to decide who we are and where we fit in the community that extends beyond our families. Teenagers must make these important decisions based on their needs and talents, not what others want them to be. Whether it's choosing a major, how to behave at a party, or how to dress, these decisions should reflect their true selves.

This is particularly true for shy teens who don't want their lives to reflect their shyness. They may try to deny that they feel insecure, socially anxious, and fearful. Consequently, they may follow the paths of others (and conform), rebel, or withdraw. Unfortunately, all of these choices work against self-awareness.

Shy teens need to come to terms with themselves and their shyness. If they are successfully shy at a young age, they will be prepared for the tasks of adulthood: expressing themselves through intimate relationships and work. We all discover who we are by interacting with others at work or at home. But if adolescents are uncertain about or quell their emotions and opinions, they will feel shackled by shy myths that can impede their growth.

In order to become successfully shy adults, teenagers must understand themselves and how shyness influences the many important choices they make.

12

Shyness in Adulthood

"I married two 'wrong' men because they picked me and I felt nobody else would want me," Marsha, an unhappily shy woman, wrote to me. "I have no social life and haven't had one since my divorce ten years ago. I'm depressed and I isolate myself. Once in a while I force myself to go to a movie alone, but that's about it. I see maybe two movies a year unless I rent one. I haven't been to a party in twenty years. I've worked for twenty-one years in a job I hate. I don't try to move up because then I would have to talk to people."

What a sad state of affairs. Marsha has chosen to isolate herself and suffers considerably. If you have not learned to be successfully shy during childhood and adolescence, shyness can become a more deeply entrenched personality trait when you grow into an adult. As in Marsha's case, over time it can become a habitual and destructive response to social situations.

You may isolate yourself and lose faith in your ability to meet new people, be confident during social situations, or conquer your shyness. You may feel this way because of your narrow comfort zone—you seem always to be caught in the same rut—and negative thoughts about yourself. The longer a behavior occurs, the harder it is to change, so you may find yourself at a loss as to how to break out of the prison of your shyness and become more socially connected.

Unfortunately, shyness in this stage of life has many negative implications. It can make it difficult for you to achieve the tasks of adulthood—finding a mate, achieving sexual satisfaction, accomplishing rewarding and challenging work, feeling satisfied with yourself, and being able to give of yourself to others.

In fact, shyness in adulthood can become not just a personality trait but a quality-of-life issue. Researchers have correlated it with loneliness, depression, substance abuse, limited career advancement, low self-esteem, self-doubt, poor coping skills, the inability to solve problems, lack of community involvement, and poor health. Shy people view challenges as threats to their sense of self rather than sources of personal growth. Consequently, they are apt to shrink from them and live in a state of social and emotional stagnation.

Marsha's sad experience seems to bear this out. Hers is but one of several equally harmful coping mechanisms shy adults use. These include isolation, an escape into fantasy life, and the use of alcohol or other forms of self-medication.

Isolation

Shy people have few friends, and loneliness can take a toll in terms of happiness. According to psychologist Richard Booth and his colleagues, lonely and shy people may experience a "happiness deficit," especially if their loneliness and shyness become lifetime conditions. Indeed, their research has shown that "lonely people tend to be shy, that shy people tend to be lonely, that lonely and shy people do not tend to be happy." That is certainly true for Marsha.

Although not usually surrounded by a large social group, most shy people do have some friends. But since they are apt to make social comparisons, they may believe that they don't have enough friends or that they need different ones. In fact, if you find yourself in this situation, you may discount the friendships you do have because you've maintained these relationships for years and take them for granted. This can be a sign that you want to expand your comfort zone, but it can also leave you feeling bereft of social connections even if you are not.

Moreover, your friendships may be in flux because shyness may have slowed the pace at which you tackle developmental hurdles. Perhaps friends who have already married and started a family have left you behind. Ironically, those who need support of friends the most have the hardest time making new ones.

It's important for you to advance professionally and socially by expanding your social network. To be successfully shy and create friendships, you must continually invite new people into your life and seek common ground with those who are already part of it.

A broad social network affords many benefits. Talking about yourself to your friends helps you gain insight into your problems and how to solve them. Shy people with small social networks tend to have poor coping abilities because they feel isolated, compare themselves with others who seem so confident, and catastrophize their problems. When you're isolated, you lose objectivity about yourself and the issues you face. Friends can help you get a grip.

But expansion of your social network may be hampered by the shy tendency to place each person into a discrete category. You may believe, for example, "Jim is my bowling buddy; Frank is my neighbor; Harvey is my coworker; Bill is my brother." If these categories never intermesh, how will you ever discover that you have more in common with the people in your life than you think? Harvey may like to bowl, or Frank might love to go to the movies with you sometime.

Jackie, a shy woman in her thirties, struggled with just this issue. For months she and her neighbor Gena worked together to solve a problem with the landlord of their apartment building. After they had resolved the conflict to their satisfaction, Jackie abruptly stopped speaking to Gena. When I asked her why she and Gena had not become friends, Jackie replied, "Oh, I could never talk to Gena in a more personal way."

Jackie had categorized Gena as a neighbor but not as a potential friend. She did not know how to network with others on a personal level to expand her social circle. But this doesn't have to be. Jackie could have easily taken the opportunity to befriend Gena following their success. Their triumph would have made a perfect excuse to celebrate with coffee or a dinner out. Then they might have explored other areas of common interest that they could enjoy together in the future. Or since they worked so well together on this project, they could have looked for another task to accomplish together. Such a social meeting would create a sense of interdependence that would nurture the relationship in the future.

Divergent thinking will help you break down these categories to create more fulfilling relationships. Creative people use this technique to link unrelated ideas and find similarities where none were initially apparent. (A divergent thinker, for instance, might link computer software with the idea of good child care and develop a child care rating service on the Internet.) Below I will provide some helpful tips to developing greater creativity in viewing relationships and expanding your conversational comfort zone.

Escape into Fantasy

"I am an extreme introvert," writes a thirty-six-year-old counselor in North Carolina.

> I do not have a social life now and have never had one. Mostly, I tend to believe that I am not a man that women could enjoy the company of. Also, I tend to have a flashback of another bad time in life as a defense mechanism for protection, so that I won't have to deal with the present pain of shyness or possible rejection. When I see some lady I think I'd like to meet, instead of introducing myself, my fantasy mind kicks in and I meet her that way. It's easier to meet her that way than an actual approach. I have tried to remind myself that other people feel the same way (probably)! But it never really helps!

As I explained in Chapter 9, being alone is necessary for taking stock of your life and developing interests and talents. An active imagination can help you safely act out scenarios and think through problems before facing them in the real world. But too much time alone can be isolating—and harmful. Withdrawing from the world and losing yourself in your fantasies cuts you off from much needed personal contact and practice at being successfully shy. You will miss out on being part of a social network. Acquaintances may think they're unwelcome in your life and not make the effort to develop a friendship. And you may forget how to relate to others in the real world. Such unproductive use of your time can lead to loneliness, diminished self-esteem, and depression. You may, in fact, have spent your time lost in fantasy since you were a child, but, sadly, nobody recognized it.

Unproductive fantasy consists of thinking about a person or situation without doing anything about it. A more productive use of fantasy would be to regard it as the first step in the warm-up process, rather than an end in itself. Artists, composers, and writers do this all the time. They visualize an idea first in their heads, then concretize it with their creative production.

When you fantasize without acting, you may distort your role in difficult situations. Because you become the center of attention in your own fantasy life, you may make more self-blaming internal attributions such as, "Don Smith will never talk to me because I'm just the little guy on the totem pole." (See Chapter 6.) Rather than focusing on your own attributes (or lack thereof), however, it is more helpful to fantasize about how you might remedy the situation. Instead of ruminating on your faults, think about what you can do to get a conversation going. Focus on your behavior rather than on your personal characteristics.

You can fantasize how you're going to talk to Don Smith at the next annual convention, and then play out the roles and scenarios in your head in a constructive way. The next step is to act, based on a scene you've constructed. Practice in front of a mirror. Then work your line of thinking into a conversation with your spouse, a neighbor, or someone on the bus. Finally, express it to Don Smith, the head of your division.

The consequences of fantasy are nil. You can play a scene out any way you want. Fantasy is practice, if you use it constructively.

Medicating Yourself with Alcohol or Other Drugs

Self-medication with alcohol or other substances is another misguided coping mechanism, one about which many shy people write to me. Alcohol is a "disinhibitor"—that is, it can loosen the lips of shy people. As a man in his mid-thirties wrote to me, "In social situations I will use alcohol moderately to relax and be less self-conscious and more outgoing."

And a female college student shared:

> When I'm with a group of people I don't or do know or am just starting to get to know, I don't say a word. Maybe I say "Hello. How are you," and "Good-bye." I can't stand it one bit because it makes me very uncomfortable and I feel frustrated. I'm afraid that if I do say something, people will just look at me like I'm an idiot or they won't respond. And there are times when I'm with people who I've just met and I say something and I blush, and then I start to get panicky and think that hopefully they won't see me blush.
>
> I do like drinking with my friends, but I notice that I tend to indulge myself in alcohol to feel more loose and more talkative when it comes to meeting my boyfriend's friends. But then when I see them sober, I feel like a loser because they just saw me the other night as a happy, talkative drunk.

Another female college student wrote to me, "Since I'm in college now, most of the social functions involve alcohol. I admit I use it as a social lubricant. If there is a social function with a large group of people that I'm uncomfortable with, I will not go unless there is alcohol."

Research has shown that shy people often use alcohol as a crutch to help them warm up. However, some studies have found that the intensely shy do not drink when in the company of others because they're so concerned about the impression they make and fear appearing sloppy or losing control of themselves. They may drink at home in the misguided belief that the alcohol is helping to mask the pain of loneliness. However, this may render them even less likely to go out and meet new people.

Moderately shy people may drink socially because they believe this is the best way to take the edge off. They are attempting to reduce their anxiety and lower their inhibitions. Those who use alcohol, whether consumed privately or publicly, to help resolve problems related to shyness must face the fact that they are grappling with the basis of a drinking problem.

I have found that shy people often attribute their gregariousness to the effects of liquor rather than the warm-up period. However, if you extend this rationale, you will find that they only allow themselves to become chatty when under the influence. Like the college student who attends large gatherings only if alcohol is served, they have willingly surrendered control of their shyness and become dependent on liquor instead. In so doing, not only do they feel that the drink helps them talk, but they also eliminate many choices and the sense of control that successfully shy people enjoy. Besides, if they're quick to take a drink, they will never experience the unadulterated magic of the warm-up period. They rob themselves of any credit for their successes if they believe the alcohol made them gregarious.

You don't need a crutch like alcohol to achieve intimacy. Time and a sense of personal control are your best allies. You can overcome your hesitations using the techniques I suggest throughout the book, especially the follow suggestions for building rapport and speaking freely and candidly.

The Art and Craft of Making Small Talk

Gloria, thirty-one, owns a hair salon in the Pacific Northwest. As a youngster she was extremely shy. "When I was really young," she explained, "and a new person came into the room, I'd cling to my mother's legs—you'd think that I was a part of my mother!" But her career choice forced her into situations in which she had to meet new people and make small talk.

"I used to be afraid of talking about myself because it meant putting too much ego out there," she admitted. "But I've worked out a routine. Now I tell my clients something personal about myself, and that can get the conversation going. First I start out with the formalities: what do they want to have done with their hair. Then I ask questions like, 'So, are you married?' or 'Do you have any kids?' or 'Do you live in town?' I try to find things I can relate to so we can talk a little bit better."

Shy people often complain that they don't like making small talk or that they can't. One man wrote to me, "I find it almost impossible to start a conversation with strangers, especially women. I cannot think of anything to talk about." In fact, Gloria also felt that way. Fortunately, a teacher recognized her talent and nurtured her small-talk skills so that she would be more confident and successful. "She'd watch me work on people," Gloria explained, "and she'd say, 'Gloria, you have to open up your mouth! Ask people things!' She told me what to talk about and what not to bring up—you know, religion, politics, that sort of thing.

"I really do believe what they tell you in beauty school. Eighty-five percent of your clients come to you because they like you and feel comfortable with you, and only 15 percent care about your skill."

Gloria has become adept at small talk, and it has served her well. Every relationship, be it business or social, begins with such chattiness—we even use it with family members and established friends when we're warming up to a conversation with them. It is therefore vital for you to become skilled at it if you are to be a successfully shy adult.

Small talk is only a temporary phase in a dialogue—a first step. If you do it well, you can move on to more intimate conversations almost immediately. Once you learn the art and craft of making small talk, you can use it in a variety of settings: work, networking, dating, at the grocery store, the beauty salon, or the doctor's office.

Practicing the basics of successful small talk will help alleviate your shyness. Your body will feel more relaxed if you become confident about how to talk to a stranger; your mind will struggle with fewer negative thoughts because you will be thinking creatively about how to build common ground with someone. Finally, in making small talk, you expand your sense of self by growing your comfort zone. Believe it or not, small talk helps you stretch socially and personally.

How Confident People Make Small Talk

It seems effortless, magical, mysterious. Some people seem to be able to talk to anyone. Philip Manning and George Ray, sociologists at Cleveland State University, analyzed interactive patterns in pairs of shy and confident college students to discover why confident people had such fluency in their conversational skills and shy people did not. They wanted to know whether confident and shy people carry on small talk differently. They found that the former use certain communication patterns that are lacking among the latter. They are as follows:

1. *Setting talk*. This is brief and consists of remarks about surroundings. Neutral statements such as "It's stuffy in here, isn't it?" or "Lousy seats, huh?" establish contact and orient partners to each other.

Setting talk has been called a "false topic" because it is devoid of intimate information and is soon exhausted. That makes it ideal for situations in which people wish to disclose as little as possible about themselves or to avoid seeming as if they are prying. But it functions as a stepping stone for the next phase of conversation. Confident people tend to keep their setting talk to a minimum. There's only so much you can say about the weather, but you have to start somewhere!

2. *Name exchange.* There's a window of opportunity at the beginning of a conversation when exchanging names is natural and polite. Early name exchange shows you are interested in getting to know the person with whom you are speaking and want him to be comfortable with you. It creates a degree of familiarity. You can exchange names later, but it becomes more and more awkward as time goes on. Confident people often exchange names at the outset of their interactions.

3. *Pretopical sequence.* After greeting a new person and exchanging names, a confident person begins to fish around for something to talk about in the same way that Gloria did. He may ask questions to see how the other categorizes himself such as, "What's your profession?" or "Oh, you're an engineer. What kind of work do you specialize in?" In his quest to find a topic, he might try a more general line of inquiry such as "How do you know our host?" If one subject doesn't pan out ("Can you believe how Congress voted to raise their own pay?"), he will offer another that may be more fruitful ("I hate these Monday-night board meetings because I miss the football game"). Confident people are willing to talk about a variety of subjects. Think of this as the warm-up period.

There are some ground rules in finding a suitable pretopic:

- Relevance. The topic must naturally fall into the conversation. You wouldn't talk to a stranger in the elevator about NASA's upcoming budget. A better pretopical question might pertain to the condition of the building's lobby or the difficulty of finding a parking spot downtown.

- Sensitivity. The topic must be sensitive to the "unsaid" background of the partners. It must relate to shared knowledge without being offensive or too familiar. For instance, two pregnant women striking up a conversation at the obstetrician's office would have certain shared experiences. Their pretopical questions might relate to how far along they each are, whether they know their baby's gender, whether this is a first pregnancy, or how they came to be referred to this doctor. They might avoid more controversial topics such as the status of the baby's father, abortion, financial concerns, or whether this was a planned pregnancy. Such questions might be deemed too personal or offensive.

How would they know if they have overstepped their bounds? An attuned conversationalist would be alert to signs of surprise or stress in the other person: averted eyes, a long pause, blushing, hesitation, or stammering. These would indicate that they have caught the other person off guard and made her uncomfortable.

- Balance. In their pretopical questions, confident people behave neither as know-it-alls nor as people desperate for companionship. They strike a balance.

How can they evaluate whether they are successful? The other person might smile or nod; she might ask questions, provide anecdotes, or contribute similar information. Her comments could overlap theirs as if she were anticipating what they were about to say. She would also be engaged in the subject.

Of course, it helps to have something to say. Here is where

social reconnaissance comes in handy. If that is impossible (say, the impromptu conversation occurs in the checkout line at the grocery store), you might take into account the fact that you're both in the same situation—stuck on line at the market. Relying on this shared *situational identity*, you might comment on the rising cost of vegetables, the way one supermarket chain is buying out the other, or the outrageous stories in the tabloids on sale next to the cashier.

4. *Taking turns.* Once the topic has been selected, confident people take turns talking. When the conversation flows smoothly, the speakers may even overlap, picking up on one another's ideas and moving forward in new directions. They give and read cues (such as eye contact, pausing, averting the head, or changing the pitch of speech) as to when they want to talk and when to relinquish the floor to the other.

5. *Banishing silences.* Confident people recognize that silence is awkward for the other person. And so they play host within the conversation. They quickly negotiate turns by selecting the next speaker with a direct, open-ended question ("So, you grow wheat. How have the rains affected your crops?") or they jump in themselves with a new topic.

This shows great social sensitivity. Because confident people are not as self-focused as those who are shy, they are able to direct their attention toward others, reading their body language for clues of boredom, discomfort, and awkwardness (strained smiles, frowns, averted eyes, fidgeting, checking one's watch, looking around the room), all signs that the other person is leaving his own comfort zone.

6. *Self-disclosure.* Confident people work at matching their partner's level of self-disclosure. This moves the speakers beyond their situational identity—two people who happen to have a doctor's appointment at the same hour—to a relationship that can be more intimate and rewarding. Appropriate levels of self-disclosure become an excellent way for individuals to find common ground. If one partner volunteers a per-

sonal anecdote about a topic ("I was referred to Dr. Meyers by my partner who had a baby last year. She helped me find good day care, too"), it is fitting to respond at the same level of intimacy. ("Day care is a big concern for me, too. My sister had a hard time finding a good sitter last year when she had a baby. What arrangements have you made?") This may open the door for an even deeper conversation.

If, on the other hand, the individual is unwilling to reveal anything about himself, it may be wise to back off, no matter how uncomfortable the encounter may feel. The other person may need more time to warm up. You may wait a few minutes and then throw out another topic, but sometimes there's just nowhere to go. Gloria encountered that situation with one of her clients. "Sometimes I'll find someone who will sit in dead awkward silence and not talk, and that's really painful. There's this one uptight guy, Kenneth. I remember asking him what he and his wife do on weekends, and he said, 'Well, that's very personal!' Then he stopped talking. And I just wanted to know, 'Do you guys go to the lake, or whatever!'" Gloria surmised that this client was arrogant, but it is also possible that he too was shy.

Often shy individuals go through the process of self-disclosure too slowly or too eagerly. If you assume that the other person has negative thoughts about you, you may be unwilling to reveal yourself for fear of boring him. You may not realize that he is interested in what you have to say. In addition, when you match the level of self-disclosure carefully, you can anticipate that the other individual won't feel you're revealing too much too soon. The key is negotiation and sensitivity.

How Shy People Make Small Talk

Drs. Manning and Ray found that shy people have a distinctly different small-talk style. Rather than trying to help the other person feel comfortable in the situation, they are motivated to avoid their own embarrassment, disapproval, and rejection. Consequently, they don't take risks in conversations by asking questions, increasing their level of self-disclosure, or discussing a topic outside their comfort zone. Instead, because they fear losing face or offending the other, they remain on what they erroneously believe is "safe" ground, reverting to short replies, lengthy setting talk, favored topics, or silence. And that's what renders small talk so uncomfortable to shy people and to those with whom they are speaking.

Shy small talk proceeds as follows:

1. *Setting talk.* Shy people rely on setting talk extensively. In Manning and Ray's research, previously identified shy individuals meeting each other for the first time in a laboratory spent an average of thirteen turns using setting talk at the beginning of their conversations (in contrast to confident couples, who only dwelled on the setting in five turns), and unlike the confident partners, they returned to setting talk later in their conversations.

We might understand this prolonged use of setting talk as an extended warm-up period. It may take a while for shy individuals to relax and respond fluently.

2. *Pretopical sequence.* The more confident participants in Manning and Ray's experiment, relying on their situational identities, quickly shifted from setting talk to pretopical questions to ask their partners about college majors and career plans. Little of that occurred among the shy. Indeed, they often rejected and batted away (with monosyllabic answers) appropriate pretopical questions. Consequently, there was insufficient information shared to develop a topic and get the conversation off the ground. Soon they reverted to nonproductive setting talk.

Sadly, this small-talk style can produce more and longer awkward silences, which you may do little to remedy. Moreover, it can make you appear rude or cold, since you seem to be keeping yourself from your partner. Why would this occur? In part, it may have to do with your fear of evaluation and rejection. You may believe the less said, the less you can be judged negatively. Unfortunately, this strategy can backfire. It puts the onus of the conversation on the other person, who may soon tire of having to draw you out. He may simply move on to a more forthcoming individual.

This only fulfills your expectations and your worst fears— that you can't make small talk, that others are unwilling to give you a chance, that you are boring, that you have nothing in common with others.

3. *Favored topic.* For the most part, shy people only develop a head of steam in a conversation when they find the opportunity to talk about their favored topic. In fact, they become overly enthusiastic about this subject, which could be anything at which they feel expert, from Ella Fitzgerald's song stylings to the Japanese art of origami to famous Civil War battles, to Internet software applications, to their work, to the latest school-board rulings.

Unfortunately, belaboring a favored topic does not constitute conversation. You are merely talking *at* someone, not *with* him. It may be a source of security for you because you know more about the topic than your partner. In fact, you may feel successful when you do this because, after all, you are talking to a stranger.

But in relying on a favored topic you may bore the other person. You dominate the conversation, allowing little opportunity for give-and-take and ignoring your partner's wishes and nonverbal cues. Moreover, you can become stuck in your comfort zone when engaged in this topic, since you are not learning anything new.

It's wise to rely on your favored topic only if the other person is asking you questions about it. Always gauge your partner's interest, checking for the signs of discomfort and boredom mentioned above. If you don't, you can be sure he will look for an easy way out of the conversation.

4. *Return to setting talk.* When the pretopical sequence and

the favored subject fail to bring about a true meeting of the minds, shy people often return to the safety and anonymity of setting talk. Frustration and discomfort mount, and soon the conversation is terminated.

Errors in the Shy Small-Talk Style

As much as you may crave conversation with others, your small-talk style may jeopardize your ability to engage in lively, fluid discourse. I have identified a series of errors in the shy small-talk style that may be the source of disconnection and may interfere with your ability to make new friends.

- Shy people don't introduce themselves early in the conversation and may not do it later either, when it's more difficult. This only delays or destroys a sense of intimacy.

- Because they don't self-disclose, shy people don't develop identities beyond the situational, if at all. Since they're not searching for common ground with the other person, they never become more intimate and as a consequence never give their partner a compelling reason to talk to them again. Therefore, it always seems as if they're talking to strangers. In such circumstances, no friendship can develop.

- Shy people fail to develop subjects of common interest. They reject proposed pretopics by responding as briefly as possible. This seems rude, and so the conversation never progresses beyond setting talk and deflected pretopical questions. It takes a highly persistent and motivated partner to cut through this barrier.

- Shy people don't ask questions other than dead-end or rhetorical queries about the immediate environment. This makes them seem uninterested in their partner.

- Shy people don't jump into logical openings in conversation or take their turn when a silence arises. They allow the silence to drag on, which forces their partner to propose a new pretopic that may also meet with rejection. According to Drs. Manning and Ray, there is an "organized pattern of silences" in shy conversations: question, brief answer, silence, new question, brief answer, silence, and so on. The other person may become bored if the shy person does not contribute to the interaction.

Why might you commit these errors? As I explained above, you may worry about being evaluated negatively. Or you may believe that silence is safer than risking a subject you believe you're unqualified to broach. Unfortunately, you can make a bad impression with this silence because it makes you seem cold, aloof, uninterested, and uninteresting.

There are many other possible reasons for this unproductive conversational style. You may believe that you're doing your partner a favor by letting him talk to a captive audience. You may believe that your thoughts are uninteresting or unimportant. ("Nobody wants to hear what I have to say anyway, so why should I put myself out?") You may lack trust in the predictability of everyday life. You may perceive conversations with strangers as risky. You may not trust that others will be kind or understanding toward you, or you may feel that others are more powerful and can hurt you. You may fear losing face. You ascribe to the belief "The less you know about me the less you can criticize me." You may be uncomfortable asking questions. That's an "approach" and therefore may feel too assertive for you. You fear you might be perceived as being "nosy" or "prying." You may rely on social loafing even in one-on-one conversations. You make your partner do all the work in a conversation by struggling to coax you out of your shell and suggesting a series of topics you might be willing to talk about.

How to Correct Your Small-Talk Style

Understanding the dynamics of successful small talk and the pitfalls you may encounter will help you become more successful at it. The following are some additional suggestions to help you become friends with new people you encounter:

Introduce yourself early. It's easier to exchange names soon after the conversation begins. If you have trouble remembering your new acquaintance's name, be sure to repeat it at least three times in your conversation or comment on it to fix it in your mind. ("Alessandra. What a pretty name. Is it Spanish in origin?")

Remember that rejection of a topic isn't personal. If you ask a question and the other person moves on to something else, he is not rebuffing you—just your topic. Perhaps it's a subject he feels uncomfortable or insecure talking about. Let it go.

Look for shared topics of interest. Be creative. For potential topics, follow major stories of the day in the newspaper, or watch the morning news shows while you're getting dressed.

Become a "host" rather than a "guest." Ask questions, and focus on the other person's comfort level in your conversation.

Elaborate on your answers. A simple "yes" or "no" leaves little room to develop a topic. Disclose something about yourself. For example, when you introduce yourself, make sure to tell a story or anecdote that relates to what you do for a living. "I work for a computer software firm that produces . . ." Try to relate your career to something in the other person's life. "What kind of software do you use in your computer?"

When in doubt, ask a question. It's an easy way to fill silences. Your question could be one of clarification and rephrasing such as, "Let me see if I have this right. Do you mean to say . . . ?" This lets your partner know that you're participating, paying attention, and looking for common ground. It also gives him the opportunity to elaborate and explain further. But make sure the question is appropriate. See above for signs of discomfort.

Avoid your favored topics. Although you might believe that a favored topic is your safety net, it can do you more harm than good. Keep away from these unless they are also your acquaintance's favored topics. Notice if he is asking you questions, interjecting personal stories, and relaying additional information. If he's not, back off with a statement such as, "Look at me dominating the whole conversation. So tell me about your favorite hobbies."

Expand your topic options. Give yourself permission to talk about subjects in which you're a novice. It's perfectly acceptable to reveal that you don't know much about deep-sea fishing or medieval painting. Your partner will appreciate your honesty and may teach you a thing or two. Besides, it will also make him feel good about himself to share new information with you. Make sure to say, "Gee, I didn't know that" or "I never really thought about it that way before" to reinforce the other person taking risks.

Pay attention to silences. Jump right in with a question or comment at a break in the conversation. Or, if you have the floor, pause periodically to give the other person a chance for a rejoinder. If she doesn't come in, perhaps she is uninterested in the topic, doesn't know what to say, or wants to talk about something else. Look for cues that she wishes to move forward or back off.

Practice the art of conversation. Try making small talk when there is little risk involved. Strike up a conversation with someone while waiting on line to see a movie. (You might talk about other films you've seen with the same star or director.) You need not see this person again, but the practice will help you become more comfortable once you find yourself in situations that feel more important. You can then move on to people you see every day at the bus stop or lunchroom. Small talk gets easier and more natural the more you do it.

Appreciate the effort it takes to make conversation. If your partner is working hard, reward him with your full attention and complete responses. (This is impossible to do if you remain focused on yourself and how you're faring.)

Lighten up. Few people are highly critical of your performance and personality in the beginning stages of conversation. Take a risk by talking instead of retreating into silence.

Joining an Ongoing Conversation

Some shy people have little difficulty making small talk once introduced to a new person but are stymied when it comes to joining a conversation already in progress. When entering a gathering in which people are already engaged in discussion, they don't know how to break in without seeming rude or inappropriate.

In Chapter 10, I explained how children successfully integrate into a group of playmates. First they hover at the edges of play, watching the interaction and mimicking their peers' activities. Soon they formulate a way to be helpful. They provide assistance to the other children, offer suggestions when the play lags, give compliments or praise, share, and generally focus on others. These prosocial acts demonstrate that they will benefit the group and can be trusted, and soon they become a valued participant in the activity. Adults can learn much from these interactions. In adulthood, the dynamics of joining an ongoing group are much the same, although the situations and one's verbal abilities change with maturity.

While adults are also capable of building trust with prosocial acts, they are more apt to do so by sharing personal details about their lives. Women tend to talk about themselves to show that they have the same experience as others, while men tend to one-up or one-down others in a group in an attempt to even out the perception of power and status.

This pattern of developing intimacy can fluster a shy person, who may either expect instant intimacy (and reveal too much) or withhold self-disclosure out of fear. In warming up, it might be helpful to revert to prosocial acts and volunteer a social grace. If you're at a party, offer to bring a plate of food. If you're at a business meeting, you might say, "Can I get anybody some coffee?" This can help break the ice, even if your offer is denied.

Waiting and hovering serves a dual purpose. It allows you to warm up to the group and assess the level of intimacy, but it also lets the others become familiar with you. Indeed, there is a reciprocal relationship between you and the group. If you jump in right away, that may disrupt the conversation, and the others may see you as domineering.

Respect and respond to the ongoing flow in communication. Make sure that others have their say. As you listen, smile and nod when you agree. A lull in the conversation provides a natural opportunity for you to jump in. Ask a question of clarification rather than stating an opinion, which could be seen as too aggressive. Let others bring you into the conversation. You want to be accepted, but it takes time to become involved.

Now imagine you've come upon four coworkers having an animated discussion. You assume its work-related, but as soon as you come within earshot, you realize they are debating the merits of your city's basketball team, a subject you have little interest or knowledge in. There is nothing wrong with excusing yourself and moving on to a different group. This is not a sign of failure and will certainly feel more comfortable to you than standing by mutely as they go on about the various players. Perhaps, later in the day, you can connect to those with whom you wish to connect in another context.

To join a group in progress:

- Stand at the edge and listen for a while.

- Offer a social grace.

- Jump into logical openings during silences or lulls.

- Ask questions at first.

- Let others bring you into the conversation.

- Provide relevant information.

- Move on if you have little to offer.

Thinking on Your Feet

According to creativity expert E. Paul Torrance, creativity consists of four major elements:

1. Fluency: The ability to think of a large number of ideas or possible solutions

2. Flexibility: The ability to think of different approaches or strategies

3. Originality: The ability to think of unusual possibilities, to get off the beaten track

4. Elaboration: The ability to work out the details of an idea and implement it

Inhibited creativity underlies many unsatisfying shy conversations. And research has shown that shy people seem to lose their verbal creativity when they believe they are being evaluated—most often during social interactions. They focus on judging themselves rather than on the task at hand. In fact, even when people aren't evaluating them, they think they are. (This explains why you can conjure sparkling repartee once you've left a meeting but not while struggling to make conversation there!) You may be unable to think of what to say or how to approach a topic from a new angle; you may be unwilling to attempt new subjects that you know little about; you may not elaborate on subjects raised by failing to ask penetrating, open-ended follow-up questions.

All of this is to say that when you're feeling shy, you may lose the capacity to think on your feet. It's hard to conceive a logical follow-up in a conversation if you are busy grappling with anxiety and excessively focusing on your internal state—the narcissistic paradox—rather than on your partner. Remember, your brain can cope with only one issue at a time. It's best to focus on the moment, not the anxiety. Once you do, you can shuffle through more information and pay attention to what is being said.

Think of it this way. A reporter who has a list of questions from which he will not deviate may miss half of what his interviewee has to offer. He may not ask follow-up questions because he's so busy taking notes and so preoccupied with his next query that he doesn't pay attention to his interviewee's nonverbal and verbal responses. He needs to have done some homework on the topic to be able to ask logical questions that will elicit the kinds of information he's seeking, but he also needs to stay focused in the moment. Just as note-taking and preconceived questions distract the reporter, so may anxiety or self-conscious thoughts distract you.

Another way to enhance creativity during conversation is to engage in divergent thinking. That means generating many new ideas or bringing together two or more that may have remote connections. For instance, you may compliment a pearl brooch your partner is wearing, then remember a documentary on pearl diving, and finally relate all of that to a vacation in the Bahamas. Taking turns in the conversation, you could ask your partner if she has ever visited the tropics or gone scuba diving. Or you could inquire about what other sports she enjoys, and so on.

Creativity is unrelated to intelligence. The following ideas can help you become more creative.

Enlarge your knowledge base. Using social reconnaissance, get more information about the people you are likely to meet at a gathering. That will help you to ask relevant questions during conversations with them and expand the potential range of topics you can discuss. Reading the newspaper or weekly newsmagazines can help in that regard.

Review your take on current friends and acquaintances. You may have fallen into the trap of categorizing people. In your Shy Life Journal, list the many people in your life and brainstorm alternative relationships you could have with them. Can you go for coffee with your hairdresser? Attend a play with a colleague? Watch a dog show with your personal trainer? Using small talk, try to discover common interests. Your personal trainer may have a picture of a golden retriever on the wall. You might say, "There's a breeder's show coming to town next week. Would you like to go with me?" If he is unresponsive, he might have a policy against befriending clients. Don't generalize from one interaction. Try again with someone else.

Associate with creative people. Observe how their minds work. Read books and interviews about them. Find out as much as possible about them and try to do what they do. The creative process includes the approach/avoidance conflict. You will find that creative people are moderate risk-takers. They typically have trouble getting started and often have a mentor.

Successful creative people are not threatened by your success. They're more than happy to share. Look for those who are content doing what they're doing—that's a good sign.

Experiment with novelty. Break out of the mold. Explore a different grocery store; try the latest clothing, hair, or makeup styles; hang different pictures in your office, or move the current artwork to new locations; eat lunch at a diner that just opened; bring home fresh flowers; take an unfamiliar route home from work, and so on.

Free-associate. You can do this in your Shy Life Journal until you feel more confident among people. Pick a topic and see where it takes you. Visualize possible scenarios. Don't censor your ideas—the wilder the better. Bring together notions that normally wouldn't go together. For example, juxtapose the role of a host at a dinner party with the role of a facilitator at a business meeting. This is a constructive use of fantasy.

Practice divergent thinking. In your Shy Life Journal, jot down every use you can imagine for a brick. Start with the obvious—building a house, paving a patio, holding up bookshelves—and advance to more creative uses such as flowerpot stands, doorstops, footrests, writing instruments, and so on. Choose new and unusual objects, and repeat the exercise. Don't evaluate your ideas as you go along. That reduces creativity. Brainstorm for fifteen minutes, and then go back to link ideas and evaluate.

Analyze conversational patterns. Recall the threads of successful past conversations, and think through how they veered from one point to the next.

Encourage creativity in others. Be supportive of others in their attempts to be creative. Disclose to them your strategies for creativity. Engage them in brainstorming or divergent thinking. Let people know that they can bounce ideas off you. Show through your actions that you encourage creativity. Relate what they're doing to other things that are going on in your life or the lives of those around you.

Don't rely on the obvious. Delve deeper; ask questions.

Creativity can occur anytime, anyplace. Once you develop a more creative conversational style, you can always pick up the threads of an old conversation and generate new questions or related topics to fill any silence. A creative conversational style has as its basis a creative thinking style. You can practice divergent thinking all the time, either through the constructive use of fantasy and or simply by being around other people, listening to their conversations, and imagining how you would respond.

A Last Word on Shyness in Adulthood

Shyness can be an issue at all stages of your life. Indeed, research has shown that adults who have been shy may have more difficulties as they age. They tend to be lonelier; have smaller and more unpredictable social and caregiving networks; have more difficulty replacing friends lost to retirement, illness, or, death; and are more likely to be institutionalized.

In many cases, adults grow into shyness and lose their old comfort zones following a divorce or the death of a spouse. The shy response alters as expectations and life circumstances evolve. In Part IV we will examine how shyness manifests itself in four aspects of adult life: in intimate relationships, on the job, in our culture, and as part of the Information Age.

Shyness in the World

The many tasks of adulthood include developing a sense of community, discovering your place in society, finding and keeping love, raising a family, and engaging in meaningful work. Sadly, many of these tasks are difficult to achieve if your shyness makes you feel like a second-class citizen.

Researchers have shown that shy people know what to do to make their lives more enjoyable but doubt their ability to carry through. For example, you may recognize that you must take a risk to begin a relationship but still worry excessively about self-disclosure, becoming the focus of attention, or rejection. You may want to make eye contact when talking with someone but feel too cautious and believe that you can't rise to the challenge. You may refrain from asking others questions because you fear you may be prying even though you know it just means you are showing an interest. You may have unreasonable expectations—you want immediate intimacy and paradoxically still expect others to draw you out.

Scientists have found that some shy people are highly anxious and may have poor emotional coping skills. They allow their feelings to run amok because they don't open up to others to seek reality checks or advice. They even deny themselves the comfort that comes from knowing that others have had the same experience. They feel lonely in new or challenging situations.

When you don't rely on friends, social anxiety and self-doubt can fester, decreasing your ability to handle problems constructively. When you're anxious, you may find yourself unable to break problems into manageable components. Overwhelmed by your troubles, you soon fall into a vicious cycle. You constantly evaluate yourself negatively but never give yourself a chance to succeed.

Indeed, in times of challenge you may engage in catastrophic, negative thinking and social avoidance and may fail to recognize opportunities for growth. Rather than solving your problems creatively, you become passive and just dwell on them. You may believe that other people can't relate to you because, unlike you, they seem so confident and able to work through their difficulties.

The result is plummeting self-esteem. Shy people constantly fail in their own eyes. They know what's expected, don't try, don't succeed, and feel miserable that they can't accomplish what they know they're supposed to.

It is easy to see how shyness, unhappiness, and loneliness are tightly interwoven. Social support is imperative for happiness. It affects the way you think about the world and your place in it. It gives you hope and the belief in your ability to change your circumstances. It enhances problem-solving skills and motivation.

Woody Allen is reputed to have said, "Ninety-nine percent of life is just showing up." In Part IV, I will help you learn how to "show up" in your own life as a successfully shy lover, worker, and citizen of the world.

The Successfully Shy Lover

"I do not attend social events like weddings or parties," a college student wrote to me. "I have never really had a boyfriend because I shy away from men when they attempt to talk to me. This is really bothering me because all of my friends are dating and I am not, due to my shyness. This is ridiculous!"

"I usually don't talk to a woman unless she talks first," admitted a thirty-two-year-old unemployed man in New York City. "I find it difficult to start a conversation."

A professor in his mid-forties wrote, "I mentally imagine everyone else at a party as being a united group, which is having a uniformly good time, rather than as a set of individuals with their own failures and rejections."

All of these people have had difficulties initiating social interactions. Paradoxically, less than 7 percent of the more than 150 letters I analyzed for a recent study claimed that shyness interfered with their intimate relationships. Unfortunately, the problem lies not in getting along once the connection is cemented but in getting close to someone in the first place.

You may struggle to meet new people, summon the courage to ask someone for a date, and behave naturally and openly on the first few dates with a new partner. Since you may have trouble approaching and making small talk with new acquaintances, this is easy to understand. But making romantic connections is not as complicated as you may believe. I will share with you the relatively few rules you'll need to remember in order to do so successfully. Some people seem to do this intuitively, but others profit from practice, patience, and persistence.

But first let's understand the many sources of the shy lover's difficulties.

The Fallacy of Instant Chemistry

Many dating-related problems derive from unrealistic expectations. Indeed, many shy people place far too much emphasis on instant chemistry, but this is understandable. If you dislike dating because of your shyness, you may hope to put an end to dating discomfort by finding your own true love. In the process, each date becomes a "superdate"—you want each new partner to be *the one*.

But instant intimacy or chemistry is a fallacy. Good relationships exist not just on the physical level but also on mental, intellectual, physical, spiritual, psychological, and emotional levels. Despite what we see in the movies, friendships and romantic attachments don't coalesce all at once. It takes time for two people to warm up and get to know each other. It's a process of persistence, patience, and progress toward intimacy.

Unfortunately, the belief in instant chemistry can put more pressure on you and make you even more anxious and less natural on a date. The stakes are so terribly high. And in the end, you will feel more disappointed when the situation or person is imperfect.

Sid, age fifty-nine, a highly successful ophthalmologist, has trouble with this concept. Having recently divorced after more than thirty years of marriage, he suddenly found himself dating again, and it felt unpleasant. "Professionally, shyness doesn't affect me at all," he explained. "I can get in front of a group and talk, and it doesn't bother me. I guess I feel I have control over the situation. I know more than they do. I can meet people professionally and I'm confident about that. Maybe I'm just shy with women. Dating isn't as good as I expected. I feel that I don't have anything to say, that people won't want to listen to me. I find it difficult to meet women. If I know someone at a party, I can mix pretty well. But if I don't know anyone there, I'll walk right out the door."

Sid has fallen victim to the approach/avoidance conflict and faulty expectations. If he can't make a connection to someone instantaneously, he runs. By avoiding, he risks nothing. But as a result, he has been unable to spend the time it requires to meet and get to know someone new.

Where the Problems Lie

Being sociable isn't a popularity contest that boosts your ego. It means making connections and helping others look good and feel appreciated. Your unrealistic expectations may get in the way. But many other issues can keep you from making a romantic attachment with someone of your dreams.

The approach/avoidance conflict. You feel attracted to someone, yet your self-consciousness and the fear of rejection is so great you fail to make your intentions known and approach. The tension lies between the fear of feeling bad about yourself and the need for a fulfilling interpersonal relationship. In Sid's case, the fear won out.

Lack of trust in yourself. You have little faith in your own social appeal. Shyness is likely to cause concern about physical attractiveness. Psychologist Robert L. Montgomery and his colleagues at the University of Missouri have found that shy people consistently judge themselves less physically attractive than those who are not socially anxious—this, *independent of their actual looks.*

You may also be oblivious to your own social worth. Remember, you can offer someone much more than what is evident in a first impression: wit, good listening skills, great cooking, passion, loyalty.

Comparisons. There are two types of comparisons that interfere with dating. You may compare yourself to others in the room. They seem so much more sophisticated than you, and more adept at connecting. A nineteen-year-old baker wrote to me, "I become jealous a lot because I wonder why I can't be like another person. I feel as if I'm worthless in my social aspects because I can't always talk about 'fun' stuff." No connection is possible if you always come out on the losing end of an unfair comparison and believe that all of your friends are better with the opposite sex than you are.

You can also compare yourself to the person you wish to approach. You may believe that he or she is too attractive, refined, cool, or intelligent to be interested in the likes of you.

Trouble with compliments. You never learned how to respond to them. When someone flirts with you, you fail to notice or brush it off as empty flattery. It's best to accept the compliment as sincere and respond with a compliment. For example, if someone remarks on your nice new briefcase at a meeting, you might reply, "Thanks. It's kind of you to notice. Most people don't pay attention to such a small detail." That keeps the connection going. From there, you might ask a question and then move into small talk.

Self-defeating beliefs. There are myriad beliefs that can stop romance in its tracks. You can't believe the person you're attracted to may like you, too. When you meet someone new, you remember and dwell only on negative past encounters. If you ask someone out and she declines, it's the end of the world. You're too ugly/fat/thin/stupid/plain/old/uninteresting for anyone to find you attractive. Once people get to know you, they won't like you. They'll think you're boring.

Limited small-talk skills. You want to be intimate with someone but are unwilling to go through the initial stages of conversation that ultimately lead to intimacy. You deny yourself all-important warm-up time. Part of the process of intimacy is uncovering information about the other. What you discover during small talk informs whether you will want to move forward with the relationship. For instance, if during your chat you discover the other person holds religious or philosophical beliefs you can't abide, you may decide to move on to someone else. Discovery takes time.

Excessive self-preoccupation. This inhibits your ability to act naturally and show your date your true self. A college student in West Virginia wrote, "I feel terribly uncomfortable at parties when someone tries to evaluate me in five minutes or less to see if I should be added to their repertoire of friends." He is assuming that all eyes are on him, and they're critical.

If you are excessively self-preoccupied, you may believe that everyone notices that you're trying to make a move or extend intimacy with someone. You become more self-conscious because you feel your behavior is on public display. Walking across a room to ask someone to dance is a public move of intimacy that requires a lot of nerve. If the person refuses your offer, you may think that people are judging you more harshly than they actually are. Most likely, if they consider you at all, they'll think, "At least that person tried" instead of "What a loser."

Problems with self-disclosure. Either you give too little or tell too much! If you withhold sharing yourself, you may appear closed, distant, and aloof. If you may reveal too much too soon, your date may run. (See Chapter 12 for signs of discomfort during self-disclosure.)

Small social networks. It's difficult to meet potential partners through friends if you have relatively few friends. You may fail to take advantage of the social contacts you do have—you don't think to invite a work associate for coffee after hours. Your low self-esteem or rigid thinking may prevent you from making overtures to the many other people in your life.

The power of first impressions. In your need to feel welcome at a gathering, you may place too much importance on first impressions. You may be relying too heavily on what is immediately discernible through social comparison—attractiveness, status symbols (expensive jewelry or clothing), and having a conversational partner. This preoccupation can prevent you from thinking about the process of being with another person. You may believe that if you've bombed, you can never recover.

But this is only a first impression and no more. Rather than trying so hard to make a good first impression, make yourself comfortable during the warm-up period so you can behave naturally.

Lack of dating experience. You become shy in the dating experience because you're out of your comfort zone. Perhaps you didn't date much in high school or are recently widowed or divorced, or getting over a long relationship. Perhaps you married your high school sweetheart—the only person you've ever dated—and now, twenty-five years later, you have no idea what to do. Recently divorced Sid explained, "There's a lot of confusion about dating. I'm new at it. I'm still trying to figure out which age group I should be dating. There are a lot of things to think about. I have a lot of inhibitions. Things are totally different now than when I married my ex-wife."

None of these problems are insurmountable. Besides, everyone has difficulties dating because it's just plain hard. It requires poise, confidence, and charm—traits that may be in short supply when you're feeling shy. You may have to take it a little slower and perceive the "risks" as being less risky. You'll find many suggestions throughout this book and especially in this chapter to help you expand your dating comfort zone and become a successfully shy lover.

Shy Women and Shy Men

Just as in adolescence, shyness affects the genders in unique ways. These differences are tied to our traditional gender roles, which are especially salient in dating situations.

Shy Women

Traditionally, it was acceptable—even expected—that women behave passively, demurely, and quietly. We have also counted on their being the more emotionally expressive of the genders. Although today it is acceptable and even highly desirable for women to be assertive, independent, and active, when engaged in the dating game they may still fall back on traditional expectations of conduct.

Shy women fit more easily into the traditional gender role. In romantic situations, a woman who is shy is perceived as coy, feminine, hard-to-get, and safe. If she is physically attractive, it's even easier for her to remain passive during social encounters. She can simply wait for men to approach her. In fact, attractive women tend to behave more shyly than those who are unattractive. The latter approach men more frequently and are generally more outgoing.

In the cycle of small talk, a shy woman is likely to shoot down one potential topic after the other. A man who wishes to make a connection with her must continually formulate new potential subjects. This is the shy woman's extended warm-up period, during which she becomes accustomed to talking to an unfamiliar man. Attractive women may do this, in particular, because they're used to men approaching them and don't want to be bothered.

In general, men take this behavior in stride. If they perceive the woman as attractive, they are comfortable with her coyness. In fact, if they believe she is playing hard-to-get, they may pursue her all the more. But a man who is not persevering may feel discouraged by a shy woman's behavior. Most likely, he will not outlast the extended warm-up period and will retreat.

Interestingly, this courtship ritual can create problems for shy women because it limits their potential partners. They may find themselves with highly persistent men who may be questionable matches for them. These men may be domineering or they may believe that they can control the woman. Moreover, the men may be surprised when the warm-up period ends and they discover that the shy, self-effacing woman they are dating is more opinionated and independent than they first believed.

Because of the persistence it requires, a shy man will rarely break through to a shy woman. He may be too timid to approach her, or he may try but give up too quickly. In addition, a shy woman may not encourage a shy man to make an advance because she's unskilled at flirting or doesn't know how to emit signals that communicate she might enjoy his company.

It might be helpful for shy women to learn how to approach shy men or, at least, make themselves more approachable. Here are some tips to help you connect to men, shy or otherwise.

- Try to be less curt during small talk to encourage a shy man to continue a conversation.

- Smile, nod, and act interested. Make eye contact instead of looking down or to the side.

- In group situations, whether professional, leisure, or social, converse with people. Make small talk. Let others know you're approachable.

- Appreciate the attention you receive. If someone tries to talk to you, answer him. Don't appear aloof.

- Make contact with others through social graces. Offer to get food or drink or help in other ways.

- Invite a man you're attracted to into a group you frequent.

- If a man approached you earlier and you rebuffed him because you hadn't warmed up yet and were feeling too shy, pick up the threads of the conversation with him when you're more comfortable.

- Try not to make the conversation one-sided. (See Chapter 12.) The art of intimacy starts with getting to know a person. As you find out more about him, you'll know which topics to pursue.

- Don't be passive. Talk.

Remember, intimacy involves risks and rewards, approach and avoidance.

Shy Men

"I had a particularly trying adolescence, the effects of which I am only recently discovering in therapy," a thirty-four-year-old musician wrote to me. "A carefree childhood in which I was the beloved 'baby' of the family was replaced by torment from an abusive older brother whose domination was not only physical, but included humiliation before peers and pressure to score with girls. I found that by avoiding potentially disastrous situations and the tests of 'manhood' I could survive—by being invisible."

This unhappy man came by his shyness through difficult experience. Another did so almost out of spite. "I have thought quite a bit about my shyness over the years," this accountant wrote to me.

I have realized that I have been shy since I was a teenager. Before then, I was relatively talkative and outgoing at school, but that changed by the time I was about twelve years old. I was told several times that soon my attitude toward women would change, and I would be attracted to them. I strongly disagreed. I am stubborn enough that I fought this mentally for a long time. I didn't seriously rethink my attitude until I was probably about seventeen. By that time, most seventeen-year-olds had a couple of years of social skills that I didn't possess because of my inexperience, so I never really pursued any

> women because I was afraid my inexperience would show.
> The social-experience gap only widened as I waited.

This man suffers from the "off-time" syndrome and now feels that he can never catch up.

It seems that in general shyness is a bigger problem for men than it is for women. The latter can retreat into traditional feminine roles when feeling shy and still be accepted (and even prized), but when men are shy, they fail to fulfill the expected male role of assertiveness, action, and confidence and do not actively initiate relationships. (The "strong silent type," on the other hand, is far from shy. He may be aloof, in control, and self-assured, but these traits are attractive to many women.) A shy man is perceived as weak, avoidant, and neurotic. There are some exceptions, however. If a shy man is handsome, women will approach him, but he must make some effort as well.

Shy men often lack confidence. Not only are they insecure about their social behavior, but they also believe they're unattractive. When they approach a woman, therefore, they feel greatly at risk and assume they will be rejected.

The cycle of unsatisfying social interaction begins with the shy man's negative attributions ("She wouldn't want to talk to a jerk like me"), which spawns his infrequent eye contact. That nonverbal cue makes the woman uncomfortable and self-conscious, and she shuts down. Both then make negative attributions. (The man: "This is all my fault. I can't talk to women." The woman: "He's not interested in me. He's not even looking at me—he's looking around the room.") This leads to unnatural interactions, more avoidance, more pauses, more conflict between staying and leaving. Communication breaks down to the level of setting talk. Eventually, the shy man's negative attributions become a self-fulfilling prophecy—the woman doesn't want to talk to him.

Not only do shy men behave contrary to the traditional expectations, but sadly, this shy behavior actually makes women feel uncomfortable and turns them off. During initial conversations, shy men fidget, have closed body language, fail to make eye contact, and allow awkward silences to grow. (When women do this, men don't seem to mind.) They don't communicate empathy to the woman. Clearly, the man is uncomfortable, but he also makes his partner uneasy. The silences and embarrassment become acute, the conversation feels forced or strained, and eventually progress stalls.

Research has shown that shy males fear the conversational aspects of dating and actively worry about what they're going to say on a date. "I never know what to say," said a typical shy man in one study. "If I ask her a lot of questions, she tells me I'm interrogating her. If I don't ask her questions, she says I'm not interested. If I talk a lot, tell stories, et cetera, she thinks I don't care what she has to say. If I don't talk much, she says I'm boring—so what am I supposed to do?" Others feel anxious when they know the conversation is dragging. Another man said, "After a while, you run out of small talk about the weather and your classes. When the dialogue dies, it's awful." This young man had not learned how to progress beyond setting talk to pretopical questions and a more satisfying give-and-take. (See Chapter 12.)

Paradoxically, however, the dates of these shy men were struggling with their unwanted sexual advances. It seems that men are too shy to talk much during the date, but they try to make a move anyway! They are oblivious to the fact that if a woman doesn't have a satisfying conversation or if she feels uncomfortable, she won't want to become intimate.

If a woman is willing to take time to let her date become relaxed and if she encourages him to talk, the relationship might progress. But you should learn how to successfully approach women yourself so you're not overly dependent on the kindness of others. When no one is willing to make the first move, two shy people will rarely connect. That leads to many missed opportunities and unrequited love, confirming your worst fears about yourself—that you are unlovable, worthless, and condemned to a solitary life.

Brian Gilmartin at Montana State studied love-shy men—those like my correspondent who have never been on a date in their lives. These lonely individuals don't have close ties to other men and had virtually no connection to females even when growing up. They have no sisters, female friends, or close relationships with their mothers or other female relatives. Consequently, they never learned how to relate to women platonically or romantically. As adults, they are at a loss when it comes to dealing with women but fantasize about them a lot and have unrealistic notions of what women are like. They are so far behind their peers when it comes to romantic experiences that they believe they'll never catch up.

If this describes you or your experience, all is not hopeless. There are many things you can do to decrease your fear of rejection.

Go on practice dates. Practice conversing with women in general. This will give you much needed experience without "practicing" on a person you might really care about. Practice dates help you get used to the process of dating relieved of the pressure of making a good impression.

Set the stage for intimate conversation. Everything good in life comes from taking a risk. The trick is to communicate your desire for controlled intimacy while minimizing the chance of rejection. You let your feelings be known by guiding the depth of the intimacy.

At a party try saying, "Can we talk in a quieter spot?" At a business function ask, "Can we meet in a less formal setting?" At the volunteer organization say, "Perhaps we can have coffee after the fund-raiser next month" or "Why don't you stick around after the meeting so we can talk a bit."

Be persistent. You have a warm-up period to work through, but so does the woman.

Take periodic breaks to perform social graces. Social graces make you seem thoughtful, and they have a secondary benefit. When you excuse yourself and come back with drinks or a snack, you give yourself and the woman time to relax and recover. Contact need not be continuous, but it should be ongoing.

Repeat your approaches. Don't invest your whole sense of self in the success or failure of one encounter. If you see a person on an ongoing basis—in class, as part of a professional or volunteer group, on the bus—whom you'd like to approach, continue to say hi and make small talk. This gives you and the woman a chance to warm up to each other. Such repetition and persistence will bring familiarity. Because you don't have the tremendous investment in any one meeting, repeated contact eases the approach/avoidance conflict. The risk is smaller.

Reframe "rejection." Think of your initial approaches as practice sessions. You don't have to succeed the first time or with the first woman. If she's uninterested, use the experience to gain insight for the next time you try. Rather than seeing a rebuff as failure or rejection, think of it as a source of information and feedback.

Assess what you did and said. Did you disclose too much too quickly? Did you make eye contact? Were you asking open-ended questions? Were you dominating the conversation with your favored topic? Was she in a hurry or interested in talking to someone else? That's her decision. Could something else (like the setting) have contributed? Explore your experience in your Shy Life Journal.

Focus on your successes. Shyness of the mind reinforces the tendency to overlook successes and focus on failures. Pay attention to what works—what you said or did that brought the woman into conversation with you. Did you ask a question about a common interest (volunteer schedule, class notes), make several approaches before starting a conversation, tell a joke, wear an attention-grabbing tie? Did you watch the news and have something to say?

Even if, after getting to know this woman, you realize she's not for you, you can use the information you've gained from your success in establishing relationships with others.

Arrange a series of dates with various people. This makes any one date seem less important. If it doesn't work out, you won't feel as devastated. There are always others to fall back on.

Talk to men and women. If you vary your contacts in social gatherings, you will feel more comfortable. Talking to men as well takes the pressure off you and the woman. It keeps the conversation at a more social (rather than an intimate) level and is less threatening to you and those around you because you're not "on" all the time.

Remember the rules of self-disclosure. If your conversation partner hesitates, stammers, or clams up, she may be anxious. These are signs that you're moving too fast.

Spread the word. Let your friends know you are interested in meeting others.

There are many benefits to being a successfully shy man. Once you become involved in an intimate relationship, you have much to offer: you may be more attentive, more loyal, and a good listener. You take relationships seriously and are considerate. Understand the nature of your shyness and how it impacts your interactions with others.

How to Meet Potential Dates

Many shy people tell me they don't know how to meet potential dates. A common strategy is to try to pick up someone in a bar or at a party. Such social "scenes" are especially hard for shy people because they're so reluctant to approach strangers. As Sid explained, "If I'm in a bar, I just can't walk over to a woman and start talking!" Being publicly rejected is especially painful.

To get around this, many shy people rely on personal ads,

Internet chat rooms, and singles groups. Although these venues may be useful in weeding out incompatible people, they have their downsides as well.

Impersonal Venues

Impersonal venues include Internet chat rooms; personal ads; and computer, video, or other dating services. They are highly mediated and relatively safe because the risk seems minimal and they require little effort. They can provide greater access to a variety of choices, help you initiate contact, save time, and furnish you with an attributional outlet—you can always blame the dating service for making a bad match if a prospective date doesn't work out.

Impersonal venues may appeal to you since often they help to avoid the awkwardness of the initial contact. With E-mail or personal-ad correspondents you don't have to think on your feet or make conversation. You can compose your messages carefully. If you feel insecure about your appearance or social behavior, you can create a new persona. In a dating service, you can ask for an ideal mate and others can make you believe they are the person of your dreams.

Chat rooms and personal ads make it easy to eliminate people. Since chat rooms are organized by interest areas, you can write at length about your favored topic and you are likely to hear from people who are equally enamored with the subject. Reading personal ads gives you an inkling of what the other person is like. This is a meeting of the minds; physical, psychological, and social aspects of a relationship need not be involved. In a sense, it shortens the warm-up period because you may feel less anxious when responding through a modem or on paper.

These impersonal venues may be acceptable initially, but they shouldn't constitute the only way you meet potential partners. Eventually you will have to meet in person, and if you are shy, you may find yourself at a disadvantage. Not only may your expectations regarding your date be too high (creating anxiety), but you may not live up to what you've billed yourself to be (creating even more anxiety). Disappointment reigns for all involved.

You may believe that a dating service is risk-free because both partners are single and available and the matchmaker has done his or her work, but pitfalls abound. Mara B. Edelman and Aaron C. Ahuvia at Northwestern University have studied computer and matchmaker dating services. They find that these can help you with searching for and matching with a potential partner but not with interacting and actually hitting it off. And even then, there are problems. They have a success rate of only 10 percent.

Why the low success? To begin with, no one takes a pledge of honesty. Clients can modify their presentation; a potential match might have "rounded up" when describing himself, or you might have been inclined to do so. Besides, if you're highly selective about who you want, you're apt to exclude many people, which defeats the purpose of the dating service. Try to be more open-minded. You may be pleasantly surprised.

Also, in matching yourself to others, you may not know or be unable to articulate what qualities you want in a mate. (Or you may delude yourself and others, saying that looks are unimportant when you're really searching for someone glamorous.) You may also have unrealistic expectations, giving up too easily because there's always someone else to try in the dating pool. In a sort of "shopping effect," you may want your money's worth and keep trying new matches for a better fit. This can be a particular problem for people who are slow to warm up and are likely to back off too quickly anyway.

Dating services do nothing to ease your difficulties once you're on that first date. Most first dates are in high-talk settings—two people sitting at a table face-to-face. (The movies, on the other hand, are a low-talk setting.) You may have problems with self-disclosure and anxiety. You may move too fast because you're impatient or too slowly because you're afraid.

Dating services only provide the opportunity to make contact with a number of individuals, nothing more, nothing less. It's your responsibility to turn this meeting into a date by establishing and creating intimacy in ways I've suggested. Dating services are efficient and formulaic, but in truth, there's no formula for a good relationship or even for finding someone who will be good for you. According to one study, most people focus on physical attributes and can overlook important variables such as religion, economic status, culture, race, and sexual needs that come through developing intimacy.

If you are inclined to use one of these services, the following tips may prove helpful:

- Honesty is always the best policy. You can aggrandize yourself in your description, but what happens when you actually meet?

- Weigh the specific against the general in the application. The information you obtain from the dating service may be inadequate. It gets you started, but you may have to make some adjustments. For instance, two applicants might respond, "I like the outdoors," but her idea of the outdoors is a gentle jog through the woods while his is mountaineering and ice fishing. A person may share your interest in theater but strongly differ from you in religious, philosophical, or political views. You can only discover the details through intimacy. Be realistic.

- Know what you're looking for. If looks really do matter, admit it. If you're looking to establish a long-lasting relationship, other factors may ultimately be more important. The ideal is not found—it's created.

- Expect to be surprised. People often make faulty or inflated descriptions of themselves. A dose of reality can startle you.

- Put some flair in your presentation. Talk about those things that are important to you. Flag your enthusiasm for vegetarianism or your job. When you tap into what excites you, your passion comes through. Let your personality shine. If you have a good sense of humor, work on an amusing opening.

- Mention "big" issues early on. Religion, socioeconomic status, education, and so on may be the most important deciding factors.

- Be realistic. Remember, only 10 percent find long-term relationships. Keep in mind that a dating service is good for meeting a large pool of prospective mates but that it doesn't help you navigate a date.

- Don't take rejection personally. People can reject quickly and move on to the next prospect. You may not have enough time to make a good first impression.

Use dating services to supplement your regular dating strategy. Keep asking people out on your own and going on practice dates. Keep letting people know that you're interested. And keep working on your social skills. That's the only way to negotiate a relationship.

Semipersonal Venues

These can include singles groups, organizations, and group dates. You meet others face-to-face, but the matchings are not random. The organizers make an effort to smooth introductions.

In semipersonal venues, you have the opportunity to practice social skills and meet others in person (rather than on paper or electronically). Often you share common interests. Singles dances or other group activities may be hosted by religious institutions or other organizations—gourmet groups, hiking or skiing clubs, alumni associations—so the people you meet might fit more closely into your comfort zone. If the organization convenes regularly, the warm-up period can occur during business meetings or other activities, even before the singles event.

But merely showing up isn't good enough. You still must approach others. Also, unfortunately, sometimes these activities can feel like a "meat market." The most charming or assertive will meet people, while the shyer may be left standing on the edges of the crowd. Moreover, if the gender ratio is uneven, shy people of the majority gender may have difficulty getting noticed or making moves.

Joan Goldstein, founder and director of Conscious Singles Connection in Manhattan, organizes singles events for individuals interested in personal growth and health and has had experience with hundreds of singles. She notes that at singles gatherings shy people tend to stand in corners or at the edges and wait to be approached—despite fact that the express purpose of the gathering is to meet other singles and that attendees have paid to get in. She offers several valuable suggestions regarding how to navigate these affairs with aplomb:

Give yourself an assignment. Commit "to talk to three strangers—they don't even have to be strangers of the opposite sex. If you think of it as homework and that you're not looking for the love of your life, it makes it easier."

Use a prop. "You should always have a prop and look for other people's props like a unique piece of jewelry or clothing, a book—something that's unusual enough so that someone could comment on it without becoming too personal. A prop gives someone the opportunity to say to you, 'Wow!

Neat tie.' And then you can say, 'Thanks. I got it when I was in Tuscaloosa.' Then you can start a whole conversation about that.

"Alternatively, if you're a shy person and you're looking for a conversation piece, and someone has a prop, then you can say, 'That's an interesting sweater. Was it handmade?' or 'Great book! I hated to finish it.'"

Get involved in the event. "This works wonderfully for shy people. If you have a job to do at a singles event like taking registration, passing around snacks, or helping the host distribute literature, it's much easier to meet people. It's not really *you* you're putting on the line when you talk to strangers. You're just doing a job. It's your role."

Personal Venues

The single most effective way to meet someone is through a friend. Sid explained, "When I get fixed up with a woman, I'm okay. The ice has already been broken because we have a mutual friend. I can build my confidence if other people I know are around or if they've fixed me up."

Meeting someone personally is also one of the most risky ways. When you approach someone one-on-one through a friend, on a blind date, or simply on impulse, you don't rely on an organization or other intermediary to make the initiation easy. As Sid admits, "It takes all of my courage to make the phone call and ask for a date."

The upside is you are more in control of the situation and accept the responsibility for the success. This in turn builds self-confidence, increases approaches, and expands your comfort zone. The downside, of course, is that you could be rejected in person. This isn't fatal, but you may exaggerate the negative consequences.

It's important to recognize the advantages and disadvantages of meeting people in these three ways. Impersonal venues are no substitute for dating. You must still meet in person, and a real relationship has to grow out of the mediated one. Semipersonal venues are good for disqualifying people and getting warmed up, but they're not an end in themselves. You must still put in effort. Personal ways are the most effective but also the most risky, so you must learn how to diminish the risk.

But whatever method you use to get things started, eventually you must personally make a date.

How to Make a Date

Dating is a learned behavior like playing tennis or riding a bike. The more you do it, the better you'll be at it. Whether practice or "for real," there are some general rules of protocol for making a date:

1. *Ask for a phone number.* It's the only way to follow up contact. A simple statement such as "I enjoyed talking to you. Would it be okay if I called you sometime?" works well.

But you may have many problems with such a straightforward question. You may fear that asking for a number seems too forward, or you may doubt that the other person is interested in dating you. (Of course, the only way to find out is to ask.)

What happens if the other person says no? You can maintain your dignity and a bit of connection by saying, "That's fine. But if you change your mind, here's how you can reach me," and offer your own number. Or you can say, "Sorry it won't work out. I still enjoyed talking to you."

Later it might be helpful to assess why the other person was uninterested. There are many possible reasons, and most don't involve you. She may already be in a relationship or may be recovering from one that didn't work out and feeling unready to date. Perhaps there are problems with children, ill family members, or work assignments that make it difficult to engage in an active social life. Maybe she is painfully shy and doesn't know how to accept an invitation without feeling overwhelmed with anxiety and doubt.

Examine your own behavior. Did you engage in small talk to discover the other person's interests? Paying attention to nonverbal cues, did you make sure she was comfortable in the interaction? Did you dominate the conversation with your exploits at the office? What lesson could you learn from this rejection?

2. *Call.* Shy people often obtain the phone number of someone they'd like to date but then fail to follow up. They second-guess themselves and wonder if the person was truly interested or was just being polite. There's nothing to be lost by calling but much to be lost by not calling. Assume the person is interested.

When you call, identify yourself. Place yourself in the context of your last conversation and reestablish the pleasant connection. Keep it short. You might say, "Hi, Nancy? This is John Brown. I met you last week at the Super Singles dance. I was the one with the funny purple tie."

3. *Arrange the meeting.* The purpose of the initial meeting is to make small talk. It helps you warm up, expands your comfort zone, and renders the approach possible.

To take the onus off a first date and make it more manageable and less momentous, don't ask the person out to dinner, the zoo, or any other meeting that will require more than a thirty-minute commitment. Go out for coffee. Offer to let the other person choose the location so that it's convenient. Make sure it's public. If there's no connection, you can get out quickly.

4. *End the conversation.* A simple "I'm looking forward to seeing you next Thursday" will do fine.

Tackling the Predate Doubting Syndrome

Anxiety may set in as soon as you've hung up the phone. You think of all of the things that can go wrong. You worry you've made a big mistake. What are you going to talk about? What will you wear? At this point it's helpful to lower your expectations. Remember, you're just meeting to get to know each other a little better, not to discuss wedding plans.

Use social reconnaissance. Go to the coffee bar a few days in advance to become familiar with it. That will help to reduce uncertainty during the date and shorten your warm-up period. You will be more relaxed, confident, and better able to concentrate on making conversation if you're comfortable with your surroundings. If you need to, peruse the menu. Order something, so you'll be able to speak with experience during small-talk exchanges. ("I've had the Sumatra coffee here. It's really good.") Observe what other customers are wearing and ordering. Anything you do to minimize the initial awkwardness will help.

Knowing where she usually hangs out tells you a little bit about your date. Also your social reconnaissance will help make your arrival seem effortless, expanding your comfort zone and further reducing uncertainty and self-consciousness.

Increase your chances of conversational success by thinking about what you're going to discuss. Compose a list of topics that include subjects you already covered when you first met. Do a little research and thinking. Perhaps you can develop some meaningful questions. Even if you don't use your list of topics, it will help you feel more secure and prepared.

Now do a little psychological work on yourself. Stop ruminating that the other person is only going out with you because of pity. The worst thing that can happen is that there will be no second date. Think of it as a practice date to diffuse its importance. Concentrate on whether you like this person and would want to add her to your social network.

If you are on the receiving end of an invitation, always give the person a chance, even if you don't feel an instant connection. Respect that it takes a lot of courage to ask someone out. If the first date is short, it won't be much of a sacrifice. Besides, you might have gotten a false negative impression when you first met (perhaps the other person was nervous), and you might find her much more interesting one-on-one.

On the Date

It's wise to show up fifteen minutes early to give yourself time to acclimate and warm up. (If both of you are shy, you may both show up fifteen minutes early! That could be an opening point of conversation.) Bring something to read while you're waiting. That can also serve as a prop. Prepare a greeting so the conversation is already started. ("I'm so glad to see you again. I had such a good time meeting you at the party.")

Follow the rules of small talk outlined in Chapter 12. Start with setting talk. Try to find common ground by asking questions and being interested in what your date has to say. Ask open-ended questions, go through your list of topics if necessary, and don't be afraid of silences—they are never as long as they feel. Match levels of self-disclosure so there's give-and-take. Your date may not enjoy feeling interrogated.

Don't assume that your date is negatively evaluating you. Recognize that he is probably nervous, too. Your goal is to discover if you like the other person. Keep your expectations realistic. Don't try to win your date over—simply spending time together is reward enough.

Ending One Date, Starting Another

Turning a beverage date into a dinner date can be a difficult transition, requiring mutual consent. To determine if coffee will develop into something more substantial, you can offer a second cup. If she assents, it means he wants to spend more time with you. If she replies, "Oh, I've had enough, but if you want more, I'll be happy to sit and chat with you," the same meaning derives.

It's easier to move from here to a light dinner. At this point, you could say, "If you need to take off, I'll certainly understand. If not, would you like to grab a bite to eat?" That implies another hour or so.

If the other person says she has to leave, that doesn't necessarily mean she isn't interested. You might say, "I'd like to call you again." Give a specific day and time. If she tells you she is going to be away from the phone or out of town, that communicates interest. If she agrees, call as scheduled. If there's no interest, it gives the person an easy way out. He or she may not pick up the phone or may have prepared something to say. If there is no answer, leave a message that you will call again and include your number as part of the message. Do call back. There are many reasons—which do not have anything to do with you—why she might not be at the phone at the prearranged time.

If you don't extend the beverage date, end it as planned, but ask if you can call again. When you call to make the second date, tell her you had a great time and bring up a few choice tidbits from the conversation. Reestablish your connection by inviting her to do something that involves your common interests like watching an adventure movie, listening to jazz, roller-blading, or indulging in Indian food.

If after an unsuccessful encounter you decide you don't want to see that person again, explain that the two of you have too little in common or that you're not looking for a relationship right now. But if you're in doubt, give her another chance and try a second date.

General Dating Reminders

You must become more active if you wish to meet someone. Here are a few more suggestions to help you date successfully:

- Have realistic expectations. Don't expect to fall in love or find your soul mate on a first date.

- Be patient and persistent. Take an active interest in your partner. Ask questions. Persevere. Know that it takes time to build rapport with someone—especially someone attractive.

- Match self-disclosure levels. Extend and elaborate on what your partner says. As you make the other person comfortable, you'll feel more comfortable, too.

- Be aware of body language. There are more ways to communicate than through words. Eye contact is crucial. It shows interest and conveys intimacy. Once it is established, the stage is set for a better interaction.

  Appropriate touching (a repeated, gentle brush of a hand) is a form of expression. If the other person lets you touch without pulling away, you can use it to communicate interest and intimacy. It's a sign that the relationship is progressing. Leaning closer also communicates intentions. If you lean toward someone and he or she moves away, you've violated a comfort zone. If he or she moves toward you, closeness is desired. But it doesn't mean that intimacy has been established, only that the relationship is progressing.

- Look for positive verbal cues. Notice if the person mentions past relationships. (Not a good sign. The person may still be recovering from the relationship.) Talking about the present and issues related to you alone, and asking you questions ("What do you think?" "How do you feel?" "What do you do?") are statements of exclusivity and a sign that the conversation is working. Watch for fewer and shorter pauses and more overlapping sentences in natural conversations.

- Be aware of your thoughts. Your negative thoughts and attributions are self-fulfilling and do impact the other person.

- The burden is on men—at least initially. But women can help shy men by being more active in the conversation and looking for common ground.

Shyness in Intimate Relationships

For the most part, once shy people become intimate, their shyness ceases to hold them back from enjoying the relationship. However, a few problems may crop up.

You and your partner may experience differing levels of shyness. For example, an eighteen-year-old college student wrote to me, "My boyfriend is very friendly, and he gets mad at me when I do not want to go socialize with him. He knows many people and feels as if I need to talk to them, too! It makes me angry that he wants to change me, but I'm also angry with myself. I cannot start a conversation with anyone. I feel bad because I'm afraid they will think I am snobby, but I just don't know what to say. Sometimes I don't want to go anywhere or be with or around anyone."

A fifty-six-year-old homemaker has difficulties with this issue as well. "Our social life is very limited, mainly because of my inhibitions and insecurities. The wife usually is the social convener, and that's where we run into problems, because that is something I cannot do. Apart from my sister and husband, I don't have any friends. My husband makes a real effort to drag me out to things he's involved in."

It's only natural for one partner to be more shy than the other. After all, if both were equally shy, who would make the first move? And often shy people want to go out with more sociable people because they find it an attractive trait—one that they would like to emulate themselves.

Unfortunately, these temperamental differences can cause some friction. Like the college student above, you may dislike or feel uncomfortable around your outgoing partner's friends or may resent having to follow their plans. Or, like the homemaker, you may hide behind your partner and fail to make social efforts yourself. Your partner may feel you're a drag because you're always reluctant to socialize. If you don't share common interests or if you subordinate your needs to your partner's, it can lead to dissatisfaction, resentment, and dependency.

Problems may also arise in the level of self-disclosure when talking about intimate issues. Revealing deep feelings or details about your life is difficult for even the most verbal of people. The risk of offending your partner or being rejected is great. Saying, "I love you," "I want to get closer to you," or "When you leave clutter around the house, it drives me crazy" can have ambiguous and unknown effects. You may think it best to keep your thoughts to yourself, but that will diminish the level of intimacy in the relationship.

Finally, being shy in a relationship can foster dependency. You may find it hard to discuss sexual needs within the relationship and may rely on your partner too heavily to make decisions about contraception or sexual activities. Moreover, when you let your partner do all the talking for you or make most of the decisions, you can lose faith in your ability to be social on your own. (This is especially true of the persistent-man/coy-woman match.)

Dependency issues are especially apparent when people start dating after divorce or the breakup of a long-term relationship. They must refurbish rusty dating behaviors and adjust to the new rules of the game. And they must renew an independent identity. If they had been social in their previous relationship, this won't pose overwhelming difficulties, but if they let their partner make all the social decisions, they might have a harder time.

Finding Courage

Successfully shy people have found the courage to leave their cocoons and meet others. Perhaps their experiences will inform and inspire you.

A businesswoman explained how she changed her shy mind. "[A seminar I attended] got me to accept that strangers were just as nervous about me as I was about them, and there was no need to be afraid of them, as we were all in the same boat, and need to get to know each other before judging. Now I rarely have a problem, although I still don't walk up to strangers and speak as if I've known them forever. But I do speak to them!"

A successfully shy college student in New Jersey wrote, "I take a good look at myself and tell myself that I have no reason to feel insecure and I can't let other people decide my life. They have no control over me and what I do."

Unsuccessfully shy people run the risk of unrequited love. They are lonely, feel unloved and unlovable, and constantly second-guess themselves ("If only I had . . . "). Successfully shy people take control, expand their comfort zones, resolve the approach/avoidance conflict, gain valuable dating experience, and find love. They use persistence and patience. They understand that dating is a process, not an act, and that intimacy, far from being a thunderbolt experience, grows slowly based on risking, expanding one's comfort zone, considering others, accepting oneself, and becoming self-aware. All of these factors make it possible for you to open up to yourself and to others. And that will make you a successfully shy lover.

14

The Successfully Shy Worker

We often think of work as a means toward an end—earning money. But a job is so much more than a paycheck. It can help you gain a sense of self-worth, promote personal growth, augment your social network, and provide recognition for your talents. It can be a source of satisfaction and pride.

Since most jobs require many social as well as technical skills, shyness can prevent you from performing at your peak. This has nothing to do with competence but involves your difficulties in dealing with the interpersonal aspects of work so critical for success. Many people have shared with me how their shyness interferes with their careers. Allen's story is one of the most representative.

Allen is a thirty-three-year-old engineer for whom shyness was a particular problem in the workplace. "In my last job," he told me, "shyness affected me to the point that I would be afraid to talk to people—even people at work who were friends. I'd avoid any sort of social interaction with them. I wouldn't eat lunch with them, or I'd avoid them in the hallways. With my boss or upper management, I'd be afraid to say things. I'd be in knots the whole time."

In fact, Allen's problem with authority figures got him into hot water. "Once I was working on an important project with a very intimidating person. I was supposed to get the project to him by five P.M. I had it done, but I didn't tell him because I was afraid to talk to him. I got in trouble the next day because he thought I didn't finish it. Shyness interfered with my job pretty badly."

The impact of shyness is often unacknowledged in the

workplace. You may believe it is peripheral to the intellectual and technical aspects of work, but this is a mistake. Think about what it takes to get ahead in today's job market. Employees must be optimistic and assertive. They should be skilled at networking, negotiating, and interviewing. Those who are most willing to explore the social side of work—the adept salespeople, managers, and office politicians—are the most likely to succeed. People who speak up are seen as competent and as leaders. *Even if their contributions are mediocre*, they steal the spotlight.

"I did really good work, and that was recognized," Allen explained. "But the only employees who got promoted were the ones who were outgoing, talkative, and sociable. That hurt me because I'm not one of those people. I was seen as a necessary person in the company but unworthy of any job that would require leadership."

A survey respondent had a similar problem. She wrote, "I'm sure I've suffered professionally because I've never been one to sing my own praises or to bring a problem to the boss's attention. So no matter how hard I work, I'm sure I can seem aloof, disinterested, and even snobby in my coworkers' eyes." You too may feel handicapped by your avoidance of the social aspects of work. You may fail to promote your accomplishments, and others may believe that you're not a team player. Such an attitude may lead to the erroneous perception that you are indifferent to your job and coworkers.

Shyness may also prevent you from volunteering or going out of your way for others. You may refrain from making presentations or engaging in other activities outside your comfort zone and job description. Moreover, you may fail to develop close relationships with your boss, peers, or subordinates, which can undermine their loyalty.

The goal of this chapter is to help you understand how shyness affects your career path, job, and relationships with colleagues and how to take steps to minimize its more negative consequences. Think of it as a surrogate mentor to help you through office politics.

A Rocky Career Path

Research indicates that shy men generally delay establishing a career. This can begin even before they hit the job market, while they are still in college. Susan Philips and Monroe Bruch at the State University of New York at Albany found that shy undergraduates tend not to seek out the information they need to make wise career choices. They fail to consult mentors, career advisers, or the campus placement center, perhaps because they must initiate these actions and promote themselves. They may experience an approach/avoidance conflict around people who can help them.

They may also lack a "vocational self-concept." That is, they don't know what they want to do with their lives. An indistinct vocational self-concept is related to low self-esteem and may be a product of poor identity formation during adolescence.

Perhaps these shy students haven't sought enough information to make a career decision, or they haven't explored—hands-on—diverse tasks and opportunities that could help them take inventory of their talents. They may hang back during this indecisive phase because they are unready to leave the comfort zone of school and take the next step. They cling to the familiarity of their student status and hesitate to move into adulthood.

For all of these reasons, when they finally do find employment, shy workers tend to be older than their peers. But because they are "off-time," they are often less satisfied in their jobs. Moreover, Avshalom Caspi at the University of Wisconsin, Madison, found that others may perceive them as less competent, forceful, ambitious, or intelligent than their on-time peers. They are thought to be less effective managers and leaders.

Once in their careers, shy men can be slow to advance. They may hang on to secure but unchallenging jobs in which they feel safe (remaining in their comfort zone) and may resist going on job interviews (falling victim to the approach/avoidance conflict). Often superiors overlook them for promotions because of their quietness.

Although Caspi's research focused on men, it is likely that the same issues arise for shy women in the workforce. Indeed, as one young woman wrote to me, "I graduate from college in May and fear entering the real world. I think getting a job is very frightening. I just dread those first few months of awkwardness and not knowing how to behave."

All of this impacts quality of life. Dissatisfaction, doubts about one's abilities, lack of self-fulfillment, and lagging behind friends can make shy workers feel bad about themselves. Like Allen, they become frustrated if they do their job well but their contributions go unrecognized. They observe peers advancing and feel left behind. They may experience a crisis of confidence, helplessness, and despair, which can lead to burnout, social withdrawal, and personal or marital problems such as drinking, communication breakdown, divorce, anxiety, and low-grade depression.

Add in the specter of downsizing, the consequences of shyness in the workplace become devastating. Shy people can find it harder to bounce back after having been laid off because of their pessimistic cognitive style, small social network (through which they would hear of job openings), poor performance on interviews, and general difficulty in dealing with new life challenges.

The following suggestions can help you overcome shy obstacles on your career path.

Decide what you want to do, not just what you don't want to do. The best way to accomplish this is through an internship or volunteer position in which you can gain experience without a total commitment. If you work full-time, volunteer in the evening, on weekends, and during vacation time. This may sound harsh, but it's better than staying in a job you hate because you don't know what else to do with your life.

Seek professional help. A career adviser, headhunter, or campus placement center will help you with career diagnosis, occupational outlooks, job listings, resumes, interview coaching, and contacts. (If you're no longer a student, you can often use college job-placement offices for a fee, or you can look to your alumni association for information.)

Increase your personal contacts through networking. Tell others you're looking for a job, attend professional gatherings, join a networking group or student organization, and talk to people in the field or related areas.

Separate the personal from the professional. Don't let personal inhibitions like shyness interfere with your career. Ask yourself if you are resisting a new job because you're truly happy in your current work or because you are fearful of expanding your comfort zone and breaking out of the approach/avoidance conflict.

Take calculated risks. Find out about new positions by using social reconnaissance and gathering information.

Rethink your views on promoting yourself. There's nothing wrong with it as long as what you say is true. If you don't promote yourself, nobody else will. Have confidence in your abilities.

Remember, social skills make you promotable. They not only help you land the job, but they also enhance your leadership qualities and advancement.

Taming the Interview Demon

Another reason that shy people get a late start on a career track may be linked to their passive behavior during job interviews. They may think, *If I show up and have a decent resume, then I don't have to do much else.* They may freeze or wait for the interviewer to draw them out instead of promoting themselves. This may be linked to fear or to shy narcissism, an attitude that conveys, "I'm here. Isn't that good enough?"

They are wrong, of course. As a shy accountant wrote to me, "I never got the job in any multinational firms. Why? Maybe I didn't come across as aggressive enough, assertive enough, determined enough, smart enough." Fighting for a job helps you to land one.

Perhaps beneath the passive attitude lies fear. Most shy people dread job interviews because they activate so many alarms. Indeed, many claim that they don't advance in their careers because they hate the process. A twenty-five-year-old woman in New Jersey wrote to me, "My avoidance of situations cost me a great many job opportunities. I would put off placing the phone calls to secure an interview, and eventually, when and if I ever got the courage to call, the response was, 'Sorry. The position has been filled.' I heard this way too many times, and I know I am the only one to blame by letting my shyness and shyness-induced fear control me."

It stands to reason that interviews are frightening. The process intensifies all of those insecurities arising from being evaluated and finding yourself the center of attention—the focus is on you alone, your history, and your potential with the company.

Interviews exaggerate the negative characteristics of the shy mind-set and can heighten your natural tendency to criticize yourself. Suddenly, objective self-awareness, pessimistic attributions, narcissism, and unfair comparisons come to the fore. The approach/avoidance conflict also looms; you must present and promote yourself, but you worry about evaluation. You must play up past successes, which can be difficult if negative self-talk interferes. You may be self-effacing, self-censoring, and self-conscious, so you refrain from blowing your own horn about your accomplishments. (You're giving yourself a compliment!) Yet that's exactly what you're meant to do in this situation.

A job interview can also force you to interact at a pace that feels uncomfortable to you; you don't have time to warm up to the situation. It's like being on a blind date—lots of small talk, concern about a favorable impression, and evaluation. If you're paying too much attention to your performance or worrying about what the interviewer thinks of you, you cannot focus on the situation. Your heightened arousal can sap most of your energy and dull your intelligence.

You may take rejection personally without assessing whether this would be a good job for you in the first place, or whether you have the skills the company needs. Indeed, your anxiety may be so great that you believe the situation is too much for you to handle at all.

But as my correspondent made clear, avoiding the opportunity to interview only creates more frustration and wastes your talent. Don't resign yourself to an unsatisfying work life just because you fear foundering during an interview. Here are things you can do to help yourself.

- Realize that just about everyone hates interviews, especially if they want the job and pressure themselves to do well.

- Go on practice interviews (similar to practice dates) for positions that only tangentially interest you. Practice will help you acclimate to the process, and you can get over the rough spots without jeopardizing an important career move. The more you interview, the easier it will become.

- Attend seminars or consult a headhunter who can advise you on how to present yourself.

- Leave nothing to chance. Research the company beforehand. Read its recent annual reports. Search newspaper databases for local or national stories about it. Check to see if it has an Internet home page. Call people you know who work in a related industry to ask what they know about the company. Find out about its mission statement and corporate culture. What does it produce? Who are its clients? All of this will help you generate ideas about how you would contribute to the company if you landed the job.

- Prepare for questions you might be asked. Write down your answers and rehearse with a friend. Expect personal as well as professional questions such as "Where do you expect to be five years from now?" "What are some of your limitations?"

- Be ready to ask the interviewer about the company and your position. Ask yourself if you would be happy in this job, instead of accepting whatever job is offered.

- Think about and verbalize what sets you apart from other applicants—community service, a history of attending seminars to further your education, excellent sales.

- During the interview focus on the position, not yourself, just as you would in social situations.

- Make the personal professional (what you bring to the job) and the professional personal (why you'll thrive on the job).

- Volunteer additional information about yourself at the close of the interview, if the interviewer didn't ask you the right questions.

- Maintain contact with the employer after the interview. Write a letter expressing how much you enjoyed the meeting and that you continue to be interested in the job. Or call to ask a question or add personal information you had forgotten during the interview. Follow up periodically about the status of your application.

- Prepare for a series of interviews rather than one. The warm-up period may work to your advantage; if you get past the first one, subsequent interviews will feel easier. Be sure to accept an invitation to a second interview.

- Keep expectations realistic. You may not be hired on the spot, and you may not be offered a job at each company.

- If possible, get feedback from the person who interviewed you, especially if you receive a rejection letter. Ask about reasons for the rejection and how you can improve your chances to get a similar job in the future.

- Bear in mind that all applicants but one will be rejected for this position. Don't take it personally.

Shy Career Choices

"My professional life, or lack of it, has been most severely hampered by lack of confidence," one woman wrote to me. "Even though I needed and wanted to work after getting married, I shrank at the thought of competition. The only work I have been able to find is part-time, as an interviewer with a market-research company. The questions are quite structured."

Research indicates that shy people gravitate to technologically oriented careers rather than interpersonal ones, and thanks to the Information Age, these technical fields are expanding. But many of these high-tech jobs are exceedingly competitive. Employees must be highly entrepreneurial (to bring in clients) or service-oriented (in areas such as computer repair, tech support, customer service, Web-page development) to get ahead.

It may be helpful to ask yourself why you don't consider a job in sales, management, or other people-related fields. Do you believe that you can't be successful at this kind of work? Are your expectations realistic, or are they the result of negative self-talk and a pessimistic attributional style? You limit yourself by being locked into one option. Being a successfully shy worker means having the ability to expand your comfort zone and seek alternative career choices.

The truth is, even if you're in a technical field, you will still need social skills. In fact, we can call these "technosocial skills"—the ability to relate technological information at a human level (making it user-friendly for the average consumer). Also, since many technology companies are large, you may have coworkers and a business hierarchy to negotiate. If you're working on your own, you must either deal with isolation (and the possible atrophy of social skills) or be sociable enough to increase your client base. How can you set yourself and your company apart if you're unwilling to woo clients and service their needs? Communication is a must.

It's unrealistic to believe that you can avoid being with people on the job. Computers are no substitute for conducting business the old-fashioned way—negotiating with others. Even if you're an engineer, computer programmer, lab technician, or interviewer for a market researcher, you will need to learn how to work with people.

Because of your social difficulties, you may ask, "Well, why can't I just chuck the social aspect of work and telecommute from home?" But what appears to be an easy out really isn't. You may believe that you can rely on your computer to do your talking for you, but technology makes personal meetings all the more important. When working at home, you may become lonelier. You have little face-to-face contact and must find alternate social outlets. The more dispersed the work group, the greater your need for social support to get through the rough spots and stay motivated. (See Chapter 15.)

Managers of telecommuters must be creative in finding ways to forge camaraderie and "face time" with their employees—weekly conference calls, periodic office meetings, employee newsletters, and so on. Newsletters may be more important and frequent now that the workplace is fragmented. If you freelance, you may want to set up a communal office so you see the same group of people every day.

You can't get away from dealing with others. Whether you work for a large corporation or yourself, advancement depends on social skills.

Talking to Colleagues in the Workplace

Okay, so you've landed your dream position. Still, knowing what to say and how to initiate communication with coworkers is vital for gaining the recognition and help you need to progress in your career. Much negotiating and jockeying for position occurs around the water cooler and before and after important meetings, so when you're out of the loop, you can miss valuable information that flows outside official channels. And these days, as job security becomes unstable, coworkers can be competitors. It's easy for your boss to fire someone who seems uninvolved.

"I stopped going to any parties whatever, even office parties," one man wrote to me. "Also, while I normally can express work-related opinions at work, I seldom make any purely social overtures (such as inviting anyone to my house or even to go to lunch). At professional conferences, I don't introduce myself to others or attend the cocktail party, but generally hide behind a newspaper. If I try to discuss anything besides work with coworkers or my boss, I remain standing, generally sweat a lot, keep it brief, and leave their offices feeling amiss, inept, and disappointed."

You too may need help navigating the roiling waters of the

work social scene. You may wait for others to approach you or fail to seek the company or advice of peers. You may fall out of the information loop that's so important in getting the job done or feel isolated, believing the coworkers whom you encounter daily are strangers. You may feel unable to share personal or professional concerns, and your job satisfaction can decline as a result.

Self-disclosure can also be a problem for you. You may rely on E-mail and memos rather than meeting coworkers face-to-face and may avoid communicating anything substantive. But, the more you depend on E-mail to communicate, the less satisfaction you get. New technology can increase social isolation. (See Chapter 15.)

All in all, you feel like an outsider at work. But your coworkers are more than merely employees—they're family. You may need support from them, especially if you have a small social network. To communicate with your coworkers:

- Approach them during informal moments at the office: as they arrive in the morning, around lunchtime, during breaks, after work.

- Following the rules for small talk outlined in Chapter 12, match their level of self-disclosure so you don't get too personal when the relationship is first and foremost professional.

- Find common ground unrelated to the workplace. You're both baseball fans, have kids, live in the same neighborhood, drive the same sports-utility vehicle, or ski. Build on those connections.

- Don't dwell on the downside of the job. Be positive and ask for courses of action when you seek advice.

- Value your coworkers as sources of support. They're familiar faces, and they confront the same burdens you do every day. With time and patience, you can warm up to them.

Dealing with Authority Figures

"For some reason, I'm mainly shy around authority figures," Allen admitted. "I guess I worry that they are judging me and they're in a position to control my well-being." If you have difficulty dealing with authority figures in any context, talking to your boss or manager is likely to be problematic. This originates in the fear of negative evaluation. Supervisors have the power—and often the duty—to appraise their employees; due to a pessimistic thinking style, you may assume the worst.

You may feel intimidated and hesitate to approach your manager unless forced to do so. Indeed, your approach/avoidance conflict may be operating at its most potent with her. You may wonder, "If I ask a question, will my boss think I'm stupid or wasting her time? How can I request feedback, a raise, or a promotion? In this time of employment uncertainty, how can I let her know how good my work is without seeming like a shark?"

You may hate being singled out or drawing attention to yourself, but if you recoil from relating to your supervisor, she may overlook you when it comes time for promotions. Indeed, you may devalue your work accomplishments as you do your social contributions. But you must build rapport with your superiors in order to be recognized for your efforts and to demonstrate your interest in your job. The following suggestions may help.

- Don't be intimidated by potential criticism of your ideas, especially if others rush to judgment.

- When your superior or colleague asks for participation, offer your services. Get involved on as many different levels as you can.

- Take leadership roles when possible.

- Track your progress, and send a note to your manager to keep her informed. Communicate that the whole company is advancing as a result of your efforts.

- Prepare for meetings by studying the agenda in advance. You'll be ready to comment intelligently on the topics raised.

- Stop exaggerating the power difference and negativity. Humanize your manager and render the situation less threatening by realizing that you're not alone in this situation. Your boss may experience the same feelings you do when talking with her boss. And your employees may feel intimidated by you.

- When speaking with superiors, focus on the content of what you're saying, not the quiver in your voice. It will pass.

How to Ask for Help

There are many good reasons to ask your supervisor or others for help. Your request for assistance can furnish needed information, increase your confidence and comfort zone, decrease your anxiety, build rapport with a coworker, help to start and maintain a relationship, and prevent bigger problems down the road. If you don't know how to ask for help effectively and therefore don't receive it, you can feel disappointed, lonely, isolated, unsupported, and mistrustful of others.

But shy people often have difficulty requesting help from

others—especially their bosses. "I feel like if I have to ask for help, someone will think less of me, that I can't do the job," Allen confessed. "I'm always worried about the approval of others." In addition, you may not want to interrupt a supervisor who looks busy. Or you may believe your needs and questions are unimportant.

You can approach your busy boss (or coworker) with a request by saying, "When can we talk about the Collins account?" or "I need two minutes of your time. Is this a good time?" Or write out the question and ask for a reply. E-mail or a voice-mail message can be useful for simple queries. Be specific about what you need. Questions aren't a sign of weakness but a deterrent to future problems. Indeed, you may be saving your job (and your supervisor's hide) by drawing attention to a potential problem. Besides, in many instances, you may not be at fault if you can't figure out what to do. (Beware of negative internal attributions.) The task itself may be faulty.

Be aware of and address your anxiety. Recognize that you have difficulties initiating contact, so just push through it. The longer you hesitate, the worse your anxiety will become. In truth, authority figures always bring out shyness in people.

Interestingly, shy people exhibit certain gender-based patterns in asking for assistance. It is difficult for shy men to ask women for help and, conversely, it is difficult for shy women to ask men for help. In fact, shy women are much less likely to seek help from their male bosses than are their more outgoing female colleagues. This can affect a shy woman's performance and advancement. Her gregarious colleague may profit from this hesitancy by creating a closer relationship with her male boss.

Shy men don't ask women for help, especially when another woman is in the room. In fact, if a shy man works in an office with many women, he may isolate himself and withhold his questions. Why is this so? Perhaps it is related to sex-role beliefs: he may find it difficult to admit that he needs help from a woman. Or maybe he doesn't want to look bad or lose face. He may expect to make a negative impression by admitting that he doesn't know how to do something. Also, he must initiate this request interaction, which he believes can only underscore his insecurities and self-doubts.

Unfortunately, if you don't ask for help, you may do your job poorly and be overwhelmed by avoidance, procrastination, and stress. In addition, you can miss out on a good opportunity to establish contact with the opposite sex. Questions initiate interaction and maintain relationships. Besides, asking for help implies that the other person is of value, and that can be flattering.

Receiving Feedback

The ability to handle feedback is at the heart of gaining competence and confidence. It's the best way to understand how others (especially your boss) perceive you. The more feedback you get, the better off your career will be.

Of course, getting good feedback is rewarding; take it at face value while asking for areas in which you can improve. Reinforce your boss's statements by adding information. For example, you might say, "I'm glad you like my visual aids. I've been working hard on adding those to my presentations. In fact, recently I bought a new graphics program for my home computer for just that purpose."

Negative feedback is never easy, but refrain from becoming defensive. You need not provide an explanation. Jot down the comments to let your supervisor know you take them seriously. Ask reflective questions for clarification such as, "What about my summary was inconclusive or vague? Was my ending too weak? Was there no direct course of action for the customer to follow? I guess if someone made the same presentation to me, I might not know which direction to take either." Show your supervisor that you're unafraid of discussing shortcomings. Ask for more feedback.

Don't take the negative feedback personally—your performance is being evaluated, not you as a human being—even though your boss may try to make it personal. Turn the negative feedback into constructive criticism by generating alternate strategies: "Next time I'll . . ." Thank your supervisor for his candor and tell him that you may have questions later. Ask for a chance to show that you can act on his comments.

Don't let personal insecurities color your work. Avoid generalizations such as "I'm a failure," "I'll never be good at making group presentations," or "I will always stammer when I get into these kinds of situations." Don't dread feedback, just dread making the same mistake again and again.

Making Presentations

A hatred of public speaking is not the province of the shy—just about everyone fears it. Unless you have a job that requires it regularly, addressing a group is outside the normal comfort zone. Typically, we don't get going until the speech is almost over (we're slow to warm up), we feel uncomfortable at the center of attention (objective self-awareness), and we want to be recognized for our work but fear a bad outcome (approach/avoidance conflict). What's worse, often we must make presentations in front of authority figures, which intensifies our apprehensions. Anxiety creeps in, so we procrastinate and prepare inadequately.

The fear of public speaking involves your whole being. Physiologically, you are in an arousal state, with all of its attendant discomforts. But if the cat's got your tongue, you will have a hard time sounding eloquent.

On the cognitive level, you may be so disturbed by the task that you think catastrophically and imagine the worst. These thoughts overwhelm you so you don't prepare sufficiently or think through what you're going to say.

Since emotion is defined through a combination of cognitive and physiological labeling, while speaking publicly you can be intensely aroused and label it anxiety or you can make a favorable attribution and label it excitement and challenge.

Behaviorally, the way you label your emotions will have an impact. If you're anxious, your presentation may be disjointed, your speech choppy, and your eye contact limited. You present scanty information because you feel overwhelmed and doomed. If you label your emotions favorably, you will be expressive, expansive, and enthusiastic.

Interestingly, people respect those who speak in public because it takes the pressure off them. The obvious solution to your oratory jitters is preparation rather than procrastination. Leave as little to chance as possible by writing down the speech and reading it out loud to your family or into a tape recorder. Place your emphasis on content, not on yourself. As an expert, you'll feel more confident and won't worry that the question-and-answer period will catch you off guard. If you're concerned with getting across your message, you will focus less on your trembling hands and more on content.

Ad-libbing or speaking off-the-cuff, on the other hand, are the worst possible public-speaking strategies for shy people, as a friend of mine, the owner of a smoke shop, discovered. "A while back I had to talk about pipe smoking in front of a group of people whom I knew," he explained. "I totally froze up because I wasn't prepared. I just wanted to think up my speech on the spot. But even though it was something I knew about, I still froze. Now, even if I don't write down my speech, at least I think through what I'm going to say, so I know what I'm going to talk about."

People often assume they can ad-lib in order to avoid thinking about having to speak. They procrastinate to avoid the anxiety. This is self-defeating. If you have nothing prepared or rehearsed, you have nothing to say, and you can't do well. And once you're on the spot, objective self-awareness kicks in. You stutter and stammer and freeze like my friend did. Even celebrities and comedians who go on talk shows know in advance what the host will ask them, or they prepare jokes. They are aware that ad-libbing is difficult under pressure, and they don't want to appear like "real people" who stumble and fumble in public.

Some ways to help you feel comfortable with public speaking include:

Taking every opportunity you can. Speak at Toastmasters, church, or on social occasions like weddings so the behavior becomes habitual. Offer to make a toast at a dinner party. Serve as an emcee at a school, company, or church function like a talent show or recognition banquet. Introduce speakers at business seminars. Make opening and closing remarks at meetings. They don't have to be long—in fact, probably they shouldn't be.

Overpreparing. When you have a wealth of information from which to draw, you will stay within your comfort zone while speaking. You are the expert.

Reconnoitering. Find out as much as you can. Ask "Who is my audience? Can I bring props? Will there be other speakers? How long can I speak? Will there be a question-and-answer session afterward?"

Greeting attendees. If at all possible, befriend some of those who will hear you speak as they enter the room. This will speed your warm-up period and give you people with whom to make eye contact during the presentation.

Creating a hook. The same rules apply as in small talk with an individual: start with setting talk, and then go into pretopical talk. Make an observation that's general to everyone—a joke about the rubber banquet chicken or an anecdote about a prior meeting. Smile and use humor to open your speech. This warms up everyone, including you. When your audience laughs, it will buoy your confidence.

Addressing your anxiety. If anxiety encroaches and you hear your voice trembling, remind yourself that you are in your warm-up period and that the discomfort will soon pass. Stop, take a sip of water to regain your composure, breathe deeply, and continue. You can even comment on or joke about your nervousness to the audience. They will understand. And talking about it will help it go away.

Using props. Slides, overhead projections, or flip charts take you out of the limelight. As you gesture and point to the visual aids, you need not make eye contact with the audience. Reading from prepared materials helps keep your speech on course. One woman wrote "crib notes" on the backs of her flip-chart boards. Although she essentially read from these, her presentation came off naturally. Props create a more interactive process. The audience is involved visually as well as auditorially, and some people retain information more effectively that way.

Participating in Meetings

"In my professional life, I miss out on participating in group discussions," a young woman wrote to me. "I feel uncertain and stupid. I force myself to appear relaxed and outgoing, but inside I'm just crawling."

Shyness may make it difficult to participate in a group interaction. You may believe that your input is unworthy, or you may have trouble asking questions because you fear others will think them stupid or that you're wasting time. If an authority figure runs the meeting, that can intensify your fears, especially if you worry about evaluations. Meetings can also be competitive if everyone is vying to advance their own views.

But your silence may be construed as disinterest or lack of enthusiasm and can lead to social isolation. It's helpful to remember that meetings with coworkers are a little easier than with strangers because you all share a body of knowledge and a sense of familiarity.

To effectively participate at meetings, ask questions or make comments of extension. Relate what is said to other issues in the meeting. For instance, you might say, "You've talked about team building being profitable for the company. How does it relate not only to our department but across other departments?" This demonstrates that you're listening to what colleagues say, and it gives them the opportunity to clarify and elaborate on their ideas. Just like children on the playground, you offer something of value to build trust.

Brainstorming sessions in particular may be difficult for you. You may generate ideas slowly because you fear evaluation and are slow to warm up. But everything you say doesn't have to be brilliant. Others will put forth unworkable plans too. That's the whole point of brainstorming: to create as many ideas as possible.

Brainstorming involves everyone's cooperation, extension, and elaboration. Because so much sharing is involved, there's actually less evaluation and fewer reasons to feel self-consciousness. In fact, sessions will work (for everyone, shy or not) if three rules are observed:

1. Ideas must be generated without evaluation or criticism.

2. Ideas should be elaborated on and extended upon by others.

3. Ideas should be linked to the ideas of others.

If you are called upon to lead a brainstorming session, set the ground rules first so people feel safe to make fools of themselves. Research shows that if you evaluate early, the quality and quantity of ideas decrease, so permit criticism only during the weeding-out process. And make sure the whole group gets credit, not just the individual. Individual ownership of ideas breeds competition and reduces cooperation and creativity. Nobody wins.

Networking

Networking is a necessary part of the business world; it provides valuable opportunities to make business contacts in a relaxed atmosphere and helps you put faces to the names of people with whom you are doing business. The overriding feature of networking is ambiguity, since it is a pseudosocial situation—neither purely social nor purely business. The protocol is unclear. Attendance is usually not mandatory, but it would look bad if one stayed away.

Not surprisingly, however, networking can be a nightmare for shy people: a room full of strangers, lots of small talk and jockeying for position, and many authority figures to fear. Indeed, the powerful people there have the opportunity to judge you, not your work. Conversations can be evaluative and superficial. If the event is brief and you're stuck in the approach/avoidance conflict or are slow to warm up, you may meet few people. Furthermore, often these meetings occur at the end of the day when energy is low. Alcohol is sometimes involved, so it may be difficult to judge what's really going on. You may feel drained because you're performing. Many people dislike this aspect of their jobs, but they must do it anyway.

Successfully navigating networking events calls for a combination of charm, assertiveness, and tact. It requires you to expand your comfort zone from social to professional situations. It is much like dating and interviewing—situations with which you are familiar. Networking is not impossible. As you become more outgoing socially, you will have an easier time dealing with socializing for your job. In a large gathering, there is a lot of room for improvement; if you don't hit it off with one person, you may do well with someone else.

The following strategies may help you through this difficult activity:

Don't find excuses. Your boss will know who shows up and is willing to forgo free time to be part of the team.

Never underestimate the power of small talk. If you believe you're poor at small talk, you may avoid it, but it's necessary to make a good impression and initial connections with others. Remember the rules of small talk, and find common ground with others. Be a host and invite them into your conversation. Excuse yourself gracefully by saying, "It was great to speak with you."

Do your research before you go. Networking becomes less intimidating when you know what to expect. Find out who will attend, and target a few people to talk to. Prepare questions, topics, and anecdotes. Carry business cards or relevant props.

Establish contact. You need not worry about talking to a person all night or closing the deal on the spot. Follow up the next day in a manner with which you're comfortable: on the phone, by E-mail, with a quick note.

Don't drink. Free drinks are tempting, but if you lose control and become sloppy at a business function, you'll make a bad impression. Liquor interferes with clear thinking.

Circulate. Talking to one person all night only defeats the purpose. After you've made contact, move on to the next.

Give yourself a time limit. The event won't feel so overwhelming if you've committed for only one hour of your life. A time limit also helps you focus on who is important to meet. You can always extend your time there if you're enjoying yourself.

Focus on your social successes. In your Shy Life Journal, note what worked. Use that information at future networking events.

Create a comfort zone. Bring a colleague along if that helps you feel more relaxed. Join professional associations and attend lectures and seminars to accustom yourself to these situations.

Becoming a Successfully Shy Manager

Management requires you to have delicate people skills while conveying a sense of authority. At the heart of a good management style is communication, which you use to exchange information in a constructive manner. You obtain what you need and explain what you want from your employees and how your company's objectives can be met. These skills help you give and receive feedback, delegate assignments, deal effectively with authority figures, mediate disputes, and foster creative expression among your supervisees.

Your position puts you squarely between higher-ups and subordinates. With those above you in the hierarchy, you must make your needs and accomplishments known, obtain the resources you require to get the job done, receive and apply feedback, and get credit where it is due. With those below, you must become comfortable making requests and giving orders, conveying authority and being assertive, providing feedback and building camaraderie. You must approach your employees often to ensure that they do their jobs and to maintain morale. For a shy person, that's a tall order indeed.

Management is one of the most difficult jobs a shy employee can undertake. You can be handicapped by underdeveloped social skills, which may erode the output and the esprit de corps of your team. You may reinforce quietness in your department. This can create a harmful model for your subordinates; denying them the opportunity to interact can lead to poor morale. Negotiation and tact can also be difficult for you. If you're negatively preoccupied with yourself, it's hard to be socially sensitive and to discern others' feelings—musts in skillful managing.

If you're inclined to lock yourself in your office, you won't get good results from your employees because you seem aloof. You may be oblivious to what's going on in your department (both the good and the bad). You may miss your employees' strengths and limitations, and others may perceive you as harsh. Finishing projects may be difficult for you either because you're poor at delegating or because your employees make empty promises. They resent being asked to put out for someone they see as uncaring and who doesn't engage in small talk with them.

Filled with your own self-doubts, negative evaluations, and uncertainties, you may also have trouble exercising authority over others. You may worry too much about your employees' feelings and not enough about the job at hand. You don't want them to take criticism personally or be offended in any way because you know how bad that feels, but if you're submissive, your employees may take advantage of you.

To be a good manager, you must concern yourself not just with the bottom line but also with building rapport in your department. You may believe that it's acceptable to communicate only through E-mail, but your workers need human contact. Inaugurate after-hours gatherings, social events, and retreats. Be sure to use your small-talk skills at these events. Try in-house training seminars at which you do the training or rotate assignments so everyone gets a chance to be in authority or in a subordinate position. Provide regular performance reviews—every few weeks rather than every six months. This helps with the warm-up process and allows supervisees to accept feedback more readily because they are used to it. Frequent performance reviews are easier for you because they're shorter.

Allen experienced an intense approach/avoidance conflict around leadership positions. "I wanted to be a manager," he explained to me, "but I didn't want it because I didn't want the feelings that went along with it—when I get shy I freeze up and can't talk real well; I stammer. I wanted the job and I avoided it. It was an inner struggle." It may help to remember that in most cases, being a manager is just an extension of your old job with a few new responsibilities.

Making Requests

Research has shown that most shy people rate themselves as ineffective at persuading others to do what they want. They go into the request with dread and expectations of failure. They may procure promises of action but little follow-through. This can leave a shy manager chronically frustrated and disappointed. Difficulty in making requests becomes yet another self-fulfilling prophecy—your thoughts do affect your (and others') behavior.

But there are effective ways to make requests of your employees. When asking someone to perform a task, you must be verbally skillful, you must think of the goal rather than the "imposition," and you cannot come across coldly. Here are some helpful suggestions.

- Practice out loud or in your head so you're fluent.

- Be specific. Tell your employee what you want and how you want it done. (This is particularly important for employees who are too shy to ask for information.)

- Set a deadline or other limit, and adhere to it consistently. Inform the employee of the consequences of being late. Follow through with those consequences, if necessary.

- Stress the importance of the task and your employee's contribution.

- Give the context of the task so employees can troubleshoot on their own and understand the ultimate purpose of their work.

- Break the assignment into smaller tasks.

- Schedule times when you will be available to take questions along the way, but mention that you'll check on progress periodically.

- If necessary, give reminders or follow-up requests.

- Ask for updates on projects during informal times in the office—when people arrive, before and after lunch, at the end of the day.

- Appreciate your employees' contributions, and thank them in writing, if possible.

Giving Feedback

Just as feedback can be difficult to receive, it may be equally difficult to impart. To ensure that your employee is ready to hear it, notify him in advance and be prepared to talk at the appointed time. Be specific about your needs and how your employee can meet them. Set up a timetable. Follow up with a written summary of conversation, and ask for an acknowledgment. The more concrete you are, the easier the process will be.

Make the feedback behavioral and not personal. Rather than saying, "You were careless," say, "You need a more specific course of action for the client." Rather than "You were unclear," advise, "Maybe more visual aids and a bulleted summary will get your ideas across more clearly." If you talk about how the employee erred, offer corrective suggestions. You won't just be complaining; you'll get results. Provide alternative courses of action so your employee will have guidelines. Temper negative feedback with praise. Give your employee a chance to improve, and keep lines of communication open.

How to Handle a Shy Employee

As a shy person yourself, you may recognize shyness in an employee. Be sensitive to the many issues he must cope with. As a result of his approach/avoidance conflict, he may hesitate to talk to you or speak up in meetings. He may need guidance but not seek it.

There are ways you can help:

- Ask for opinions from employees who are rarely vocal, and let them know that you value them and that they can trust you.

- Vary the modes of communication. Don't just rely on written comments. Use E-mail, phone, and memo messages, but also meet with shy employees one-on-one. Vary the location—your office, her cubicle, over lunch. This shows you're willing to talk at any time and in almost any circumstance. Follow verbal feedback with written or electronic confirmation or written feedback with a phone call or personal contact. This helps get shy employees out of the habit of communicating via E-mail exclusively. You are modeling new behaviors.

- Be respectful of the warm-up period. A shy employee may initially resist change. Persist, and give him time to adjust.

- Open the lines of communication. Encourage shy employees to make their needs known to you.

- Be a mentor—take a shy employee along on sales calls so he will have an example to emulate.

- Recognize how shyness may affect an employee's performance. His people skills and not his work skills may be holding him back.

Positive reinforcement does wonders for shy employees—eventually. They rate themselves more favorably after a success. However, research has shown that they need more than a single success and more encouragement than their nonshy colleagues to feel confident. Perhaps they see the first achievement as a fluke or good luck. Perhaps they are slow to warm to the idea of doing well. Continue to encourage shy employees with positive feedback, and in time you will both reap the rewards.

A Last Word on Successfully Shy Workers

Work interactions are no different from interactions in other areas of your life. The same rules apply. As you become more successful socially, your skills will easily translate to the workplace. If you're shy at work but relaxed with friends and family, make your coworkers friends. By the same token, the lessons you learn at work can transfer to your personal life. If you're confident at work but not at a party, think of the party as a job. Learn what's expected, prepare, ask questions, make contacts.

Allen found a way out of his shyness in the workplace. With the advice of a psychologist, he used "positive cognition activities." "Whenever I had a negative thought I wrote it down, and then I would write a positive thought to replace it. At first it didn't work—actually it would have, but I didn't do it enough. Then I persevered and became consistent, and it finally worked. I forced myself into situations that I wouldn't have been in before. The more I did it, the easier it got. As I did this, my confidence grew."

Today Allen has an engineering sales position. "Not only do I have to go out and get new customers, but I have to keep the customers we already have." That takes people skills, and Allen seems to have acquired them.

"A lot of people think that there is no cure for shyness," he continued. "But a lot of people don't realize that it takes time to get over this problem. Shyness and anxiety are habits that form over years and years. You can't change that overnight. It takes years to unlearn. I'm proud that I've come as far as I have."

15

The Successfully Shy Global Citizen

Jonathan works from his home. He's involved in a multinational import-export business, mostly in Asia, and deals with all of his clients through phone, fax, and computer.

Kevin grabs a six-pack of beer and logs onto the Internet after work Friday night. He spends most of his free time these days on-line, roaming from one chat room to the next.

Candace pulls into the driveway of her condo complex, activates the automatic garage door without leaving her car, enters her apartment, calls in for Chinese take-out, turns on the TV, and settles in for a long night at home without having to speak to a soul.

All of these people lead lonely, shy lives. Their experiences teach us not only about how shyness impacts our individual behavior, but also about shyness in our society. In this chapter we will explore the widely differing attitudes toward shyness in various cultures and how Western society, through increasing fragmentation and the use of technology, seems to reinforce and augment it.

Shyness and Culture

Shyness impacts us beyond our personal identities or interpersonal relations. Because it is a personality trait, it exists universally. Interestingly, however, it is neither defined nor experienced in the same way from one culture to the next, but varies from culture to culture and among ethnic or geographic groups within cultures. Some societies encourage shyness, while others discourage it. Shyness, although universal, is still a relative, culture-bound phenomenon.

How can you discern the role of shyness in your own culture?

It's difficult without an external point of reference. You can only understand your society in relation to others. Researchers, therefore, have studied how other cultures view shyness and encourage or discourage it among their members. They have been able to trace the roots of shyness back to attributional patterns (how one characterizes failure and success), social norms (what is considered acceptable in terms of personal space or social graces), and cultural ideologies (whether the culture prizes the group or the individual) within each society.

The Role of Attribution

In his cross-cultural research, Philip Zimbardo found that there were differing levels of shyness in the various ethnic student populations he tested at Stanford University. Japanese-American and Taiwanese-American students consistently expressed the highest levels of shyness, while Jewish students expressed the lowest.

Based on these clues, Zimbardo traveled to Japan, Taiwan, and Israel to study college students in their home environments. His on-site investigations revealed even greater cultural differences than were evident in the American survey. In Israel only 30 percent of college-age students reported being shy, while 60 percent of those in Japan and Taiwan admitted to this trait.

From conversations with foreign colleagues and parents, Zimbardo acquired insights into the cultural roots of shyness. One of the keys was attributional style. As you recall from Chapter 6, attribution is the way we explain behavior to ourselves and others. Zimbardo examined how parents heaped blame or praise on their youngsters' performance. When a child tries and fails at a task, who is rebuked? When a child tries and succeeds, who is commended?

He found that in Japan, if a child does well, his parents get the credit. So do his grandparents, teachers, coaches, and even Buddha. If there's any praise left, only then does the child receive it. But if the child fails, he is fully culpable and cannot blame anyone else. An "I can't win" belief takes hold, so children of this culture neither take risks nor attempt acts that attract notice. As the Japanese proverb states, "The nail that stands out is pounded down."

A low-key interpersonal style results from this cultural attitude. Children are likely to be modest and quiet. They do little to call attention to themselves and are much less likely to speak or act up in a social gathering. (In fact, Asian-American students score lowest in studies of the tendency to behave in ways that make them stand out or seem unique.)

Israeli children grow up with the opposite attributional style. If a child tries, he will be rewarded regardless of his success. Consider the Yiddish term *nachas*, which means deriving great pleasure and pride from one's *child*'s accomplishments. If a child tries to build a kite, his parents experience *nachas* and point out what a great little engineer he is. If the kite doesn't fly, parents blame the wind. If a child tries and fails in a competitive setting, parents and others might reproach the coach for faulty training. In such a supportive environment, a child senses that failure costs little—and so is willing to take risks.

With such a belief system, a person is likely to develop chutzpah, the audacity that emboldens one to venture forth— with or without the talent. Children growing up with such a value system are more apt to speak up in class or ask someone to dance at a party without overwhelming self-consciousness. Of course, this is not to say that no Jewish children are shy, for certainly shyness exists among all of us. It is a safe bet, however, that a shy Israeli would not be considered shy in Japan.

The Role of Social Norms

A Frenchman would think little of greeting a male friend with kisses on both cheeks, while an American man might be horrified at the thought. Individuals on the East or West Coast of the United States may feel freer to hug a new acquaintance or offer some intimate tidbit of information than those living in more conservative areas of the Deep South or the Midwest. These social norms are the unwritten rules within a society designed to facilitate and govern day-to-day social interactions. They include behavior such as maintaining personal space and eye contact, touching, and adhering to a certain level of self-disclosure. Each culture has its own set of rules, and these vary within cultures from one geographic area or subculture to the next.

Harvard psychologist Nancy Snidman studied social norms in relation to child-rearing in Ireland and the United States. She found no differences in the degree of nervous-system reactivity in four-month-old babies from both cultures, but at age five the Irish children didn't talk as much, nor were they as loud as the Americans.

The difference lies in the cultural norms expressed in child-rearing. Using American norms of social behavior as the standard of comparison, the normal Irish children would be labeled shy. But in their own culture, with their own norms of behavior, they are not. By the same token, the Irish may perceive American kids as boorish.

Similarly, studies of Hispanic children have shown that those raised in Caribbean cultures are encouraged to be sociable and expressive, while those raised in Peruvian Inca homes are taught to be quiet and reserved.

Sometimes social norms differ among ethnic groups within one culture, and that can cause relational confusions. Consider the issue of eye contact, which, according to experts, is often responsible for problems in cross-race interactions among blacks and whites in the United States. William Ickes at the University of Texas at Arlington explains that blacks tend to consider it "rude, confrontational, or disrespectful to maintain eye contact with a person who is speaking, whereas whites tend to consider it evasive, inattentive, or disrespectful not to do so." As a result of these differing social norms, both African-Americans and Caucasians can experience their visual interaction as "somewhat awkward and uncomfortable."

It is easy to misinterpret what others are feeling if you base your reading of their nonverbal cues on your own social norms, rather than theirs.

The Role of Cultural Ideologies

Cultural norms relate to behavior, but ideology refers to a culture's underlying philosophy. Indeed, attributions and norms derive from a culture's ideology. Two distinct ideologies have been identified: one that stresses the importance of the group and one that emphasizes the individual.

Collectivism

In the late 1990s, as businesses in Asia failed due to a downturn in the economy, executives of bankrupt corporations paced outside their insolvent companies wearing sandwich boards on which they had written personal apologies. What would cause a CEO to take personal responsibility for financial ruin that had its roots in government policies? The cultural ideology of these countries is one of collectivism, and this philosophy explains behavior that can seem odd to those unfamiliar with it.

In a collective culture, the group is more important than the one, people must cooperate to keep society together, and communication is restricted to maintain the status quo. Expression of individual wants and needs is suppressed if it conflicts with group desires. The welfare of family, hometown, employer, and country surpass personal freedoms. This type of culture often arises when physical space is limited: people are concerned about offending others because it is so very easy to offend.

An individual is careful to preserve his relations with these institutions because when he draws attention to himself, it reflects badly not only on him, but also on his social network. One eschews controversy to avoid embarrassing one's family.

Shyness and related characteristics like modesty are encouraged in collective cultures. They keep the fabric of society tightly woven. Individuals refrain from speaking out, erupting in rage, or asserting their needs unless the group encourages it, and the group rarely encourages it unless it benefits the group. Individuals are reticent in order to spare their group adverse attention.

Shame—remorse for having violated the group's norms—is a salient emotion in these cultures. Negative behavior brings shame to families, employees, customers, countrymen. An airline executive, for instance, will publicly cry and hang his head after a plane crash, stressing how awful it makes him feel to bring disgrace on his company and nation.

People in collective cultures act shy, not because they worry about self-evaluation (as Westerners do), but because they fear extended evaluation. They might reason, "If I do badly at this party, people will think my parents didn't raise me well," rather than "People will think I'm a fool."

As we have seen from Dr. Zimbardo's work, the Japanese experience a high degree of what we call shyness. This comes from internal negative attributions, as I've noted, but also from the use of shame or *haji* to regulate public behavior. *Haji* is central to how the Japanese organize their society and involves the feeling of always being watched by the "eyes of other people." It makes one feel inferior and decreases the chances of stepping out of bounds. The "eyes" are always evaluating members of society, preventing them from breaking taboos. They are symbolic of increased objective self-awareness, social comparison, and evaluations.

The Japanese follow the norm to become more reserved. We label their behavior shy because their reticence and self-consciousness looks like shyness to us. Indeed, what they perceive as boisterous and overly social behavior may be friendliness to us.

By their discipline style Japanese mothers instill and encourage this attitude in their children at a very young age. Rather than saying a certain behavior is "bad," a Japanese mother may scold her child by claiming that his behavior will bring shame on her or that others will ridicule him for it. From this, children learn that others are always observing and evaluating their behavior.

In fact, shyness in the form of restraint is so desirable, Japanese mothers claim they can detect it in their five-month-old infants, and they try to encourage it in their children. This early training leads to staunch loyalty to family, school, or corporation. You would not want to shame them by acting out or rebelling.

Because they are so oriented to the collective rather than to the individual, the Japanese are likely to suffer from ego uncertainty or lack of a proper independent identity. This can lead them to be more passive and restrained but also kinder and more flexible. Shame keeps individuals in line by fostering bad feelings about independent thoughts, making one's own way in the world, or leaving an employer.

There are various ways in which Japanese people alleviate their identity uncertainty. They depend on some group—family, school, company, sports teams—to provide them with a sense of identity. They are highly conscious of status and acutely aware that others are evaluating them. And they conform and strive for perfection to leave no room for criticism.

American shy people are also highly conscious of status, and they strive for perfectionism, too.

In India, the concept of shame is not advanced as much as that of modesty and shyness. Indian women are encouraged to cultivate *layja* or modesty in order to develop and maintain relationships. Similarly, they are discouraged from expressing anger, which disrupts relationships. This submissive attitude keeps society intact, since only a few people can give orders or act out their hostility. Emotional restraint and modest clothing keep women in their traditional "place." Silence is encouraged in such collectivist societies.

Individualism

In contrast to collective societies, where personal needs are subordinated to the group, members of individualistic societies place more emphasis on themselves. People identify themselves based on internal factors (personal interests, individual advancement, and personality traits such as shyness or aggressiveness) rather than on their participation in a group. They may speak out with little regard to shaming their family, town, or employer.

Gary, a young man in Idaho, decided to become a chef rather than take over the family farm, as his family wanted. That would shame a family in a collective culture. But in an individualistic society Gary can express his sense of self and feel less concerned about the collective. However, in this society, it's not enough to know who you are. You must also act on that self-knowledge. Self-assertion is paramount, and great importance is placed on making your own way without group restrictions.

Guilt becomes the overriding emotion. It is a sense of personal failure and means that an internal rather than a group norm has been violated. When you feel guilty, you seem compelled to explain or account for your shortcomings. Personal failure leads either to face-saving defensive attributions—you explain what happened by blaming others ("I was a victim") or pessimistic attributions—you blame yourself ("Something flawed in me caused this to happen"). Shy people use the latter.

Shyness is discouraged in individualistic cultures, where members are expected to be independent and bold and to pave their own way.

The United States is the most obvious example of an individualistic society. Our culture was established on the principle that individuals have the right to seek their own version of happiness—anything from practicing religion to speaking out to leaving their hometown for another city. Our founding fathers were rejected for their religious beliefs, so they took great pains to assure the freedom for all of us to speak our minds. Today we value boldness and individuality. "Talkers" are perceived as influential and become role models. We place a great premium on verbal ability, courage, and candor.

Shyness is part of the human condition, so a certain number of people will feel shy no matter what culture they live in. What differs is how shy people interpret their shyness, which is largely due to cultural influences. For example, if you are shy in Japan or India, you may feel perfectly at ease, since your culture supports and encourages this behavior. However, because shyness is frowned upon in our society, if you are shy you may believe that you're not living up to the norm or the ideal. You don't boldly act out your inner self like the most successful individuals in our society—people like John F. Kennedy or Donald Trump. Because your personal identity may be inconsistent with the cultural ideal, you're more likely to feel negativity and pain about your shyness. The belief that you don't fit into the standards of our culture lowers your self-esteem.

Moreover, since social networks are loose and transitory in an individualistic society, shy people are often left without stable comfort zones and the security of family members or long-term friends for support. As a retail salesman in his early thirties wrote to me, "Personal situations are more awkward than they should be. I have recently relocated to another state with no family or friends. I am having a hard time making new friends without the social comfort base that my friends provided back home."

If you're shy, you may not be as assertive as people are encouraged to be. Anxiety comes from having to take risks without guidelines from an intact group, a natural source of support in a collective society but one that can be sadly lacking in an individualistic society.

The Best of Both Worlds

Can a culture be built on self-focused people? I believe that there is such as thing as too much individualism. Our society would do much better with an integration of individuality and social relatedness. I believe we should encourage more social interest so we anchor our identities on what we share with others: community involvement, ethnic affiliations, and prosocial action. Common interests bind us together.

The following are ways to use the best of this culture within your family or group of friends.

Praise successes. At the personal level, don't just ruminate on failures, focus on what you do well. When raising children or dealing with employees, recognize accomplishments.

Minimize failure. Learn to reframe "failure" as a learning experience for yourself. Offer social support to others, particularly in times of defeat.

Encourage moderate risk-taking. Expand your own comfort zone slowly, and encourage the same in others by praising success and minimizing failure.

Increase tolerance of ambiguity. Ambiguity comes with change and expanding your comfort zone. Realize that, initially, trying new activities will involve frustration and confusion for you and others. Be patient.

Accept diversity. If you are to become a successfully shy global citizen, you must be willing to expose yourself to new ideas, new people, and new situations. At a cultural level, it's important to be aware that there is a wide range of individual differences. Learn to tolerate and accept diversity not only in yourself (good as well as unfavorable information about yourself) but also in others.

It's a challenge to be shy in an individualistic society, but you need not give in to the pressure to be an extrovert. Just because others are rude and noisy, you don't have to be. Rather than practicing individualism—self-centeredness—I believe it's advisable to practice what the eminent psychologist Gordon Allport called "personalism"—understanding the unique nature, operation, and expression of your personality within the culture and how it can best serve you.

Knowing how cultural ideologies and norms influence your shyness and expressing it in your own unique ways will make it easier for you to live the successfully shy life. You don't have to be the life of the party to have a good time. It may be more "personalistic" for you to talk to a wide variety of people at the party, rather than try to make everyone focus on you, as the extrovert might.

Why Shyness Is on the Increase

Studies show that between 1975 and 1992, shyness increased in the United States. Despite this surge, however, it is becoming increasingly difficult to be shy. The push toward individualism has intensified in America over the last fifty years. Norms have shifted from a society anchored in stability and continuity to one touting transition and instability. There's more "willful self-assertion," increased concern with the self and less with others, and greater narcissism. We turn away from defining ourselves in terms of formal roles and broad social values and turn toward our inner needs and traits.

Since we show less interest in maintaining tradition, we have been experiencing the loss of extended family and neighborhoods. As our lives become more unstable and uncertain, we tend to look toward our own self-interest. We become ruder, angrier, less tolerant.

In addition, our society is becoming more socially fragmented. More people are living alone (in 1940, only 8 percent of all households consisted of one person, while today about

25 percent do). Couples marry later, have fewer children, get divorced quicker, and think little of moving across the country. Fragmentation seeps into our daily lives. Our more transient relationships breed social isolation.

Suburbanization also decreases connection. People move to the suburbs to find stability, predictability, and community, but today they live in homogeneous pockets: gated communities, planned subdivisions, and condo complexes where diversity disappears. Neighborhoods become balkanized as people shrink into comfort zones of sameness. Such segmentation is an example of people living alone collectively. When the crime and drugs of city life find their way to these pristine communities, residents isolate themselves further, fleeing to the wide-open spaces of Montana and Wyoming.

Not only do the old social networks fall away, but also we must quickly establish new ones. Few people still live in the communities in which they were raised. The lack of a solid social network (comfort zone) can increase shyness, at least temporarily. The breakdown of social norms means that the level of uncertainty is heightened and shyness grows.

Consider what happens when you attend an old friend's wedding. You will probably know many of the guests, and you'll feel comfortable about how you're expected to behave. Contrast this to trying a restaurant in the neighborhood to which you just moved. You're unfamiliar with the waitress, disinclined to talk to strangers (unless you're very gregarious), and constantly checking your behavior against that of others. The uncertainty renders it unlikely you will feel relaxed enough to strike up a conversation and make a new friend.

In the current social climate, we create friendships we can't always count on; even our new friends can move away. We continually cope with people coming and going from our lives.

Moreover, we may encounter more people in the media than we do in real life. Indeed, the media becomes the glue that holds society together. But social comparison can become skewed if we lose sight of our peers. On TV we only see extremes—Dennis Rodman, Jenny McCarthy, Rosie O'Donnell. We compare ourselves to them and feel inferior. Even on run-of-the-mill television, nobody is at a loss for words because of editing and scripted dialogue. When we fumble in real life, we scold ourselves for being less witty and articulate than those who live out their dramas in the media. We become dissatisfied with our family and friends—no one matches up.

The average sitcom is based on hostile humor and put-downs. This leads to decreased patience and civility; we forget that others have feelings. As our culture becomes more fragmented and depersonalized, it becomes easier and more acceptable to turn aggressive and nasty.

Although women have come a long way in creating options for themselves (they can be either traditional or independent), to a large extent men don't have as many alternatives. While there has been much talk about men who are "in touch with their feelings" and who don't have to pretend that they're invulnerable (most shy men fit into this category), such men receive little respect from male peers, some women, and the media.

If shy people accept these cultural norms, they may have a hard time. They don't "willfully assert" themselves but rather sink into their shyness ever more deeply as they find themselves lost in this aggressive society. They become mired, basing their identities on personal attributes (as others in our culture do) but unable or unwilling to assert themselves in ways they are expected to. As others become louder, ruder, and more impatient, shy people are deprived of the decency and the adequate warm-up period they need. During these chaotic times, they may feel guilt that others don't feel (they are not living up to their own standards). When people are rude and angry, rather than thinking society is falling apart, they blame themselves and feel inadequate.

The more fragmentation we see, the greater the number of

shy people. The breakdown makes them anxious and self-conscious, so they avoid and retreat. As the clamor becomes more tumultuous, stronger people grow louder, but those who are reserved grow quieter. Fragmentation is divisive.

The Role of Technology

People don't think of shyness and technology as being related, but they are. Reflect on my own experience, writing this book in isolation. Within the small comfort zone of my study, dressed in my pajamas and listening to my favorite music, I had a computer, fax, phone, and E-mail—everything I needed. Everything, that is, but human contact. When, in this isolated world, I received phone calls unrelated to work, I found myself relishing the contact. I engaged in small talk even when it was unnecessary to the task at hand. The more I thought about this and read about technical advances, the more I saw that our technological society can promulgate and reinforce shyness.

As our culture increasingly isolates us and thwarts our tendencies to become close to others, mistrust grows. We become more competitive and less likely to take an interest in our communities. Consequently, we may spend more leisure time relating electronically—a seemingly safe way out.

The apparent absence of self-consciousness, the anonymity, the ability to "meet" more people or to limit personal interaction on the Internet do seem to make social contact easier for the shy. Since you're not approaching someone "in person," it's easy to avoid the anxiety caused by fear of rejection and the approach/avoidance conflict. If you are slow to warm up, you can lurk in chat rooms without contributing and still feel as if you've made contact with others. You can also communicate on-line but delay meeting in person. You can choose to whom you talk and you can rely on your favored topic in the chat room of your choice to remain safely ensconced in your comfort zone.

But far from being a cure-all for shy people, technology is a double-edged sword. It's easy to hide behind the Internet and use it as an excuse to avoid meeting people. When this happens, your social skills may decline and personal contact becomes more difficult. Indeed, relying on technology limits contact with others, and this has further implications for our culture. It depersonalizes, which can lead to more hostility. Computer users tend to be more outspoken on-line and can lose patience with those who aren't as quick. It's easy to reject or "flame" someone when you don't know who he is.

An even more disturbing potential is what I refer to as "electronic cleansing." On-line, you can eliminate, delete, or simply ignore the input of those with whom you don't agree or who are different from you. It's easy if they're just an E-mail name to you. But that leads to a loss of tolerance for diversity and ambiguity. Much like ethnic cleansing, electronic cleansing creates an environment that excludes people who are different. There is no need for negotiation or compromise. It's easier to avoid than approach, to restrict the comfort zone rather than expand it. But approach, negotiation, and expanding comfort zones create civility and community.

Technology is acceptable as long as you use it to *supplement* your personal contact. It isn't a crutch, and it shouldn't be more important than getting out and being with people. Remember, overcoming shyness doesn't just mean being able to talk to strangers. It also means being free enough to maintain close relationships—and you can only accomplish that in person.

The influence of technology can manifest itself in three ways: cocooning, telecommuting, and teledating. Let's look at these more carefully.

Cocooning

Cocooning occurs when you meet most of your personal needs within your home with big-screen TV, pay-per-view movies or videos, Internet chatting, food delivery, and shopping on the Internet.

Unfortunately, when you satisfy all of your needs within your home, you lose the spontaneity of social contact. Your social skills may weaken, and your tolerance for frustration decreases. You may be rude to a waitress, talk in a movie theater, or become highly impatient if you must wait in line. You may forget to consider others' needs.

If you already have the tendency to avoid social situations, you may believe that cocooning is a viable solution to your problems. Unfortunately, there is no substitute for human contact. You still crave the companionship of others. But as more people retreat into their homes, you will have fewer social opportunities. Moreover, if you're isolated all day (either at home or working with taciturn people), cocooning offers no respite from the grind of everyday life. You need more balance.

Cocooning is only valuable as an occasional retreat from the demands of the world. As Carl Jung pointed out, we must try to seek balance between internal and external, introversion and extroversion. If you've been working all day by yourself, you need to offset that with a social life. On the other hand, if you're dealing with the public all day, you might need to withdraw at night.

Also, if others have become more impatient as a result of their own retreat into the home, they may not grant you time to warm up in a social situation. Attention spans shorten if we become accustomed to satisfying our needs immediately.

The obvious solution is to log off the computer. Become acutely aware of the balance in your life. One night of cocooning per week is enough—don't stretch it to six or seven evenings. Stay home if you're engaged in a constructive activity, such as talking to your family, phoning friends, and reading, but watching TV or surfing the Net nightly for hours are passive endeavors that can interfere with social contact.

How will you know if you're too deeply embedded in your cocoon? Answer the following questions:

- Do you purchase products over the Internet because you hate going to crowded stores?

- Do you have more mediated contact (e.g., watching TV, surfing the Net, or using ATMs) than personal contact?

- When was the last time you took a walk around your neighborhood after dinner rather than sit in front of the TV?

- Do you know more about some celebrities' lives than about your family members'?

- Do you wait for movies to come out on video rather than seeing them at the theater?

- Do you screen your phone calls?

- Would you rather get take-out than eat in a restaurant?

- Do you see socializing as stressful rather than stimulating?

The more of these questions you answer in the affirmative, the more you are engaged in the process of cocooning. It may be time to pull the plug.

Telecommuting

True telecommuters work at home in isolation. They communicate mostly by phone, modem, or fax. They work their own hours and go into the office only occasionally for a big meeting, a crisis, or a holiday party. They may also work in an office but carry out most of their projects alone or with people who are physically absent.

While ostensibly convenient, telecommuting has many drawbacks for shy people. If you're already a cocooner or are socially avoidant, it can reduce the precious little human contact you receive every day. If your comfort zone has hardened to the small space of your home office, you may become anxious when you see people. Besides, if you only communicate in person when there's a crisis, there's no warm-up period, and that can worsen an already stressful situation. Furthermore, telecommuters can lack a sense of community; when a problem arises, there's no one around to pitch in. And it's easier for bosses to downsize unfamiliar faces.

Just like cocooning, telecommuting is a poor strategy for shy people. Social skills decline when you're out of touch with others. At meetings with "coworkers" you must be unusually aggressive to make your needs known. The less time you spend with others, the less confident you become, and the more important any time spent is. Indeed, you might work yourself into a telecommuting funk, losing interest in your social life or activities outside your home. Here are the signs:

- Low-grade depression. You don't feel "up to" going out with other people or taking care of yourself. Exercise, personal hygiene, and even health suffer.

- Unwillingness to try new activities. You'd rather watch TV than try a new restaurant or attend a play.

- Loss of concentration and poor time management. It's easy to let the workweek slide into the weekend if you don't have regular hours or if you procrastinate until just before a deadline.

- Loneliness. You can become isolated if you don't know other people with your schedule.

- Pessimistic social outlook. It's hard to make conversation with others if you've spent the day alone, especially if you see social interactions as difficult and unpleasant, or if others are unable to relate to what you do in isolation. There's no office gossip.

- Lack of exercise. Why bother if nobody sees you?

- Increased recreational time alone. You watch more television, spend hours surfing the Net, and so on.

- Drinking. You may drink to overcome loneliness and boredom or to cope with the low-grade depression.

Dealing with a telecommuting funk can be difficult if you're shy because you'll have to make a greater effort to reach out and meet your need for human contact. Part-time telecommuting can be a viable solution. It involves going to a satellite office on a regular basis, say, once a week. There you come into contact with other workers in your area. This works well, since people who labor at home often become lonely and need to share space, equipment, and regular interactions with others.

Here are some other strategies for dealing with telecommuting.

- Schedule one social event per day. Make sure you get out. Have lunch at a restaurant, take a class, go to the market and the bank, meet a friend in the evening.

- Join professional associations. It can help you personally and professionally by expanding business contacts as well as your comfort zone.

- Meet with your manager or clients as often as possible. It's not enough to communicate by E-mail or to talk on the phone.

- If you manage people who work in their homes, make sure to increase face-to-face contact. Hold weekly meetings, maintain a regular phone schedule, publish employee newsletters more often, and schedule frequent social gatherings.

Teledating and Telefriendships

Teledating and telefriendships occur when most of your interpersonal contact is through Internet chat rooms, E-mail, bulletin boards, mindless Net surfing, or interactive role-playing games.

The upside is that you may become emboldened to communicate with people once freed of the worry associated with social anxiety or making a good impression. It's easier to become acquainted with those who are generally interested in the same topics you are. You can filter out people based on your favored topic or by relying on a computerized matchmaking service. You have time to compose your thoughts on E-mail, so you say exactly what you want to.

The downside is that chat rooms can be electronic meat markets akin to singles bars. And someone's ability to con you on-line is much greater than occurs in face-to-face meetings. (Men can masquerade as women and vice versa, people can lie about their age, and so on.) Besides, if you rely on these "relationships" to meet your social needs, you may be fooled into thinking they are real friendships. In truth, Internet buddies aren't companions who will go out with you. Once you turn off the computer, you're alone again.

There is no substitute for a real, live companion. Besides, when you meet someone in person that you've only known on-line, the shyness may return. You may have to experience the approach/avoidance conflict and the warm-up period all over again.

The fact of the matter is, shy people can even be shy on the Internet. They can *lurk* in chat rooms, reading others' communications without contributing their own. This behavior manifests all of the characteristics of real-life shyness: waiting and hovering, warming up, approach/avoidance, passive observation, and social comparison. Often a few people dominate the conversation and the others struggle to send in their messages.

Why do people lurk in chat rooms? I suspect it's for the same reasons that they are shy in person. In chat rooms one must jump into discussions promptly before the conversation moves on to the next topic. You may get performance anxiety if you fear you could be rejected ("flamed"), and you must think on your feet. Others may have low tolerance for those who don't write in quickly and may feel little remorse for rejection, since no personal connection is at stake. And it's easy to leave a chat room if you're uninterested in the topic or don't want to expend the effort to get involved. If there's no reason to stay and warm up, you only avoid and hover. Besides, the leap from one chat room to another is effortless.

People are people no matter what the medium. Small talk and evaluations still occur. It's easy for others to lie when they only have a screen name to identify them, and you may become lost in the anonymity of cyberspace. You may also be more vulnerable to taking these relationships seriously because Internet friends can seem more real than your real-life friends. And if you're surfing the Net excessively, you may be "cheating" or denying your real-life partner time and affection.

Keep your involvement with on-line acquaintances in perspective. Chances are you won't make lasting connections. You may be able to find someone to chat with or an answer to a problem but nothing more. Focus on developing ties with those with whom you're in daily personal contact.

Creating Social Interest

As all of these cyberspace issues become more common, how will the new generation—those raised on technology from an early age—behave? Will they be able to gain social skills if they spend so much time alone? What will happen to those who don't understand what it's like to stand in line at the bank or to work with a group of people in an office?

They may lack the social skills of the older generation and be more impatient with those who are slower—shy people. They may also miss a sense of belonging to a larger community and spend more time pursuing isolated hobbies like computer games or electronic pets. They may be more easily misled into thinking that Internet friends are people upon whom they can rely.

The solution is to create a sense of community and, in Alfred Adler's words, "social interest"—the development of the healthy self through helping and being involved with others. If you volunteer, you not only help yourself escape constant thoughts about your own problems, but you also consider the needs of others.

As the older generation stresses the importance of reaching out to others, our children will benefit by the example. Generosity through social interest helps the community and our children.

Being a Successfully Shy Global Citizen

When people find themselves among those of different cultures and races, they begin to feel more salient, more self-conscious, as if they are sticking out like a sore thumb. In fact, their behavior becomes more guarded and reserved. Those in the majority seem to watch what they do and attribute more responsibility to them for negative outcomes. Indeed, whether shy or not, once perceived as part of a minority, people become situationally shy. They leave their comfort zones and feel disquieted.

This was brought home to me recently when a friend told me about her experience at a Los Angeles manicurist's shop staffed by a group of young Vietnamese women. As Louise and another client—a stranger—sat waiting for their nails to dry, the six manicurists chatted excitedly among themselves in their native tongue. They seemed relaxed and happy in their small enclave. The other customer turned to Louise and said in hushed tones, "You know, I feel like I'm in a foreign country here." Her discomfort was evident.

Louise replied, gesturing toward the Asian women, "I'll bet most of the time they feel the way you do right now."

Understanding how people of different cultures interface becomes increasingly important as communication and mobility have opened us all to contact with those of many lands. But we need not look to intercultural domains to grasp these issues. If you are the only female engineer in an office filled with men, the only disabled person in a class of able-bodied, the only black person in a restaurant full of Hispanics or whites, the only teenager in a group of your grandparents' friends, you too are likely to feel uncomfortable and situationally shy. You will believe, perhaps rightly so, that all eyes are on you, and you will react accordingly by becoming self-conscious, self-evaluative, and guarded. It's human nature to do so, but these are also the characteristics of a shy person.

Social psychologist Kay Deaux at City University of New York found that in such situations people practice the art of *remooring*—connecting to other like-minded individuals to create a new comfort zone. A Mexican-American student attending a predominantly white college, for example, might join a Latino club. An employee transferred to another city might seek out his religious community or a chapter of his service organization. Recent immigrants live in proximity to others from their homeland, forming ethnic pockets—Little Italy, Chinatown, Germantown, Little Saigon, the Lower East Side in Manhattan.

These associations are not ends in themselves, but serve as stepping stones in the adjustment process toward further assimilation. They help individuals make the transition into the larger culture and speed the warm-up process. Those who have come before explain the rules of the dominant society to the newcomers and show them how to accommodate. Soon the émigrés begin to blend in. The student in the Latino Club, for instance, may eventually feel comfortable enough to join a nonethnically oriented political science or writing group and move into the culture at large.

These intercultural dynamics—the need to feel comfortable in awkward, shyness-provoking situations—help us understand why people limit their comfort zones and become clannish. All of us should be aware of these natural human impulses. If you find yourself in the majority, be sensitive to others' discomfort. And if you are in the minority, give yourself time to adjust. A successfully shy person of the world is able to move with relative ease from one cultural context to the next based on this awareness.

As the world gets faster, people tend naturally to withdraw and avoid. But as a successfully shy global citizen, you may have no need to do that. Because you grasp the basic concepts of your shy personality—approach/avoidance, the comfort zone, and slow to warm up—you are in a better position than most to deal with all of these changes personally as well as in your culture. And you will recognize how to incorporate these fundamentals into the ever-changing world around you.

Epilogue

Shyness is not just about shyness. It's about living a successful and full life brimming with self-awareness, self-acceptance, and self-confidence. Rather than turning you into an extrovert, my goal has been to ensure that the negative side of your shyness no longer limits your choices. I never said you had to change, only that you needed to make better choices that will open to you many potential rewards.

The successfully shy life should be no different from any other. All of the processes that we've talked about—shyness of the mind, body, self; slowness to warm up, limited comfort zones, and the approach/avoidance conflict—are fundamental principles of human nature. They just seem to be more salient issues for shy people.

These processes are fluid and dynamic. They are constantly changing within you and your world. But now, because you understand the underlying dynamics of shyness, you're well-prepared for these changes. In fact, because you have self-awareness, self-acceptance, and self-confidence you may be better off than many nonshy people who lack these strengths.

Remember that personal change comes neither easily nor quickly. You must be realistic, patient, and persistent. Your situation may worsen before it improves as you experience the growing pains inherent in an expanding comfort zone. But you need not fear change because you now understand how you react and adjust to it. You are now blessed with self-awareness instead of self-consciousness; self-acceptance instead of self-criticism; self-confidence instead of self-doubt. If new difficulties arise in your life, you can rely on the Four *I*'s—the fundamental problem-solving strategy—to help you on your way.

By now you have acquired much information about your own shyness and how it affects you throughout your life. The next step is to reach beyond your own comfort zone and use what you have learned to help others with their shyness. In this book I've talked about you, but you can substitute the word *friend, coworker, spouse, child, neighbor, classmate, relative.* Share these ideas with others along with your new sense of self-awareness, self-acceptance, self-confidence. Show them the value of a successfully shy life.

In reading this book, you have empowered yourself to help not only your shy loved ones, but also others in the world at large. Social interests, volunteering, and service to your community help you to step out of your own comfort zone and the confines of your shyness into the world's comfort zone. And it helps others in their lives.

As one successfully shy woman wrote to me:

> I find the best way to overcome shyness is to take the first step and face the fear that brings on the shyness. It isn't easy; I still get my heart racing and beating so loud, I almost feel the person next to me can hear it pounding. I volunteer for presentations and get involved in projects I enjoy. Interestingly, I found that I was not shy during my volunteer work for the World Cup soccer games. I believe the reason is because I did something from my heart. So perhaps the way to overcome shyness is to do something one really loves, and little by little the shyness will be diminished by the act itself.

Sage advice, indeed.

I hope *Shyness* will make it possible for you to greet the world on your own terms. I cannot stress enough the value of social skills, social graces, and small talk. They help you relate to others more gracefully, but they also help society function more smoothly. They make people feel more comfortable. When they aren't anxious or distressed, they can behave much more naturally instead of reactively. Living a successfully shy life is good for you and for those around you. It makes the world a better place.

I have heard from many people who are dealing successfully with their shyness. They're not trying to be extroverts, but they are aware of who they are and are incorporating their shyness into their lives. Let them serve as sources of inspiration to you:

> I've been keenly aware of my shyness my whole life. I watched my older sister go through an incredibly painful teenage period. She never socialized properly and to this day has social problems. I've made a conscious effort to assert myself in situations. When I meet a new person, I try to ask them about themselves and draw them out, or try to find common ground with them. I find trying to reach out to other shy people is much less intimidating than trying to make conversation with the loudmouths.

> The technique I usually use is to announce my inner turmoil and tell the other person to be gentle with me because I am shy. Naturally no one believes me, but it does take a lot of pressure off and it allows me to size up the situation.

> I overcame my shyness when I realized I was a smart person and could talk and give my opinion without being put down.

> I tell myself: "Nonshy people get rejected, too." "Failure at a party won't make people despise me." "People are probably not noticing anything odd." "I don't look any more ridiculous or eccentric than anyone else." "Many other people are shy, too." I try to keep in mind my good qualities, the fact that some people like me.

I have tried to overcome it by joining the church choir in which I ended up singing solo. I have forced myself to introduce myself to others at school and start conversations. I took a public-speaking class and have made several presentations in other classes.

Joining the high school forensics team has helped me to feel comfortable in front of people and with myself in general. You meet many different people and get a chance to talk in a low-pressure atmosphere. Another thing was my summer job. I worked as a cashier in a food stand. Just talking with different customers every day showed me how easy it is to start conversations. I feel I am only 10 percent as shy as I was five years ago.

As you turn this last page, remember, this is not the end of *Shyness*, but merely the beginning of *your successfully shy life*. Good luck, take care, and keep in touch.

Best regards,
Bernardo J. Carducci, Ph.D.,
Director

The Shy Life Enrichment Institute
P.O. Box 8064
New Albany, IN 47151-8064
www.carducci.com/shylife

Selected References

Adamec, R. E. (1990). Role of the amygdala and medial hypothalamus in spontaneous feline aggression and defense. *Aggressive Behavior, 16*, 207–222.

Adamec, R. E., & Morgan, H. D. (1994). The effect of kindling of different nuclei in the left and right amygdala on anxiety in the rat. *Physiology and Behavior, 55*, 1–12.

Alderman, M. B., & Ahuvia, A. C. (1991). Mediated channels for mate seeking: A solution to involuntary singlehood. *Critical Studies in Mass Communication, 8*, 273–289.

Alfano, M. S., Joiner, T. E., Jr., & Perry, M. (1994). Attributional style: A mediator of the shyness–depression relationship. *Journal of Research in Personality, 28*, 287–300.

Allen, O., Page, R. M., Moore, L., & Hewitt, C. (1994). Gender differences in selected psychosocial characteristics of adolescent smokers and nonsmokers. *Health Values, 18*, 34–39.

Arcus, D., & Kagan, J. (1995). Temperament and craniofacial variation in the first two years. *Child Development, 66*, 1529–1540.

Asendorpf, J. B. (1990). Beyond social withdrawal: Shyness, unsociability, and peer avoidance. *Human Development, 33*, 250–259.

Asendorf, J. B. (1993). Abnormal shyness in children. *Journal of Child Psychology and Psychiatry, 34*, 1069–1081.

Bell, I. R. (1992). Allergens, physical irritants, depression, and shyness. *Journal of Applied Developmental Psychology, 13*, 125–133.

Bell, I. R., Jasnoski, M. L., Kagan, J., & King, D. S. (1990). Is allergic rhinitis more frequent in young adults with extreme shyness? A preliminary survey. *Psychosomatic Medicine, 52*, 517-525.

Briggs, S. R. (1988). Shyness: Introversion or neuroticism? *Journal of Research in Personality, 22*, 290–307.

Bruch, M. A., Heimberg, R. G., Harvey, C., McCann, M., Mahone, M., & Slavkin, S. L. (1992). Shyness, alcohol expectancies, and alcohol use. *Journal of Research in Personality, 26*, 137–149.

Bruch, M. A., & Pearl, L. (1995). Attributional style and symptoms of shyness in heterosexual interaction. *Cognitive Therapy and Research, 19*, 91–107.

Calkins, S. D., Fox, N. A., & Marshall, T. R. (1996). Behavioral and physiological antecedents of inhibited and uninhibited behavior. *Child Development*, *67*, 523–540.

Carducci, B. J. (1998). *Psychology of personality: Viewpoints, research, and applications*. Pacific Grove, CA: Brooks/Cole.

Carducci, B. J., & Clark, D. L. (1997). *The personal and situational pervasiveness of shyness: A replication and extension of the Stanford Survey on Shyness 20 years later*. Indiana University Southeast Shyness Research Institute, New Albany, IN.

Carducci, B. J., Marion, C. R., Lynch, D., Dosch, M. M., & Boley, A. L. (1997, July). *What shy individuals try to do to overcome their shyness*. Paper presented at the meeting of the International Conference on Shyness and Self-Consciousness, Cardiff, U.K.

Carducci, B. J., Ragains, K. D., Kee, K. L., Johnson, M. R., & Duncan, H. R. (1997, July). *What shy individuals say about the pains and problems of shyness*. Paper presented at the meeting of the International Conference on Shyness and Self-Consciousness, Cardiff, U.K.

Carducci, B. J., & Zimbardo, P. G. (1995, Nov./Dec.). Are you shy? *Psychology Today*, 34–41+.

Carey, W. B., & McDevitt, S. C. (1995). *Coping with children's temperament: A guide for professionals*. New York: Basic Books.

Caspi, A., Bem, D. J., & Elder, G. H., Jr. (1989). Continuities and consequences of interactional styles across the life course. *Journal of Personality*, *57*, 375–406.

Caspi, A., Elder, G. H., & Bem, D. J. (1988). Moving away from the world: Life-course pattern of shy children. *Developmental Psychology*, *24*, 824–831.

Cheek, J. M., & Melchior, L. A. (1985, August). *Are shy people narcissistic?* Paper presented at the meeting of the American Psychological Association, Los Angeles, CA.

Cherny, S. S., Fulker, R. P., Corley, R. P., Plomin, R., & DeFries, J. C. (1994). Continuity and change in infant shyness from 14 to 20 months. *Behavior Genetics*, *24*, 365–379.

Chess, S., & Thomas, A. (1995). *Temperament in clinical practice*. New York: Guilford.

Davis, M. (1992). The role of the amygdala in fear-potentiated startle: Implications for animal models of anxiety. *Pharmacological Sciences*, *13*, 35–41.

Davis, M. (1994). The role of the amygdala in emotional learning. *International Review of Neurobiology*, *36*, 225–266.

Davis, M. (1996). Differential roles of the amygdala and bed nucleus of the stria terminalis in conditioned fear and startled enhanced by corticotropin-releasing hormone. In T. Ono, B. L. McNaughton, S. Molotchnikoff, E. T. Rolls, & H. Nishijo (Eds.), *Perceptions, memory, and emotion: Frontiers in neuroscience* (pp. 525–548). Oxford, U.K.: Pergamon.

DePaulo, B. M., Dull, W. R., Greenberg, J. M., & Swaim, G. W. (1989). Are shy people reluctant to ask for help? *Journal of Personality and Social Psychology, 56,* 834–844.

DiLalla, L., Kagan, J., & Reznick, J. S. (1994). Genetic etiology of behavioral inhibition among 2-year-old children. *Infant Behavior and Development, 17,* 405–412.

Dodge, K. A., Schlundt, D. C., Schocken, I., & Delugach, J. D. (1983). Social competence and children's sociometric status: The role of peer group entry strategies. *Merrill-Palmer Quarterly, 29,* 309–336.

Eisenberg, N., Fabes, R. A., & Murphy, B. C. (1995). Relations of shyness and low sociability to regulation and emotionality. *Journal of Personality and Social Psychology, 68,* 505–517.

Fox, N. A. (1989). Psychophysiological correlates of emotional reactivity during the first year of life. *Developmental Psychology, 25,* 364–372.

Fox, N. A. (1991). If it's not left, it's right. *American Psychologist, 46,* 863–872.

Fox, N. A., Rubin, K. H., Calkins, S. D., Marshall, T. R., Coplan, R. J., Porges, S. W., Long, J. M., & Stewart, S. (1995). Frontal activation asymmetry and social competence at four years of age. *Child Development, 66,* 1170–1784.

Garcia, S., Stinson, L., Ickes, W., & Bissonnette, V. (1991). Shyness and physical attractiveness in mixed-sex dyads. *Journal of Personality and Social Psychology, 61,* 35–49.

Gilmartin, B. G. (1989). *The shy-man syndrome: Why men become love shy and how they can overcome it.* Lanham, MD: Madison Books.

Hendin, H. M., & Cheek, J. M. (1997, July). *Shyness, hypersensitivity, narcissism, and shame.* Paper presented at the International Conference on Shyness and Self-Consciousness, Cardiff, U.K.

Herberner, E. S., Kagan, J., & Cohen, M. (1989). Shyness and olfactory threshold. *Personality and Individual Differences, 10,* 1159–1163.

Hill, G. J. (1989). An unwillingness to act: Behavioral appropriateness, situational constraint, and self-efficacy in shyness. *Journal of Personality, 57,* 871–890.

Jasnoski, M. B., Bell, I. R., & Peterson, R. (1994). What connections exist between panic symptoms, shyness, Type I hypersensitivity, anxiety, and anxiety sensitivity? *Anxiety, Stress, and Coping, 7*, 19–34.

Jones, W. H., Cheek, J. M., & Briggs, S. R. (Eds.). (1986). *Shyness: Perspectives on research and treatment.* New York: Plenum.

Kagan, J. (1994). *Galen's prophecy: Temperament in human nature.* New York: Westview Press.

Kagan, J., Arcus, D., Snidman, N., Feng, W. Y., Hendler, J., & Greene, S. (1994). Reacitivity in infants: A cross-national comparison. *Developmental Psychology, 30*, 342–345.

Kagan, J., Arcus, D., Snidman, N., & Rimm, S. E. (1995). Asymmetry of forehead temperature and cardiac activity. *Neuropsychology, 9*, 47–51.

Kagan, J., & Gortmaker, S. L. (1997). Day length during pregnancy and shyness in children: Results from Northern and Southern hemispheres. *Developmental Psychobiology, 31*, 107–114.

Lewis, M., Sullivan, M. W., Stranger, C., & Weiss, M. (1989). Self-development and self-conscious emotions. *Child Development, 60*, 146–156.

Manning, P., & Ray, G. (1993). Shyness, self-confidence, and social interaction. *Social Psychology Quarterly, 56*, 178–192.

Melchior, L. A., & Cheek, J. M. (1990). Shyness and anxious self-preoccupation during social interaction. *Journal of Social Behavior and Personality, 5*, 117–130.

Miller, R. S. (1995). On the nature of embarrassability: Shyness, social evaluation, and social skill. *Journal of Personality, 63*, 315–339.

Montgomery, R. L., & Haemmerlie, F. M. (1986). Self-perception theory and the reduction of heterosocial anxiety. *Journal of Social and Clinical Psychology, 4*, 503–512.

Montgomery, R. L., Haemmerlie, F. M., & Edwards, M. (1991). Social, personal, and interpersonal deficits in socially anxious people. *Journal of Social Behavior and Personality, 6*, 859–872.

Page, R. M. (1990). Shyness and sociability: A dangerous combination for illicit substance use in adolescence males? *Adolescence, 25*, 803–806.

Page, R. M., & Hammermeister, J. (1995). Shyness and loneliness: Relationship to the exercise frequency of college students. *Psychological Reports, 76*, 395–398.

Parks, M. R., & Roberts, L. D. (1996). Making friends in cyberspace. *Journal of Communication, 46*, 80–97.

Phillips, S. D., & Bruch, M. A. (1988). Shyness and dysfunction in career development. *Journal of Counseling Psychology, 2*, 159–165.

Pilkonis, P. A. (1977). Shyness, public and private, and its relationship to other measures of social behavior. *Journal of Personality, 45*, 585–595.

Reznick, J. S. (Ed.). (1989). *Perspectives on behavioral inhibition.* Chicago: The University of Chicago Press.

Roberts, P. (1995, May/June). Father's time. *Psychology Today*, 48–55+.

Rosenberg, A., & Kagan, J. (1987). Iris pigmentation and behavioral inhibition. *Developmental Psychobiology, 20*, 377–392.

Rubin, K. H. (1982). Nonsocial play in preschoolers: Necessary evil? *Child Development, 53*, 651–657.

Rubin, K. H., & Asendorpf, J. B. (Eds.). (1993). *Social withdrawal, inhibition, and shyness in childhood.* Hillsdale, NJ: Erlbaum.

Scharlott, B. W., & Christ, W. G. (1995). Overcoming relationship-inhibition barriers: The impact of a computer-dating system on sex role, shyness, and appearance inhibitions. *Computers in Human Behavior, 11*, 191–204.

Schmidt, L. A., & Fox, N. A. (1994). Patterns of cortical electrophysiology and autonomic activity in adults' shyness and sociability. *Biological Psychology, 38*, 183–198.

Schmidt, L. A., & Fox, N. A. (1995). Individual differences in young adults' shyness and sociability: Personality and health correlates. *Personality and Individual Differences, 19*, 455–462.

Tangney, J. P., & Fisher, J. P. (Eds.). (1995). *Self-conscious emotions: The psychology of shame, guilt, embarrassment, and pride.* New York: Guilford.

Triandis, H. C. (1994). *Culture and social behavior.* New York: McGraw-Hill.

Turner, S. M., Beidel, D. C., & Townsley, R. M. (1990). Social phobia: Relationship to shyness. *Behavior Research Therapy, 28*, 497–505.

Wakshlak, A., & Weinstock, M. (1990). Neonatal handling reverses behavioral abnormalities induced in rats by prenatal stress. *Physiology and Behavior, 48*, 289–292.

Zimbardo, P. G. (1977). *Shyness: What it is, what to do about it.* Reading, MA: Addison-Wesley.

Index